China's New Rulers: The Secret Files

SECOND, REVISED EDITION

To Darrell from Kel Xmas 2003

"With each passing year, China and its mandarinate become a little less opaque. The reports summarized in this volume represent another giant step forward in penetrating the old veil of secrecy that once shrouded China and its political processes with a virtually impenetrable screen. Whatever may follow, these documents provide a fascinating look behind that screen and help us understand how China's leaders interact and govern this most consequential of countries."

—Orville Schell, Dean of the Graduate School of Journalism,
University of California, Berkeley

"*China's New Rulers*—based on the Chinese book *Disidai*—provides a peek inside the black box of the highest levels of the Communist Party of China (CCP). It gives the outside world by far its most detailed and most reliable account of the men who are likely to rule China in the next few years. It sheds new light on the plots that brought them to power in the 1990s and on tendencies in what they think, or at least appear to think. We observe a peaceful transition to power—a first for the CCP—but see as well an entrenched political culture in which the views of superiors count for nearly everything and the opinions of ordinary citizens for almost nothing."

—Perry Link, Princeton University

"*China's New Rulers* has enduring value because of its vivid picture of the party's procedures in selecting new leaders."

—*Foreign Affairs*

"A remarkable book...the best guide we shall get...essential reading for anyone involved with China in the broadest sense."

—*The Sunday Telegraph*, London

"Fascinating for the account...of how the party leadership selects and perpetuates itself; and revelations of what kind of men the new leaders are...."

—Jonathan Mirsky, *Times Literary Supplement*

"It gives an acute account of the men who will oversee [China's] immediate political future—revealing some intriguing personality quirks along the way—and provides important insights into the problems and solutions that the new rulers are contemplating."

—*The Guardian*, London

China's New Rulers: The Secret Files

SECOND, REVISED EDITION

Andrew J. Nathan
and Bruce Gilley

NEW YORK REVIEW BOOKS

New York

THIS IS A NEW YORK REVIEW BOOK

PUBLISHED BY THE NEW YORK REVIEW OF BOOKS

CHINA'S NEW RULERS:
THE SECRET FILES
SECOND, REVISED EDITION

by Andrew J. Nathan and Bruce Gilley

This edition published in 2003
in the United States of America by
The New York Review of Books
1755 Broadway
New York, NY 10019
www.nybooks.com

The photographs on pages 14–22 appear courtesy of Xinhua News Agency.

PUBLISHER'S NOTE:

The first edition of *China's New Rulers* was published on November 8, 2002. This second, revised edition brings the story of the Chinese succession through the end of March 2003, when the process was completed. The ages of the leaders are given as of the end of that month, except where the context specifies otherwise.

Library of Congress Cataloging-in-Publication Data

Nathan, Andrew J. (Andrew James)
 China's new rulers : the secret files / Andrew J. Nathan and Bruce Gilley.
 —2nd, rev. ed.
  p. cm.
 Includes index.
 ISBN 1-59017-072-5 (pbk. : alk. paper)
 1. China—Politics and government—1976– 2. Politicians—China.
I. Gilley, Bruce, 1966– II. Title.
 DS779.26.N382 2003
 951.06'092'2—dc22

                     2003019501

ISBN 1-59017-072-5

Printed in the United States of America on acid-free paper.

October 2003

1 3 5 7 9 10 8 6 4 2

Contents

I

THE FILES AND THEIR CONTENTS

AT A TIGHTLY scripted press conference in Beijing's Great Hall of the People on the morning of November 15, 2002, a new Chinese leadership was introduced to the world. The brief appearance of nine men in dark suits signaled the climax of an intensely fought succession struggle which by the vindictive standards of Communist China was remarkably civilized. Little is known outside top Party circles about that struggle. Nor does the outside world, or the Chinese people, know much about the personal character of the new leaders or the story that lies behind each man's rise to the top.

Much of the relevant information is contained in lengthy internal investigation reports prepared by the Party's highly trusted Organization Department, which were used to evaluate the candidates for membership in the Chinese Communist Party's Politburo Standing Committee, China's highest governing body. Because of the Communist cult of secrecy, the Chinese have always been chary of publishing information about their leaders. The reports remained off-limits to all but a small number of people involved in the process of selecting the new leading group.

In late 2001, as preparations for the succession intensified, persons in Beijing decided to reveal the contents of the reports to the outside world. Substantial portions of the dossiers on each candidate, still in draft form, were conveyed to a Chinese writer living outside China whom the officials in Beijing trusted. They asked that he use the dossiers as the basis for a book that would tell the world the inside story of the new rulers. This Chinese-language book, *Disidai* (The Fourth Generation), was published in New York under the pseudonym Zong Hairen in November 2002.[1]

With the author's cooperation, we read the manuscript of *Disidai* before its publication and questioned him at length about it. On that basis, we prepared the first edition of this book. After it appeared in November 2002, Zong Hairen published a series in the Hong Kong newspaper *Xinbao* (Hong Kong Economic Journal) and provided some articles for broadcast on Radio Free Asia, which described further political maneuvers through March 2003, when the National People's Congress completed the succession by electing the new leaders to the government posts that most of them hold in addition to their Party positions. We consulted these articles (they are listed in the appendix to this chapter) and discussed their contents with Zong, enabling us to complete the story of the succession for this second edition of our book.

In what follows we describe in detail what the internal files say about the new leaders' personalities, how they came to power, and what they intend to do in office. For many, our portrait will be reassuring, since it shows the new leaders to be determined modernizers, intent on integrating China's economy with the rest of the world and on maintaining good relations with the United States. They are competent managers with wide experience in China's complex party-state bureaucracy and pragmatic technocrats who are capable of keeping order and promoting development in the world's most populous country. Some of them are willing to subject the ruling Chinese Communist Party to more political competition and to trust the state-

---

1. Mirror Books.

controlled Chinese media, including the press, radio, and television, with more freedom to criticize the performance of lower-level officials.

For others, however, the portrait will be frightening. This is a group of men who believe in authoritarian control as a precondition for pushing their country through the turbulent passage to modernization. They believe in stopping dissent against Communist rule before it gets started and in deterring crime by widespread use of the death penalty. They believe that their government has been more than generous to the residents of Taiwan, Tibet, and Xinjiang, and have little sympathy for the grievances of the people in these places. Although they share many Western economic values, they share fewer Western moral values. They expect strategic competition with the West, and intend to resist American dominance, yet they believe that the West will eventually have to cooperate with China because of common economic interests. For the West, the new leaders present a dilemma: it will be economically and strategically necessary to deal with them, but many Western policymakers may also feel a moral obligation to oppose their methods of rule.

Either way, the evidence from the internal reports of the Party's Organization Department allows for a major advance in our understanding of Chinese politics. Until now, the drama of high-level politics in Beijing has been reliably revealed only rarely, and always after the fact. The chief examples are the biography of Mao Zedong's wife, Jiang Qing, based on interviews she gave to an American historian,[2] the memoirs of Mao Zedong's personal physician,[3] the memoirs of aides to deposed Party secretaries in the 1980s,[4] the documentary

---

2. Roxane Witke, *Comrade Chiang Ch'ing* (Little, Brown, 1977).

3. Li Zhisui, *The Private Life of Chairman Mao* (Random House, 1994).

4. Ruan Ming, *Deng Xiaoping: Chronicle of an Empire* (Westview, 1994); Wu Jiang, *Shinian zhi lu: he Hu Yaobang xiangchu de rizi* (The Ten-Year Road: My Days with Hu Yaobang) (Hong Kong: Mirror Cultural Enterprises, 1996); Wu Guoguang, *Zhao Ziyang yu zhengzhi gaige* (Zhao Ziyang and Political Reform) (Hong Kong: Pacific Press, 1997).

account of the leaders' deliberations during the 1989 Tiananmen protests,[5] and the insider account of Premier Zhu Rongji's activities during the tumultuous year of 1999, when China's leaders dealt with Falungong, the American bombing of the Chinese embassy in Belgrade, and heightened tensions over Taiwan.[6] *Disidai* is remarkable in being the first insider account to describe how the processes of contemporary Chinese politics have actually worked so soon after the events it describes. Through it, we understand not only how a new generation of Party leaders has emerged, but also how they intend to govern and where they are likely to guide China in the coming decade.

We hope that this information will help the West evaluate the stability of the new ruling group, their potential as partners and competitors on the global stage, and the changes they are likely to bring to the Chinese economy and political system.

China's political system. Just northwest of Tiananmen Square in central Beijing is a large complex, surrounded by oxblood-red walls and strewn with security cameras, called Zhongnanhai (Central and Southern Lakes). It was once part of the imperial palace, used for fertility and harvest rites. Today it houses the highest offices of the ruling Chinese Communist Party (CCP) and the compound of the top state (that is, government) administrative body, the State Council.[7] The offices of the top military command are nearby. The physical connection of these three centers of power reflects a simple fact: while the Party, the government, and the military are separate on paper,

---

5. *The Tiananmen Papers*, compiled by Zhang Liang, edited by Andrew J. Nathan and Perry Link (PublicAffairs, 2001).

6. Zong Hairen, *Zhu Rongji zai 1999* (Zhu Rongji in 1999) (Mirror Books, 2001); English translation edited by Andrew J. Nathan in *Chinese Law and Government*, January–February and March–April 2002.

7. See frontispiece maps in *The Tiananmen Papers*.

they are inseparable in reality. It is the Party's overarching power that fuses them.

What is known as the "Party Center" occupies the southern sector of Zhongnanhai. This consists of the offices of the general secretary and the other members of the Politburo Standing Committee (PBSC), the Party Secretariat, which coordinates Party activities, and the Central Office, which handles administration for the other south Zhongnanhai offices.[8]

The Chinese Communist Party is a secretive, selective organization of about sixty-five million members who have positions of influence in all sectors of Chinese society, whether as village leaders, university officials, factory managers, newspaper editors, or bureaucrats in charge of everything from public health to police intelligence. The Party's national congress consists of about two thousand persons divided into provincial delegations, elected by Party members throughout the country. It meets once every five years to elect a Central Committee, currently of about 370 persons (including members and alternates).

The election of the Central Committee is important because being a member or an alternate member is a necessary qualification for the most senior positions in the Party, the government, and the military.[9] In the past, Party congress delegates ratified a list of names prepared in advance by the Party's Organization Department—which handles appointments and promotions—under the guidance of the senior leaders. Since 1987, the congress has been allowed to vote on a list of candidates slightly larger than the number of Central Committee

---

8. The full name of the Central Office is the Chinese Communist Party Central Committee General Office (*Zhonggong zhongyang bangongting*). It is often referred to in English as the General Office.

9. Alternate or candidate (*houbu*) membership in a Party body like the Central Committee or the Politburo signifies in theory that the alternate would take the place of a regular member if the regular member's seat became vacant. In practice, alternate membership serves as an honorific designation. The person can attend meetings but not vote.

seats. This means that a small number of candidates fail to be elected, an advance for inner-Party "democracy" in the eyes of reformers. The leaders usually accept the verdict of the congress, but sometimes they improvise—in one case recounted below, by creating an extra seat so that a favored candidate could be elected to it.

Once elected, the Central Committee approves a Politburo of twenty or more persons, the makeup of which has been agreed upon in closed-door bargaining among Party elites. Five to nine of those members are designated as the Politburo Standing Committee, which meets weekly and runs the country. The highest-ranking member of that group is the general secretary.[10]

On paper just a Party organ, the PBSC in fact makes all important decisions on the economy, social policy, foreign affairs, defense, science and technology, education, and culture—national policy in every sphere of life. It can deal with any issue it wants. No other organ of the Party or government has the power to contradict its decisions. The only exception to this general rule was a group of highly esteemed former Politburo members, sometimes called the Party Elders, headed by Deng Xiaoping, who from 1987 to 1997 exercised behind-the-scenes veto power over major decisions.[11] But since Deng's death in 1997, retired senior leaders have not exercised such power.

Each member of the PBSC takes on other important responsibilities. Some supervise crucial activities in which the Party exercises authority. Among these are internal security, including the police; high-level personnel management for jobs in the Party and government;

---

10. The general secretary is the head of the Party. The position of Party chairman, held by Mao Zedong, was abolished in order to stress the equal rank of PBSC members.

11. We use the capital E when referring to the group of eight Elders who played an important role in 1989: Deng Xiaoping, Chen Yun, Li Xiannian, Peng Zhen, Deng Yingchao, Yang Shangkun, Bo Yibo, and Wang Zhen. Never before or since have elders operated as such a well-defined corporate group.

propaganda; and other work carried on by the powerful Party Secretariat and high-level Party committees or commissions. Others hold top positions in the state apparatus—as state president, premier, vice-premier, or chairman of the national parliament. But those roles are secondary to their positions as PBSC members. Members of the Politburo may hold similar posts or may serve as Party secretaries of major provinces or provincial-level municipalities.[12]

The northern sector of Zhongnanhai contains the state offices, including the offices of the premier and those of his vice-premiers and state councilors, who are senior members of the State Council, or cabinet. Numerous cabinet-level ministries and commissions have offices outside of but not far from Zhongnanhai.

While the Party has the power to make decisions, the state is its organ for implementing the decisions. The two have separate, highly developed, and partly overlapping organizational structures. Party members occupy the top government posts, and those who hold Party posts are more powerful than the state officials in the same sphere of government activity. For example, a provincial Party secretary, referred to as "the first hand" (*diyi bashou*), ranks above the provincial governor.

The military is an independent system. Its top organ is the Central Military Commission (CMC), which appears on the organization charts of both the Party and the state. Yet in practice the military is linked to the other two pillars of power only at the top. The commission consists entirely of serving generals except for its civilian chairman, who frequently is also the head of the Party (for example, Jiang Zemin from 1989 to 2002), and sometimes a civilian vice-chairman who is the heir apparent in the civilian Party bureaucracy (Hu Jintao from 1998 to 2002). In addition, two or three generals normally serve in the Politburo, and one serves in the State Council as minister of

---

12. Four municipalities—Beijing, Shanghai, Tianjin, and Chongqing—have provincial-level administrative status directly under the central government.

defense. The officer corps consists entirely of Party members, and both officers and troops are required to study Party ideology and declare loyalty to Party principles. Yet the military's internal Party system is distinct to it rather than a branch of the civilian Party bureaucracy. The military is thus a self-governing hierarchy, with a thin layer of civilian control, coordinated with the Party only at the top.

China's constitution calls the country's parliament, the National People's Congress (NPC), "the highest organ of state power." Yet its location outside Zhongnanhai reflects its subordinate status. It is largely a device to legitimate one-party rule by giving it a theoretical claim to be based on popular sovereignty. In fact, its three-thousand-odd delegates (there are also three lower levels of people's congresses from the provinces down) are mostly Party members and have never rejected a proposed piece of legislation or a government appointment. The NPC has an even weaker cousin, the Chinese People's Political Consultative Conference (CPPCC), in which respected members of academe, business, and the professions, many of whom are not CCP members, are invited to show their support for CCP rule and offer suggestions for improving government.

In short, the Chinese system is a version of the classical Leninist party-state, in which the ruling party penetrates and directs the work of the state. It has also at the same time been a form of personal authoritarianism, in that for most of the PRC's history one leader has held highest authority in all three systems of power—Party, state, and military. The country's would-be democratic institutions, the NPC and the CPPCC, have until recently been virtually powerless.

The Fourth Generation. Chinese call the outgoing group of leaders, headed by Jiang Zemin, the Third Generation and the new group, headed by Hu Jintao, the Fourth Generation (hence the title of Zong Hairen's book). The idea of numbering generations of leaders came from Deng Xiaoping, China's leader from 1978 to 1997. He identified the First Generation as that of Mao Zedong, who ruled from the founding of the People's Republic in 1949 until his death in 1976. The Second Generation was Deng's own. Deng called Jiang the "core" of the Third Generation, which places today's top leader, Hu Jintao, at the head of the Fourth Generation.

This numbering system is useful as a rough guide to the political history of post-1949 China. Mao's generation built Communist China and then half-destroyed it with the decade-long Cultural Revolution between 1966 and 1976. Deng launched China's pragmatic, market-oriented reforms but headed off any accompanying political freedoms with the crackdown on the 1989 Tiananmen pro-democracy movement. Jiang's group presided over China's emergence as a major world power, tying its economy to the world trading system and gaining a strategic role in Asia and in relations with the West. Now a new generation will make its mark.

Hu Jintao's accession to the post of general secretary was the centerpiece of the succession. Although the state presidency used to be held by another official, Chinese leaders now agree that the core leader must be given this position as well if he is to have full powers. Thus Hu became president of China at the March 2003 meeting of the NPC. (All top state offices are formally assigned by the NPC, even though they have been decided in advance by the Party leaders.)

Hu did not, however, in March assume the chairmanship of the Central Military Commission, as he was expected to do. Jiang Zemin continued in that post, breaking with the norm that all three top positions should be united in the hands of a single leader. In retaining this office, Jiang followed a model enacted only once before in CCP history, from 1981 to 1989, when Deng Xiaoping held the military commission chair without heading either the Party or the state. Hu Jintao's hold on power thus remains incomplete. For the Fourth Generation to take full control, it will be necessary for Hu to accede to this post. Doing so will ensure that the military does not become a separate power center for ambitious officers or political rivals to Hu.

As shown in Table 1, PBSC members are assigned protocol ranks, which govern how they are treated on formal occasions, at public meetings, in photographs, and the like.[13] Protocol rank is not the same as real power. Drawing on Zong's documents, we will show that Hu Jintao is unlikely to be as powerful a leader as his predecessor Jiang Zemin, and that strong influence will be exerted by third-ranking member Wen Jiabao and fifth-ranking member Zeng Qinghong. We introduce these three men in Chapter 3.

The other members of the new PBSC are all technocrats. Although not striving for overall power to chart China's direction, they will enjoy unchallenged authority in their respective spheres of responsibility. We describe their backgrounds in Chapter 4. Chapter 5 describes other important figures in the top policy circles, including the representatives of the Fifth Generation, the elders, and female leaders.

The arrival of the Fourth Generation represents a thorough renewal of leadership in China. Eight of the nine PBSC members and all fifteen regular members of the Politburo are new to those ranks. The entire top uniformed leadership of the military is also new. The Fourth Generation is not only younger, averaging an age of sixty-one at the PBSC level as of November 2002 compared to seventy for the former PBSC, but more technocratic in training and more pragmatic in their thinking than their predecessors. Their rise to power has been smoother and more deliberate than the turbulent political careers of earlier generations. Although only one of them, Luo Gan, has studied outside China, fewer than in the Third Generation, the Fourth Generation is more aware of international opinion and modern economic and technical trends. Yet they are also strong nationalists. As we will see, the Fourth Generation is united on many issues, but they disagree on

---

13. Below the PBSC level, other Politburo members' names are normally listed in stroke-count order, that is, by the number of strokes of the pen or brush required to write the Chinese characters for their family names.

Table 1.

Members are listed in order of rank, according to protocol

15th PBSC (1997–2002)

1. Jiang Zemin (also General Secretary, Chinese Communist Party; President, People's Republic of China; Chairman, Central Military Commission)
2. Li Peng (also Chairman, Standing Committee of the National People's Congress)
3. Zhu Rongji (also Premier of the State Council)
4. Li Ruihuan (also Chairman, Chinese People's Political Consultative Conference)
5. Hu Jintao (also Vice President, People's Republic of China; Vice Chairman, Central Military Commission)
6. Wei Jianxing (also Secretary, Central Disciplinary Inspection Commission)
7. Li Lanqing (also Executive Deputy Premier, State Council)

16th PBSC (2002–2007)

1. Hu Jintao (also General Secretary, CCP; President, People's Republic of China)
2. Wu Bangguo (also Chairman, Standing Committee of the National People's Congress)
3. Wen Jiabao (also Premier of the State Council)
4. Jia Qinglin (also Chairman, Chinese People's Political Consultative Conference)
5. Zeng Qinghong (also Secretary, CCP Secretariat and Vice President, People's Republic of China)
6. Huang Ju (also Executive Deputy Premier, State Council)
7. Wu Guanzheng (also Secretary, Central Disciplinary Inspection Commission)
8. Li Changchun (managing propaganda and ideology)
9. Luo Gan (also Secretary of the Central Politics and Law Committee, in charge of political, security, and intelligence affairs)

HU JINTAO

WU BANGGUO

WEN JIABAO

JIA QINGLIN

ZENG QINGHONG

HUANG JU

WU GUANZHENG

LI CHANGCHUN

LUO GAN

some important questions, including the pace and scope of both economic and political reform.

The composition of the new leadership is the outcome of a long power struggle that we describe in Chapter 2. The key issue was whether Jiang Zemin would give up all three top posts—those of Party general secretary, state president, and chairman of the Central Military Commission—to Hu Jintao, or whether he would try to hold on to the military chairmanship in the same way that Mao Zedong did until the end of his life and Deng Xiaoping did until late in his life, in order to continue to exert influence over major decisions. In the end, Jiang kept the military commission post and, drawing on Zong's information, we will explain how he did so and why it matters.

That Jiang, his colleague Li Peng, and others of their generation nonetheless retired from all their other offices in an orderly way marks a significant change in Chinese elite politics toward more routinized forms of political conflict in which the stakes are not as high as they were in the past. This did not happen without some struggle. Yet the upshot was that the succession process, for the first time in the CCP's history, was conducted in a way that was deliberate, peaceful, and—by the lights of a Communist system—constrained by self-imposed rules of political conduct.

Much was at stake in the choice of the new leaders. The range of issues, which we discuss in Chapters 7 and 8, can be summarized with respect to two visions for China's future, one reformist and one conservative. The terms "reformist" (or "liberal") and "conservative" (or "hard-line") first gained currency in China when Deng Xiaoping launched his marketizing and open-door policies in the late 1970s. They remain useful, although their meanings have evolved. Today, reformers want to run China's economy according to market principles; they want to reduce the number of state-owned enterprises, make methods of social control more fair and efficient, and integrate China more fully into the world economy. Conservatives do not disagree with these ideas, but stress that the state must retain a dominant guiding role in the economy. In their view, the Party's enemies must not be allowed to take advantage of more moderate means of social control in order to escape punishment. The Party must take measures to counteract the harmful influences of globalization, whether political or cultural.

Conservatives favor stronger ideological and social restrictions in order to prevent challenges to the Party's power. Those identified as liberals or reformers believe that the Party will gain more popular acceptance, be more informed about changes in society, and extract better work from its own "cadres"—the standard term for Party and state officials—if it tolerates freer expression.

The effective spectrum of open policy debate is relatively narrow. Everyone in power in both the old PBSC and the new, and the great majority among business and intellectual elites, favor what Deng Xiaoping called "reform and opening"—running China's economy largely according to market principles, rationalizing methods of social control, opening the country to Western trade and investment, and engaging with other nations as a power that, for the most part, accepts the international status quo. No faction in the leadership (or even in substantial numbers among Chinese intellectuals) wants to displace Communist Party rule, at least in the foreseeable future, in favor of competitive, multi-party electoral democracy. Nor is there any longer a substantial group that wants to return to the Maoist model of a state-owned economy, economic autarky, ideological mobilization, violent mass movements, and foreign policy isolation.

Specific disagreements over policy among members of the Fourth Generation are nonetheless important. They include, in the economy, how great a role should be preserved for state-owned enterprises, how much to depend on foreign versus domestic demand to bring about economic growth, and to what extent environmental concerns should make the leadership cautious about huge developmental projects. On the relations between Party and society there are disagreements over how much leeway to allow the media in making constructive criticism, especially of local and regional officials, and how rapidly to promote competitive elections for Party and state offices.

On ethnic relations there is debate about how to deal with complaints of repression by the Tibetan and Uighur populations. In foreign policy, there are different views on how assertively China should deal with the United States and Japan. As a whole, the debates over policy define several possible futures for China, ranging from a more repressive to a less repressive version of authoritarianism; from a stronger to a weaker version of state-led development; and from a foreign policy that is more optimistic about the intentions of the United States and Japan to one that calls for measures to deter US and Japanese threats to Chinese security.

Zong Hairen, the investigation reports, and this book. The dossiers on which *Disidai* is based are highly confidential, prepared for the exclusive use of the members of the outgoing Politburo, whose agreement was needed to establish the slate of candidates for the new Politburo and its Standing Committee. Within the Politburo, the views of the highest-ranking leaders carry the greatest weight. They tend both to speak first at meetings, setting their tone, and to speak last, summing up.[14] More junior Politburo members defer to them. Still, no matter how strong a candidate's factional backing, he cannot be promoted without a record of administrative achievement and a good rating in popularity among the Party rank and file.

These qualifications are constantly studied by the Party's powerful and secretive Organization Department, which starting in 1999 was headed by Jiang Zemin's masterful ally and political adviser Zeng

---

14. One sees this phenomenon at work in meetings of the PBSC and the Elders in *The Tiananmen Papers*. See, for example, the Elders' meetings of May 21 and May 27.

Qinghong.[15] The Organization Department is the body in charge of investigating candidates for high-level political appointments and promotions. It is a trusted group of senior Party officials who are chosen for their reliability and ability to assess the work of others. They are given full access to information on the careers of the highest-ranking officials. The department submits reports (*kaocha baogao*) to the Politburo for its use in deliberating on succession arrangements. The complete reports they produce are not shown to the Central Committee members who cast their votes for the new leadership. The members receive only the candidates' short résumés.

Whenever a candidate is considered for a high-level post,[16] the Organization Department creates a team of investigators, typically headed by a retired official holding full ministerial rank or above. Besides officials from the Organization Department itself, the team may include experienced officials from relevant Party departments like the Central Disciplinary Inspection Commission, the Propaganda Department, and the Central Office, government departments like the Ministry of Personnel and the Ministry of Supervision, and often a few from the General Political Department of the People's Liberation Army (PLA).

The team reviews the investigation reports that were compiled on the candidate in connection with his earlier promotions. They also visit the places where he has recently worked to conduct fresh interviews, and, as necessary, revisit the locations of his earlier assignments to investigate issues that may have newly arisen. "Public opinion" toward the candidate is assessed by speaking with many

---

15. The following information on the report system was provided by Zong Hairen.

16. All candidates for the Central Committee and for important jobs in the Party and government bureaucracies go through a version of this process, but the following description applies to candidates for the Politburo and the PBSC. In the case of investigations into serving Politburo members, the investigation team is headed by another serving Politburo member.

who know him among the top two or three hundred Party officials around the country.

In its fieldwork, an investigation team conducts confidential interviews and reviews documentary records. Its members speak to the candidate's superiors, colleagues, and subordinates. They solicit the views of senior retired leaders who worked with him earlier in his career. On the basis of these materials they compile a book-length dossier consisting of a report and an appendix. The report includes a curriculum vitae, a detailed narrative of the candidate's life and career, summary evaluations (*pingjia*) by superiors, and finally the conclusions reached by the investigation team itself (*kaocha xiaozu jielun*). The appendix consists of excerpts from statements the candidate has made recently (*yanlun*), usually at inner-Party meetings and in unpublished speeches.

A candidate whose career has come this far is not likely to be seen as having glaring faults. Indeed, there is something of a built-in momentum toward issuing favorable reports, especially if higher leaders are determined to see a candidate promoted. An example is the glowing report issued on one of Jiang Zemin's female friends, Huang Liman, when she was a candidate for Party secretary of the open city of Shenzhen.[17] On the other hand, when a candidate is strongly supported by one faction, other factions' critical views are likely to find their way into the report. (An example in this book is the account in Chapter 5 of Li Keqiang's work in Henan.) Some mention of at least a few shortcomings is expected, or a report will not be considered a serious effort. At a minimum, colleagues or former superiors might be quoted as saying that a candidate works too hard, worries too much about small issues, is not approachable, or does not spend much time with ordinary people.

---

17. *Disidai* tells the stories of several female personal friends of Jiang Zemin, but never states explicitly whether any of these relationships was physical. See Chapter 6.

In other cases, criticisms are veiled by faint praise. Few cadres interviewed by an investigation team about a high-ranking leader being considered for promotion would respond with a direct attack, but negative opinions can be made clear by following the principle "If you have nothing good to say, say nothing." Based on both formal assessments of cadre opinion toward candidates and what they learn from their informal networks, the Politburo has a good idea of whether or not a potential candidate is broadly popular in the upper bureaucracy and why.

By tradition, an official's personal habits and sex life, and the behavior of his relatives, are considered irrelevant and are left out of the report, even though such issues do erupt into real politics from time to time. (See, for example, Chapter 5 on the wives of Bo Xilai and Xi Jinping and the children of Li Peng.) An investigation report is unlikely to contain allegations of corruption, since someone officially suspected of corruption will not have risen far enough to be a candidate for Politburo standing. The report may, however, evaluate how well, or badly, an official handled corruption cases that occurred when he was in authority, or mention corruption cases that were discovered after the candidate had already left a post, as in the case of Li Changchun and the city of Shenyang, where he was formerly Party secretary (see Chapter 4).

The completed investigation report goes to the Politburo Standing Committee and later to the full Politburo. (If the report's subject is a Politburo member, he does not get to see it.) The contents are not likely to surprise the people who read it, since they already know the candidates well, and the findings are not likely by themselves to doom a candidacy. But the investigations are important nonetheless. They play a part in the Politburo's effort to form a consensus about which candidate is best suited for which specific post. For example, Chapter 2 describes how in 1992 the search for a consensus by officials rummaging through the dossiers of candidates was critical to the elevation of Hu

Jintao to the PBSC and thus to the position of heir apparent. Besides, reading the reports carefully is one of the Politburo's responsibilities, even if it ends up confirming appointments that were expected.

Despite China's gradual opening, the secrecy that has always surrounded the leadership has if anything increased in recent years, because of revulsion within the Party against the personality cult that was created around the state's founder, Mao Zedong, and to a lesser extent around Deng Xiaoping and Jiang Zemin. While taking office in a period of unprecedented openness and interaction with the world, China's new rulers and their stories remain largely a mystery, not only to the foreign public but to people in China.[18]

In late 2001 and early 2002 Zong Hairen was provided with long sections of the then working drafts of these internal investigation reports. He tells us that these materials form the basis of his book, and that he has supplemented them with his own and his associates' observations and analysis. The chapters in *Disidai* are, on average, about one fifth the length of the investigation reports on which they are based. They follow the general structure of the investigation reports —curriculum vitae, a summary of the candidate's career, and excerpts from the subject's inner-Party statements. Zong's chapters mix passages of original language from the investigation reports with passages of comment and analysis in the words of Zong and the associates who provided the files to him. These two kinds of passages are not distinguished in the text of the Chinese book, but their style is sufficiently different so that a reader fluent in Chinese can tell which is which. We could have separated the two types of passages and translated

---

18. We know of only one book-length biography of Hu Jintao published in China, and according to Zong Hairen this is actually a pirate edition of a foreign work. Its contents are of little value but its illegal publication reflects the interest in Hu's life inside China. See He Zhongshi, *Hu Jintao: Zhongguo kuashiji lingdaoren* (Hu Jintao: China's Cross-Century Leader) (Hohhot: Yuanfang Press, 1998).

the former in quotation marks, but their bureaucratic diction and arcane references would have made them indigestible for all but specialist readers. For general readers, we have opted to rephrase all the material in more accessible English, indicating, where we thought it mattered, whether the source was an official report quoted in *Disidai* or a comment added by Zong and his associates.

In separate sections of each chapter, Zong Hairen made a subselection from the investigation reports' selections of the leaders' recent statements. He concentrated on political and economic reform and China–US, China–Russia, and China–Europe relations. (He says that he has added a small number of statements derived from other sources, including his own and his associates' personal conversations with the leaders involved. These quotations are not distinguished from the others in his book.) With a few exceptions, no sources are given for the excerpts either in the original investigation reports or in *Disidai*, and we accordingly give no sources here. In Chapters 7 and 8, we have rearranged a large amount of material from the leaders' statements, which Zong presents speaker by speaker, into a discussion of specific issues. By summary and selection, we have tried both to show how the new leaders think as a group about each issue and to highlight individual views that we think are noteworthy.

Disidai is written for Chinese readers and assumes much knowledge of Chinese personalities and institutions. To make Zong Hairen's information accessible to non-Chinese readers, we have selected, rearranged, restated, and explained his material. We have added historical and institutional information that is not mentioned in Zong's book, but that reflects the background knowledge that Chinese readers will bring to it. In doing so, we have tried not to impose our own opinions or analyses (except for a few comments in footnotes), but to make Zong's information and views as clear for Western readers as we believe they are for Chinese readers. Certain issues that concern us, such as the widespread and continuing abuses of human rights, do not figure prominently in the dossiers, and for that reason they are not extensively treated here.

Zong's chapters are written from the perspective of elite politics in China, which some readers may find insular and insensitive. Many passages are devoted to how particular leaders get along with other leaders and to the bickering, back-stabbing, and rumor-mongering inside Zhongnanhai. Little attention is given to the leaders' relations with constituencies in society, still less to the hopes, demands, and visions of those not at the center of power. The people of China, when they surface at all, appear as groups of suffering peasants and laid-off workers whose problems need to be solved by policymakers, or as the monolithic and lovable "masses"; they are not seen as citizens with a role in guiding the state or as stakeholders whose views should be respected. Zong's book retains this perspective, both because it is the perspective of the reports and because it is the perspective of Zong himself, and we have remained faithful to that perspective in recasting Zong's material in English.

Much in the book that is intended to be complimentary to the new leaders may be seen by outside readers as objectionable. Thus, Luo Gan is praised for overseeing the killing of more criminals—15,000 a year—than any previous internal security leader. Several top leaders, Hu Jintao and Zeng Qinghong in particular, are quoted at length as expressing insulting views of the democratically elected president of Taiwan, Chen Shui-bian, and the spiritual leader of the Tibetan people, the Dalai Lama. We have retained the original tone of such information as contained in the dossiers.

We have condensed or omitted material on subjects that we think will concern our readers less, such as the family trees and early careers of the candidates. We have transferred some of the material from the biographies into separate chapters on the power struggle that took place before the 16th Party Congress in November 2002 (Chapter 2), on the politics of the Jiang Zemin years from 1989 to the present (Chapter 6), and on domestic and foreign policy issues (Chapters 7 and

8). We have brought Chapter 2 up to date with information supplied by Zong Hairen about events that occurred up to the time this second edition of our book went to press in August 2003.

The issue of authenticity. Disidai is full of surprising details about elite politics in China. It reveals, for example, the patronage relations that brought each member of the new Politburo to the top. It describes how the careers of several officials suffered setbacks when delegates to Party congresses did not elect them to seats on the Central Committee. It discusses successes and failures in local administration by members of the new leadership in their earlier careers, and reveals details of policy proposals offered by rising leaders in high Party councils. The book does not evade such issues so as to leave room for error, a common ploy of ill-informed China-watching. It states a host of concrete facts unambiguously. The inclusion of such specific and important facts, which could have been quickly and easily refuted if wrong, is the first of several reasons why we consider the book to be authentic.

Second, our work with the details of the material gave us confidence. Zong came to Andrew Nathan with the project, and Nathan recruited Bruce Gilley to help write it. Nathan is a scholar of Chinese politics and foreign policy with experience in projects of this kind, having advised the publisher of *The Private Life of Chairman Mao* and written that book's preface, served as co-editor of *The Tiananmen Papers*, and edited the translation of Zong Hairen's *Zhu Rongji in 1999*. Gilley, a doctoral student in politics, covered Chinese politics and society for the Hong Kong–based Dow Jones weekly *Far Eastern Economic Review* from 1995 to 2002 and has published two books on China, including a biography of Jiang Zemin. We, like other China scholars and journalists, followed the process of succession as outside observers while it unfolded.

As we worked with the manuscript and with Zong, we came to believe that Zong's version of Chinese politics was consistent and made sense. We were seldom able to cross-check or corroborate his information, because hardly any reliable independent evidence was available. Some of his information was consistent with that circulated elsewhere, much went beyond it, and some contradicted it. Where his information conflicted with that provided in other sources, we discussed the contradictions with him and satisfied ourselves that his information was accurate. In doing so, we learned a great deal that we did not know before. Based on our previous knowledge as China specialists, the new things we learned made sense both in their details and in their general sense of how Chinese politics works.

A third reason for believing in the authenticity and importance of Zong Hairen's material is that *Disidai* is not Zong's first publication. The first work to appear under his name was an article in the respected Hong Kong newspaper *Xinbao* (Hong Kong Economic Journal), in March 2001,[19] that criticized Luo Gan, the Party security chief, for giving an overly alarmist picture of threats to domestic stability in a secret speech at a national conference of security officials in early 2001. Zong's article revealed a number of previously unknown actions that Luo Gan had taken in connection with the crackdown that was then underway. This was followed by a number of other articles by Zong in the Hong Kong press that also revealed inside information about Party leaders.

In October 2001, Zong published a book that drew on secret speeches and meeting transcripts from the top level of Party leadership. Entitled *Zhu Rongji zai 1999* (Zhu Rongji in 1999), this work described conflicts between Premier Zhu and Party chief Jiang Zemin which had taken place during 1999 over such events as China's bid to enter the World Trade Organization, the crisis following the American bombing of the Chinese embassy in Belgrade, and the eruption of the Falungong religious movement into Chinese political life. China

---

19. "Luo Gan jianghua suowei helai?" (Why Is Luo Gan Speaking and Acting as He Is?), *Xinbao*, March 6, 2001, p. 9.

specialists generally regard this book as reliable. Zong Hairen's publication record thus lends credence to the authenticity of this latest work.

Fourth, we have been able to learn a good deal about Zong Hairen and to satisfy ourselves that he was in a position to receive the material from the draft investigation reports, to add informed views in rewriting the material, and to answer our questions. Unfortunately, in order to protect Zong's security we cannot give the details of his background and personal conduct that have led us to conclude that he is trustworthy.

Fifth, the response to Zong Hairen's *Disidai* and to the first edition of this book have strengthened our confidence in the materials. Officials in Beijing never commented on either book, although according to Zong they did launch an investigation into the disclosure of the materials and briefly detained one man wrongly suspected of involvement.[20] We are aware of two critical reviews of *Disidai* in the Chinese-language press. One asserts that the materials are authentic but questions the motives behind them.[21] The other questions the work's authenticity, but in ways that we do not find convincing.[22] Among English-language publications, one detailed critique of the first edition of *China's New Rulers* was forthcoming when this edition went to press. We responded in the same journal in which it appeared.[23]

---

20. Zong Hairen, "Cha loumi caomu jiebing, wei biyao fanyun fuyu" (Mobilizing All Forces to Investigate the Leak of Secrets down to the Grassroots, Overturning the Wind and Rain to Prevent Rumors), *Xinbao*, November 7, 2002, p. 10.

21. Zhang Weiguo, "Xiaoma da bangmangde 'Disidai' he zixu wuyoude disidai" (The Book "The Fourth Generation" that Praises with Faint Blame and the Modest Fourth Generation), online at www.ncn.org, accessed December 13, 2002.

22. Chen Hongzheng, "Zhe shi shenme jimi wenjian" (What Kind of Secret Documents Are These?), *Xinbao*, March 15, 2003, p. 25.

23. Alfred L. Chan, "China's Fourth Generation: The New Rulers and the Secret Files" and Andrew J. Nathan and Bruce Gilley, "Response," *The China Journal*, No. 50 (July 2003), pp. 107–119, 121–125.

Without recapitulating the arguments, this process of critical reception and review has made us more confident in the materials themselves as well as in the decisions we made about how to present them to the English-language readership.

We have set aside other pressing projects to bring his information before the English-reading public because we think that what Zong has to say is important. We hope that a better understanding of China's new leaders will help the world deal more successfully with this rising great power at a time of transition.

The motives of those who provided the material to Zong Hairen are unclear to us. They may be essentially the same as ours—to provide more accurate information about China's new leaders to the outside world so as to prevent miscalculations. Perhaps elements of the new leadership think that they deserve better images than they already have, either individually or as a group. Perhaps they want to make the point that they are more self-assured and united than the world usually believes, and that the West has to be prepared to deal with them. Perhaps they think that the Chinese information apparatus is too cautious and tradition-bound, or too discredited, to serve as a credible conduit for such views.

Alternatively, the leaking of this material might be part of a factional struggle that started even before the new leadership took power, with some leaders seeking to damage the images of others. Though the underlying materials are favorable in tone, they demonstrate weaknesses in the records of some of the new leaders. As supplemented and interpreted by Zong Hairen and his colleagues, they also reveal Machiavellian maneuvers that some of the new leaders engaged in during their ascent to the top.

Such uncertainty about motives raises the question of whether some of the material released to Zong was tampered with before he got it, or whether Zong, in recasting it, introduced distortions of his own. We do not think so, however, for two reasons. First, damaged versions of the truth would be detected by readers and critics, discrediting the project. Second, we relied on Zong Hairen's insider knowledge, our own knowledge of recent Chinese history and politics, and our previous work with inner-Party materials to detect signs of falsification, and we did not find any.

This is not to say that Zong Hairen does not have a point of view. So, for that matter, as already noted, do the investigation reports that he worked from. Both Zong and the authors of the reports write from within the traditions of the Party elite, valuing certain sorts of skills and scorning certain sorts of weaknesses. Zong expresses complex attitudes toward the Fourth Generation. In his author's preface, he describes them as more cautious, more colorless, and as commanding less authority than previous cohorts of leaders, although he finds them more open-minded, reformist, and democratic. His biographies describe the new leaders as having impressive qualities: he sees them as dedicated, hard-working, qualified, and competent, although some more so than others. The only members of China's top circles to whom Zong is clearly hostile are Jiang Zemin and Li Peng, both of whom were targets of his previous book, and about Jiang at least he also has some good things to say. Zong's generally dispassionate tone adds, we think, to the book's value, establishing a position from which he can give honest analyses of the flaws and assets of the Fourth Generation.

To say that the materials are authentic, and that they have been transmitted without tampering and then fairly summarized, is not to say that they are without error or bias. Our underlying sources—to repeat—are long portions of drafts of Party investigation reports on candidates for the Politburo. In compiling its reports the Organization Department did not take up many questions that Westerners might have posed. There may have been facts about the new leaders that the investigators never discovered, and facts that they discovered and decided not to write about. The documents may contain errors.

Their final versions may differ in some respects from the drafts. Whatever the omissions, silences, and blind spots, we do not think that they compromise the value of Zong's materials.

Zong's manuscript was completed in February 2002. By that time, most of the major issues relating to the succession had been decided. It was, however, still not clear whether the senior reformist leader Li Ruihan would have a seat on the new Politburo Standing Committee and whether Jiang Zemin would yield the post of Central Military Commission chair. Several lesser issues were also still open: among them, whether a Fifth Generation member would have a seat on the PBSC and whether the new PBSC would have the same number of members as the old one, or more. Based on information provided by Zong, in Chapter 2 we describe how these issues were resolved, some in the final weeks leading up to the Party congress and one, the question of Jiang's role, in the period between the Party congress and the March NPC meeting.

APPENDIX

ZONG HAIREN'S NEWSPAPER ARTICLES USED AS ADDITIONAL SOURCES FOR THIS EDITION

All were published in the *Xinbao* (Hong Kong Economic Journal) except for those identified as RFA, which were broadcast in Chinese on Radio Free Asia. For serialized articles, the title is that of the first in the series. The list does not include serializations of *Disidai* published in *Xinbao*.

"*Cha loumi caomu jiebing, wei biyao fanyun fuyu*" (Mobilizing All Forces to Investigate the Leak of Secrets down to the Grassroots, Overturning the Wind and Rain to Prevent Rumors), November 7, 2002.

"*Li Ruihuan tuixiu neiqing*" (Inside Story of Li Ruihuan's Retirement), December 17, 18, 19, 20, 2002.

"*Aimei de quanli jiaojie*" (Ambiguous Power Transfer), January 13, 14, 15, 2003.

"*Xianghu liyong er you huxiang qingya de zhengzhi fenzang*" (A Conniving Yet Contentious Division of Political Spoils), January 20, 2003.

"*Huiqi de Tianjin*" (Unlucky Tianjin), January 21, 2003.

"*Chenlun de Hainan*" (Sinking Hainan), January 22, 23, 2003.

"*Mamu de Hebei*" (Numb Hebei), January 24, 2003.

"*Chenxin de Jiangsu*" (Satisfied Jiangsu), January 25, 2003.

"*Shiluo de Fujian*" (Disappointed Fujian), January 27, 2003.

"*Shengqi de Zhejiang*" (Rising Zhejiang), January 28, 2003.

"*Guishun de Henan*" (Allegiant Henan), January 29, 2003.

"*Tongtian de Sichuan*" (Sichuan with a Channel to the Top), January 30, 2003.

"*Li Ruihuan de zhengzhi jiaodai*" (Li Ruihuan's Political Valedictory), March 3, 2003.

"*Zhu Rongji tandang miandui tuixiu*" (Zhu Rongji Easily Faces Retirement), March 4, 2003.

"*Tuixiu zhi ji hua Li Peng*" (Talking about Li Peng at the Moment of Retirement), March 5, 2003.

"*Jia Qinglin yu shijie quanguo zhengxie*" (Jia Qinglin and the 10th CPPCC), RFA, March 15, 16, 2003.

"*Wen Jiabao yu xinyijie guowuyuan*" (Wen Jiabao and the New State Council), RFA, March 17, 18, 2003.

"*Wu Bangguo yu xinyijie quanguo renda*" (Wu Bangguo and the New NPC), RFA, March 19, 20, 2003.

"*Jiang Zemin yu xin yijie zhongyang junwei*" (Jiang Zemin and the New Central Military Commission), RFA, March 22, 23, 2003.

2

A RESTRAINED STRUGGLE FOR POWER

THE ELECTION OF a new Politburo Standing Committee at the end
of the 16th Party Congress marked the conclusion of a long, complex
battle for positions at the top of the Chinese Communist Party, which
has ruled the world's most populous country for more than half a century. Yet compared to earlier succession struggles in the turbulent history of the Party, this one was markedly restrained. Despite the
surprises that marked it at the end, it was the most orderly succession
in CCP history.

As in the past, factions and personal loyalties shaped the process.
But conflict was muted by a consensus in the upper ranks that the
Party could not survive another battle as destructive as the clashes
over ideology that took place during the Mao years, or the purges
that characterized struggles among the elite during the Deng years.
The conflict over succession was also constrained by a balance of
power among the factions. For all his apparent dominance and self-
promotion, Jiang Zemin was relatively weak compared to his predecessors Mao and Deng. Both of these men named their own successors
(several times, in fact). Jiang could not by himself assure the appointment of any single member of the Politburo.

The new power-holders are all the beneficiaries of a process of
meritocratic winnowing started in 1980 by Deng Xiaoping. This was

the "Four Transformations" program, which aimed to produce Communist leaders who, as Deng put it, were "more revolutionary, younger, more knowledgeable, and more specialized." In response to Deng's call, in the early 1980s senior officials around the country searched for people about forty years old who had college educations, technical backgrounds, Party membership, and good administrative skills. In the arid northwestern province of Gansu, for example, local Party secretary Song Ping found the young Hu Jintao working on the staff of the provincial construction commission and promoted him several ranks to the position of deputy head of the commission. Such quick promotions were then, and still are, rare among China's bureaucrats, who are obsessed with seniority. The same kind of accelerated selection advanced the career of Huang Ju, who was made a deputy manager of a large state-owned petrochemicals equipment factory in Shanghai. Among others who benefited from such advancement were Wen Jiabao, Wu Bangguo, Luo Gan, and Wu Guanzheng, all chosen as Standing Committee members in 2002.

In 1982 the Organization Department arranged for the election of the most outstanding members of this group of young cadres as alternate members of the 12th Central Committee, and in 1983 it put their names on a list of officials considered qualified for future appointments to high-level posts in the Party and government. Many on this list have since risen to key positions. Thus the pool of candidates for today's Politburo Standing Committee already existed twenty years ago. Top leaders had to create their personal networks by drawing on names from this list if they were to have any hope of promoting their followers to higher offices.

Over a period of about two years leading up to the 16th Party Congress, in November 2002, most decisions on the succession were gradually made by consensus. Once decisions were reached, they were hard to change. By the middle of 2002, much of the succession was settled. Five of the nine members of the new PBSC, including the most powerful ones, were agreed on. The final lineup was settled in the two months before the November 8 opening of the congress.

Although the possibility of a last-minute rupture loomed right up until the announcement of the new PBSC on the morning of November 15, the weight of pressure for a smooth succession proved strong. Only the surprise retirement of liberal Li Ruihuan (and its repercussions on other appointments) in November and the decision by Jiang Zemin to hold on to the military commission chairmanship in March 2003 disrupted the consensus arrived at during the previous summer. In other respects, in particular the promotion of Hu Jintao to be the new top leader in place of Jiang and the elevation of Wen Jiabao to premier, the consensus stood. At the Party congress of November 2002 and then at the March 2003 National People's Congress, the transfer of power took place largely as planned.

The fact that Deng's decades-old plan to elevate able young cadres unfolded as intended is testimony to how far the Chinese Communist Party has come since the chaotic days of Mao. A revolutionary party now acts more like a governing party, with agreed-upon norms of process and promotion. Those norms are new and thus somewhat fragile. But they worked in 2002 and 2003. That transformation may help explain why the CCP remains in power more than a decade after Communist regimes collapsed in Eastern Europe and the USSR.[1]

While the emergence of the new cohort can be explained as the working out of Deng's "Four Transformations" policy, this does not explain the fate of specific individuals. Some lost power after the Tiananmen events because they supported the protests. Others found the competition for the handful of top posts too intense. Those who made it to the top required more than just ability: luck and connections

1. For an elaboration of this argument, see Andrew J. Nathan, "China's Changing of the Guard: Authoritarian Resilience," *Journal of Democracy*, Vol. 14, No. 1 (January 2003), pp. 6–17.

with patrons were no less important. The Fourth Generation, then, exemplifies all that is new, and all that is not, in the politics of modern-day China.

Hu Jintao's selection. The emergence of the unassuming Hu Jintao as paramount leader was a result of both formal institutional planning and informal factors like patronage and politicking. A hydropower engineer, Hu was initially selected for special promotion by Gansu's First Party Secretary Song Ping, an old economic planner of conservative views. In response to Deng's call to promote talented young cadres, Song looked over the ranks of the mid-level officials in his province around the age of forty and in 1980 decided to elevate Hu Jintao above more senior cadres to the post of deputy head of the province's construction commission. Soon, Hu was made secretary of the provincial branch of the Communist Youth League. At Song Ping's suggestion, the central Party authorities then invited him to Beijing to study in a class for promising young cadres at the Central Party School.

From there, Hu was transferred to the Communist Youth League in Beijing and then to assignments as Party secretary of two of China's poorest provinces, Guizhou and Tibet (see Chapter 3). He achieved no outstanding record of accomplishment in either place. His service in Tibet was marred by the declaration of martial law in Lhasa in March 1989, the first time that this had ever been done in the People's Republic. This set a precedent for the same declaration in Beijing two months later.

Yet in 1992, when Deng Xiaoping wanted to promote someone under fifty to the PBSC as a way of showing that China's succession process was capable of long-term stability, he chose the forty-nine-year-old Hu. This surge to prominence was attributable to the intervention of Song Ping, who by then was serving on the PBSC and as head of the Organization Department, which has responsibility for reviewing the records and qualifications of China's high-level officials. Song was one of four men charged with putting together the list of candidates to be elected to the new Party leadership at the 14th Party Congress, scheduled to meet in October 1992. Their recommendations went to Deng and other top leaders for final decision.

Hu Jintao's name was one of four that Song and his associates considered to become the representative of the younger generation on the PBSC. The others were Wu Bangguo, Wen Jiabao, and Li Changchun —all members of the Politburo Standing Committee chosen in 2002. Wu and Wen were eliminated when the top leaders decided that the candidate had to be under fifty at the time of the Party congress.[2]

Song was able to make the case for Hu over Li because of a minor dispute concerning the transfer of another provincial official. One of many planned changes was the reassignment of the governor of the huge province of Sichuan, a man named Zhang Haoruo, to a position in Beijing where his rank would be lower than that of a colleague who had been governor of a smaller province. Zhang regarded this as an insult and refused the assignment. The four Party officials, including Song, who were busy putting together a long list of candidates for many posts were furious at such insubordination, all the more so because it came soon after the Tiananmen crisis, when many mid-level Party officials had disobeyed the leaders by supporting the pro-democracy demonstrators. This was, moreover, only a few months after a bruising battle within the Party over military appointments that had raised questions about the loyalty to Deng Xiaoping of some of his most trusted supporters (see Chapter 6).

---

2. Hu Jintao was three months shy of fifty at the time of the congress. Discussion of his age led to an amusing incident at the press conference to introduce the new PBSC. When General Secretary Jiang Zemin introduced Hu by saying, "This young person is only forty-nine," the interpreter translated "young person" (*nianqingren*) as "young woman." Agence France-Presse reported tongue in cheek, "China nearly elected its first-ever woman to the top ranks of the CCP leadership." AFP, October 19, 1992.

In this atmosphere, Song emphasized Hu Jintao's record of never refusing an assignment from the Party and his willingness to serve in China's poorest and harshest regions. The others agreed to recommend Hu, hoping to send a message to the Party ranks about the supreme importance of loyalty.

Hu's elevation to the PBSC ahead of his contemporaries made him the presumptive successor to Jiang Zemin.[3] By annulling the traditional right of the incumbent, Jiang Zemin, to make and unmake his own successor, Deng Xiaoping laid the basis for a new norm of stability in arrangements for succession. This standard of conduct survived the next decade of inner-Party politics and limited Jiang's options even after Deng died and Jiang built up greater personal power.

In the five years from 1992 to 1997, Hu was not granted much real power, but he did survive as heir apparent. He offended no one, showed respect for Jiang, and made no signs of grabbing for power prematurely. After his reelection to the PBSC in 1997, his status as successor became more conspicuous, even though he was never officially referred to as such. Pressured by a Party elite determined to see the succession come off smoothly, Jiang appointed Hu vice-president in 1998 and vice-chairman of the Central Military Commission in 1999.

When arrangements for the 2002 succession began to be seriously discussed in 2000, Hu had the air of an inevitable candidate. Nothing happened subsequently to change his position as the top-ranking member of the Fourth Generation. It would have required a purposeful initiative by someone with great influence to displace Hu as Jiang's successor. Although many inside China and out doubted that Hu could

---

3. The following year, the pro-Beijing press in Hong Kong quoted Party elder Wan Li as saying that the selection of a "Fourth Generation leadership" was now underway in line with the expressed wishes of Deng, the first known reference to the Fourth Generation. However, Hu has never been officially designated as the core of the Fourth Generation. See Bruce Gilley, *Tiger on the Brink: Jiang Zemin and China's New Elite* (University of California Press, 1998), p. 373, n. 60.

keep a grip on the successor's position for ten years, or that the CCP could break with its historic tradition of power struggles, Hu played the successor's part to perfection. Even during the last-minute battle over Li Ruihuan and its aftermath, he remained studiously on the sidelines, confident that whatever else happened, his promised mantle was beyond the reach of factional battles. In November 2002, Hu was elected Party general secretary, and in March 2003, he took over as state president.

The protégés. In addition to Hu Jintao, four other members of the new PBSC were agreed upon well in advance of the Party congress. The four men—Wen Jiabao, Wu Bangguo, Luo Gan, and Zeng Qing-hong—are, along with Hu, the most powerful members of the new PBSC. They were qualified for high office by their achievements and experience, of course. However, factional considerations also played a part in each case. They could only have been displaced by a power-ful initiative backed by irrefutable evidence of their unfitness for office. Their promotions were the result of a subtle and intricate pro-cess in which antipathies and rivalries were played out over several years in a grand chess game of elite maneuvers.

Wen Jiabao's position as a PBSC member and future premier was consolidated as early as 2000. A former geologist, Wen was Zhao Ziyang's right-hand assistant during the Tiananmen protests of 1989; after Zhao was purged, he managed the feat of remaining in office by making a convincing self-criticism and then becoming an expert on economic issues, the new route to prominence in Chinese politics.

Wen's career faced its biggest obstacle in 1993, when his promo-tion to a vice-premiership was blocked by Premier Li Peng. He had the good fortune, however, to spend the next two years assisting then Vice Premier Zhu Rongji in managing China's agricultural sector. In that period he won Zhu's praise and trust. When the tough, reformist Zhu became premier in 1998, Wen was elevated to vice-premier and handed the heaviest assignments.

Wen's cabinet portfolio included rural affairs, poverty relief, flood control, reforestation, development planning, and financial affairs. These were jobs in which one could make a mark, as well as learn about issues that would be important in the PBSC term starting in 2002. By contrast, Zhu assigned Jiang Zemin's and Li Peng's favorite for the future premiership, Wu Bangguo, who was senior to Wen, a set of portfolios dealing with the failing state sector—a part of the economy in which even a brilliant administrator would have trouble distinguishing himself, and in which experience has been less and less relevant to China's economic future.[4]

Zhu promised in 1998 to serve only one term as premier, an early indication of his intention to abide by the age limit of seventy on Politburo members, since the premier is normally a member of the Politburo. In the autumn of 2000, Zhu told a Politburo meeting that Wen was the most capable person to succeed him. No one was in a position to challenge this assessment. Neither Jiang nor Li Peng, despite efforts, could find any reason to argue that Wen was unfit for the post. Their own favorite, Wu Bangguo, had been sidelined by Zhu, while another of their candidates, Guangdong Party Secretary Li Changchun, had been tarnished by corruption scandals and other issues that caused friction between him and Zhu (see Chapter 4). As a result, Wu was given a consolation prize of promised inclusion in the new PBSC, and eventually emerged as chair of the NPC.

Luo Gan's selection for the PBSC was virtually inevitable as early as 1998. The oldest member of the new PBSC at age sixty-seven, Luo studied steel processing in the former East Germany before beginning his climb up the Party hierarchy. Luo was the key aide to Li Peng during the 1989 Tiananmen crisis. Li wanted to leave Luo in control of the country's security apparatus after his retirement, to maintain his

---

4. For work assignments at the first meeting of Zhu's State Council, see Zong, *Zhu Rongji zai 1999*, pp. 178–180.

legacy of legal repression and prevent any reconsideration of the Tiananmen events.

To achieve this, Li Peng moved step by step. In 1993, he obtained Luo's appointment to the position of deputy secretary of the Central Politics and Law Commission (CPLC), the nerve center of the Party's internal and foreign security operations. Since 1987, the CPLC had been under the stewardship of the relatively liberal PBSC member Qiao Shi, whose protégé Ren Jianxin replaced Qiao as its secretary in 1992. Jiang engineered Qiao's retirement at the 15th Party Congress in 1997 on the grounds that he was over the age of seventy but in fact because Jiang saw him as a threat to his position (see Chapter 6). Li Peng then had the opening to recommend Luo for the CPLC secretary-ship to replace Ren.

The sole challenge to Luo's ascent appeared at this time. Uneasy at the accumulation of police power in the hands of a follower of Li Peng, Jiang Zemin proposed that Luo become foreign minister, making flattering references to his "foreign experience" (in the former East Germany) and "unwavering principles." This appointment would have required Luo to leave the Central Politics and Law Commission. But the proposal was opposed by Li Peng and by outgoing foreign minister Qian Qichen. Qian may have seen that it would be a disaster for China's diplomacy to be put in the hands of someone so closely linked to the Tiananmen repression. Luo was confirmed as CPLC secretary in 1998.

Since he was already the government cabinet member in charge of these same agencies (see Chapter 4), Luo's control over the security sector through both state and Party channels was now rendered complete, even though for the time being he still worked under the nominal supervision of PBSC member Wei Jianxing, who had taken over from Qiao Shi as the Party's top official responsible for security affairs. With Wei's retirement at the 16th Congress, Luo had no competitor for successor to the PBSC seat concerned with security. Jiang tried at the last minute to offer Luo the position of head of the Chinese People's Political Consultative Conference, but the gambit failed as it was rejected out of hand by Li Peng. If there was one realm that Li Peng was determined to see in safe hands after his retirement it was internal security.

In using both Party and state offices to climb his way up, Luo had become an inevitable choice. In the new leadership, Luo remains CPLC secretary and is the point man on domestic security and international intelligence issues. Given his age, Luo will serve only one term on the PBSC, a fact reflected in his formal bottom ranking on the new body. But his real power far exceeds his protocol rank.

Zeng Qinghong's rise appeared more sudden, but actually was as smooth as those of Wen, Wu, and Luo. Zeng is the son of an early CCP leader and hence has many connections among the Party elite and their privileged children, known as the "princelings." He was the only official Jiang Zemin brought with him to Beijing from Shanghai in 1989. A skillful political tactician, Zeng was the mastermind behind Jiang's brilliantly managed consolidation of power (see Chapter 6).

During the 1990s Zeng served as head of the Party Central Office, and developed wide support in the political elite because of his competence and personal connections. The Organization Department's annual reports on his image were always favorable. By 1997, it was easy for Jiang to make him an alternate member of the Politburo. That was the minimal ranking Zeng needed to take over the powerful Organization Department in 1999 when the incumbent director retired.

Rumors that Jiang tried and failed to promote Zeng faster are untrue. As recounted in Chapter 3, his failure to rise more quickly reflects his preference for quiet power over formal position. In late 2000, as arrangements for the 16th Party Congress began to be seriously discussed, Zeng's name was promptly considered, and support for his promotion grew stronger with time. His appointment to the new PBSC was a virtual certainty by late 2001. Although Jiang Zemin was not able to name his own successor, he was at least able to name his favorite to the PBSC. Zeng became the new senior member of the Party Secretariat, in charge of managing the day-to-day administrative affairs of the PBSC. He also gained formal control over Party personnel and organizational affairs, although he had enjoyed de facto control over these areas since 1993. In December 2002, Zeng replaced Hu Jintao as president of the Central Party School, a training academy for new cadres. In March 2003 he was elected state vice-president, a largely titular position that nonetheless indicates his growing importance in foreign affairs.

The apparent ease of these four appointments in the final phase of the selection process should not obscure the battles that lay behind them. As in a game of chess, the real battles for the future of each man took place long before the 2002 congress, when each was put in a position that would make his future promotion inevitable. To oppose their final ascension as detailed planning began for the 2002 congress would have been too late, unless there were striking new considerations, such as involvement in a corruption scandal.

Zeng Qinghong is the only one of the four who never faced a substantial fight for his future. The reason is obvious: he never gave anyone an opportunity to block his rise by seeking contested offices. He took over the Party Central Office, a post normally reserved for an ally of the general secretary, only in 1993, four years after Jiang's accession. At the 15th Party Congress in 1997 he became a mere alternate member of the Politburo, even though he had by then eliminated any significant opposition to Jiang's authority. He waited a further year and a half before taking over the Organization Department when the incumbent reached retirement age. If Zeng has been a master in the consolidation of Jiang Zemin's power, he has been no less skillful in arranging his own career.

Thus, by the early summer of 2002, the choice of five of the nine members of the new PBSC—Hu, Wen, Wu, Luo, and Zeng—was already settled. In June 2002 Wen and Zeng appeared alongside Hu at a Party meeting on rural ideology—an event seen as a "return to the heartland" in the tradition of CCP politics—without any of the outgoing leaders in attendance.[5] This was as clear a sign of consensus on their appointments as puffs of white smoke from the Vatican.

The Fifth Generation and Li Changchun. Although the 16th Party Congress was to mark the ascension of the Fourth Generation under Hu Jintao, its preparation was also an occasion for the leadership to begin thinking about the Fifth Generation that would follow.

In late 2001 and early 2002 most senior leaders thought that one official should be promoted to the new Politburo to represent the future leaders. As in 1992 when Hu Jintao was selected, this person should be under fifty and should be chosen from cadres working as ministerial-level officials, provincial governors, or Party secretaries. By designating a Fifth Generation leader, or a slate of potential leaders, the CCP leadership hoped once again to reduce the instability caused by succession politics. The chosen heir would be under sixty when he took over in 2012 and still below the informal retirement age of seventy when he finished two terms in 2022. However, by mid-2002, two aspects of this decision remained unresolved: who the person would be and whether rapid promotion to the Politburo or PBSC was advisable.

In selecting candidates, the Organization Department under Zeng Qinghong put emphasis on men who were both loyal to the Party and effective administrators. The strongest candidates were a princeling and a commoner—Fujian governor Xi Jinping, age forty-nine, the son of a revered Party elder, and Henan governor Li Keqiang, age forty-seven, a product of the fading Communist Youth League system. A

---

5. They spoke at a meeting held in the lake city of Hangzhou to hail the impact of Jiang's Three Represents campaign (see pp. 84, 193–194) on rural areas; *Xinhua*, June 24, 2002.

second princeling—Bo Xilai, the fifty-three-year-old governor of Liaoning province—came in for discussion even though he was over the age of fifty, because in the long run he was still a rival of the two younger men.

Despite his aristocratic background and marriage to a beautiful singer, Xi Jinping has an easy, businesslike style that makes him popular with ordinary people. He was the leading candidate to head the Fifth Generation as early as the 15th Party Congress in 1997.[6] At the leadership's behest, Xi was appointed as an extra alternate member of the 1997 Central Committee after he failed to secure enough votes from congress delegates to win one of the 150 regular alternate seats (see Chapter 5). Xi subsequently remained under intense scrutiny from Beijing. Every one of his speeches, policy decisions, and interviews was sent to the capital for inspection. The evaluations were invariably positive.

An obstacle to Xi's candidacy was the political record of his father, Xi Zhongxun, who died in May 2002, after having been purged no fewer than three times by the CCP since the 1930s. Many surviving elders, especially the hard-liners Bo Yibo and Song Ping, had strong differences with the elder Xi and had approved his being sidelined in 1987. That made them fear retribution if Xi Jinping gained higher office. Song Ping was a promoter of Party orthodoxy of the type

---

6. Xi Jinping's candidacy to be the leader of the Fifth Generation may have been known as early as 2000. See "Xi Jinping: Zai xiwangde tianyeshang chicheng" (Xi Jinping: Galloping on the Field of Hope) in *Zhonggong disidai lingdao jiti da jiemi* (Revealing the Secrets of the CCP's Fourth Generation Collective Leadership), edited by Lin Hua (Beijing: Dadongfang Press, 2000), pp. 94–96. In the months prior to the congress, his name was mentioned in some overseas media reports as a possible successor. For example, Yi Ming, "Zhonggong diwudai yinran chengxing" (The CCP's Fifth Generation Takes Shape), *Qianshao* (Frontline Magazine, Hong Kong), May 2002, pp. 8–9. When a Reuters correspondent asked him about his chances for promotion during a news conference in Fuzhou on July 1, 2002, "he came close to choking. His eyes went wide, he flushed, he nearly spilt his drink." He then replied: "Are you trying to give me a fright?" Reuters, July 3, 2002.

supported more strongly by Li Keqiang than by Xi Jinping. Bo Yibo had an additional personal reason to be cool toward Xi Jinping—the hope that his own son, Bo Xilai, would eventually rise to the top. Since Bo Xilai was too old to be designated as the Fifth Generation successor, the Bo family's interests could best be served by seeing that the less formidable Li Keqiang rather than Xi was chosen, if anyone was. Bo had reason to expect some deference from Jiang Zemin, whose consolidation of power he had helped secure in the 1990s (see Chapter 6). Yet neither Bo Yibo nor Song Ping retained much influence by the time of the preparations for the 2002 congress.

Jiang Zemin liked both Xi Jinping and Bo Xilai but he could count on the allegiance only of Bo. Since 1997, Xi had been conspicuously unwilling to join the Jiang faction, as indicated by his lukewarm response to Jiang's "Three Stresses" (*sanjiang*) campaign (to stress study, politics, and healthy trends). Bo, by contrast, had cultivated Jiang ever since he helped him to purge liberal PBSC member Qiao Shi in 1997. Bo was the first local leader to erect a massive billboard displaying a picture of Jiang, which he did in 1997 in the center of the city of Dalian. But those actions only strengthened the reluctance of other PBSC members to support Bo.

Bo had a few other problems. He has been criticized for an unseemly eagerness to get media attention and for his wife's trading on his family's name to advance her career as a lawyer. He failed to win election as a delegate to the 15th Party Congress in 1997 from fellow Party members in Dalian, where he was mayor. Because of this earlier setback, elevation to the 2002 Politburo would have required unconventionally bypassing three intermediate steps.[7]

The real alternative to Xi Jinping for appointment as the Fifth

---

7. The promotion from non–Central Committee member to alternate member would count as one step, to full Central Committee member as a second step; to alternate member of the Politburo as a third step; and to full member of the Politburo as a fourth step.

Generation core leader was Li Keqiang.[8] Li had the advantage of being a close protégé of Hu Jintao, having served under Hu in the Communist Youth League system in the mid-1980s. Like Xi, he had no open detractors. His legal background made him attractive to some who believed that younger leaders should be professionals rather than ideologues or engineers. Li enjoyed the support of Song Ping, who had given his approval to a Maoist-style campaign to bring cadres to the villages that Li ran in Henan in 2001. As a potential core member of the Fifth Generation since 1997, Li, like Xi, worked under the close scrutiny of Beijing. Future Fourth Generation leaders Wen Jiabao, Luo Gan, and Zeng Qinghong all made visits to Henan during Li's tenure.

But Li had some burdens that Xi Jinping did not. His years as governor of Henan were marred by industrial disasters, economic scandals, and an AIDS crisis (see Chapter 5). Some leaders feared that if Hu Jintao's protégé and heir apparent was seen as a weak leader, it would weaken the authority of Hu himself and the stability of the new ruling group.

Alone among the senior leaders, Jiang had all along opposed the idea of promoting a Fifth Generation cadre. None of the candidates had enough experience in the provinces, he argued, and the Party should not commit itself so far in advance to the details of the 2012 succession. However, he had not pressed his views strongly. In mid-2002 he reopened the issue. At the time, Li Ruihuan was still slated to remain on the PBSC and five other members were already chosen. That meant there was only one seat left on the body if it was to remain at seven members. Jiang wanted the last slot for Li Changchun, his

---

8. Some outside reports said that Li was the leading candidate for Fifth Generation core. See for example Wu Jiaxiang, *Jiaoli shiliuda* (Fighting for the 16th Congress) (Mirror Books, 2002), p. 201; also Tian Ping; "Diwu dai hexin zhengduo zhan jiekai xumu" (The Prologue to the Struggle to be Fifth Generation Core), *Qianshao* (Frontline Magazine, Hong Kong), October 2002, pp. 12–14.

failed candidate for premier.[9] Short of creating additional PBSC seats, the only way to ensure that was to delay the promotion of a Fifth Generation cadre to the PBSC.

At a Politburo meeting on October 10, Jiang argued that the Fifth Generation candidates should not even join that body. He may have been motivated partly by the desire to discredit what he attacked as "political rumors"—presumably a reference to Zong Hairen's book *Disidai*, which had been serialized in early October in the Hong Kong newspaper *Xinbao*. Its discussion of the issue of the Fifth Generation succession had become widely known among higher-level officials in China. The Politburo sided with Jiang. It was agreed that the Fifth Generation leaders should remain in the provinces and that Li Changchun should join the PBSC.

Contrary to the normal rule of not revealing appointments until after the Party congress, Xi Jinping's transfer from Fujian to the adjoining coastal province of Zhejiang was announced by the official Xinhua News Agency on October 12.[10] Li Keqiang stayed in Henan, rising to Party chief, while Bo Xilai remained as governor of Liaoning. All three remain top contenders for future promotions.

The purge of Li Ruihuan.[11] In contrast to the comparative smoothness of the accession of Hu, the four protégés, and Li Changchun, the remaining arrangements did not fall into place so easily. The two

---

9. For an outside report of this fact, see Lu Fei, "Li Changchun zhengzhi hangqing jixu kanzhang" (Li Changchun's Political Prospects Continue to Look Good) in *Shiliuda qiaweizhan* (The Struggle for Positions at the 16th Party Congress), edited by Xiao Chong (Hong Kong: Xiafeier Press, 2002), pp. 216–221.

10. He was made acting governor there until after the congress, when the new Central Committee appointed him provincial Party chief.

11. This and the next two sections draw on Zhang Liang, "Lun Jiang Zemin de liuren" (On Jiang Zemin's Continuation in Office), *Xinbao*, March 18, 19, 20, 2003.

major unresolved issues were the complete retirement of Jiang Zemin and the fate of Jiang's liberal rival Li Ruihuan.

Jiang's retirement was connected to the issue of Li's future. The two engaged in a long dance of shadows as the congress approached, knowing that their respective fates would have profound implications. Whether they both stayed or both retired or one stayed and the other retired would materially affect the new leadership and the course it would take. The pair circled each other like skilled fighters until the issue came to a climax in mid-October, three weeks before the Party congress opened.

A former carpenter and mayor of the northern port city of Tianjin, Li was sixty-eight at the time of the congress. He was in good health, full of energy, and widely liked. Those who charged that he spoke too freely were countered by others who said that his blunt style was the basis of his popularity and a crucial quality for good policymaking. The preliminary arrangements called for him to stay in the PBSC and to move from the chairmanship of the Chinese People's Political Consultative Conference to the chairmanship of the more important National People's Congress.

Under Li, the NPC could have become a powerful platform for political change. This would have been the case especially with Jiang out of the way. Li's influence in the new leadership would have been greater than that of Jiang's favorites, Zeng Qinghong, Jia Qinglin, and Huang Ju. He would potentially have been in a position to reverse Jiang's conservative political course and to undermine his historical image.

There had been a history of personal animosity between the two men since 1989, when Jiang was brought in as general secretary over Li's head. Once Li became CPPCC chairman in 1993, he used his speeches to that advisory body to criticize Jiang's showy and egotistical style of leadership, although not by name (see Chapters 5 and 6). Alluding to Jiang's propensity to formulate grand theories, he remarked that "the more some people talk, the less substance there seems to be." On another

occasion he noted, "Since history will judge us, we should avoid personal interest-seeking, petty angers, and useless faultfinding and praise."
Jiang was determined that if he was to retire, Li should go too. In 2001 and early 2002, some in Jiang's camp, in particular the ever-loyal Huang Ju and Wang Huning (a former professor and Jiang adviser), suggested the importance of "a complete succession" (*chedi jieban* or *quanmian jieban*), meaning that everyone from the Third Generation should retire to create a clean slate for the Fourth Generation. This implied that Li, who like Jiang had served two and a half terms on the PBSC, should move on.

Relations between Jiang and Li, already cold, worsened during 2002. Their staffs arranged their out-of-town trips in such a way that they almost never had to attend the same PBSC meeting. Jiang sent the Beijing rumor mills into action in the first half of 2002 in an attempt to discredit Li's reputation. The rumors claimed that Li was a dissolute womanizer and that his brother and former subordinates in Tianjin had done business deals by trading on their mentor's name.[12]

---

12. Briefly, the rumors claimed that Li Ruihuan protected former Beijing Executive Vice Mayor Zhang Baifa, allowing him to escape from the wide-ranging purge on corruption charges of the Beijing municipal leadership in 1995–1996; protected former Executive Vice Minister of Culture Gao Zhanxiang from charges of corruption and womanizing; had an illicit affair with an unnamed Beijing Opera star; carried on a dissolute lifestyle like that of his mentor, liberal party elder Wan Li; protected the rich businesswoman Chen Lihua, who had embezzled state assets; protected actress Liu Xiaoqing, who as a result evaded taxes; and protected Yu Zuomin, the former head of the rich village of Daqiuzhuang near Tianjin, who was jailed on several charges of corruption and obstructing justice in 1993. The corruption rumors filtered into the Hong Kong press as well. One article claimed that Li's brother Li Ruilin had won property construction contracts in Tianjin through his connections, while Li Ruihuan had spent RMB80 million to build himself a mansion in the city on Horse Track Road (*Machang dao*). See Wang Haitao, "Li Ruihuan chuju mixin" (The Secret Struggle over Li Ruihuan's Purge), *Kaifang* (Open Magazine), December 2002, pp. 17–19, p. 18. Another repeated several of the rumors discussed by Zong Hairen and added others. See Tian Ping, "Zhonggong shiliuda quandou neimu" (The Inside Story of the Struggle for Power at the 16th Party Congress), *Qianshao* (Frontline Magazine), December 2002, pp. 10–14.

Li met the calumnies with contempt. Yet they forced him to adopt a low profile from mid-July onward so that he would not attract more attention. The elders Wan Li and Qiao Shi found an opportunity to give Li a show of support when a former liberal senior staff member of the State Council died on August 8, 2002. The staffer, Chen Junsheng, had been pushed aside from his State Council post by Li Peng when he fell ill in 1988 (see Chapter 4). He symbolized the weakened liberal forces whose most powerful standard-bearer was Li Ruihuan. In a show of support for Li's remaining in office, Wan and Qiao exceeded protocol requirements and attended Chen's funeral. They heard Li read the eulogy in his capacity as chairman of the CPPCC, of which Chen had been a vice-chairman.

The succession was not formally discussed at the annual late July to mid-August meetings of Politburo members at the seaside resort of Beidaihe.[13] However, other issues were aired there that had a bearing

---

13. Beidaihe was long favored by European missionaries and Japanese officers as an escape from the dry, baking heat of a summer in Beijing, 160 miles away. Mao began the tradition of holding summer work conferences at the resort in the 1950s. Deng refrained for a few years after Mao's death in order to play down the imperial pretense of the "summer capital." But Deng began making trips there again in 1985 and the tradition revived. While central leaders usually spend only three to four weeks at the resort together, from late July onward, meetings are conducted there from June through September. Elders usually spend longer at the resort, and other state leaders come and go as they please. Villas are rented for each visiting state leader. Meetings are held in the mornings. The afternoons are less organized. Leaders hold private meetings, or rest, or go swimming. Staff from Party, State Council, NPC, and CMC organs find the arrangements burdensome because they have literally to create an entire office in Beidaihe, including, crucially, the encoding equipment to handle the minutes of meetings. The Organ Affairs Management Bureaus of the Central Office and the State Council are in charge of the daily itineraries and accommodations for visiting state leaders. During years in which there is no Party congress, most of the discussion is about policy issues. The relaxed nature of the setting may obscure the fact that it is frequently the site of the most intense political battles. It was at Beidaihe in the summer of 1988, for example, that then premier Li Peng launched a withering attack on the rapid economic reform policies of Zhao Ziyang, prefiguring the hard-liner backlash of the following spring. See Gilley, *Tiger on the Brink*, p. 106.

on the leadership. Most important was the timing of the congress. The congress had been held every five years since 1977, but the month varied. Most Politburo members—including Zhu Rongji and Li Ruihuan—favored holding the meeting in early September, as in 1997. That would allow the new leadership to appear at the annual National Day celebrations on October 1.

But Jiang stalled for time in order to build a stronger case against Li Ruihuan.[14] He met secretly with Li Peng and Hu Jintao to persuade them to delay the congress. Hu was eager to protect his succession while the conservative Li Peng shared Jiang's antipathy toward Li Ruihuan. The matter was formally decided at a Politburo meeting in late August when Hu Jintao proposed a congress opening date of November 8. Hu gave as his reason the fact that the summer flood waters in central China would not have receded in time for a September meeting. In heeding Jiang's wishes to delay the congress, Hu demonstrated perfect behavior in the role of successor, deferring to Jiang's wishes and hiding any eagerness to consummate his long rise to power.

In early September, Jiang dispatched an investigation team of the Party's internal anti-corruption body, the Central Disciplinary Inspection Commission, to Tianjin to look into the charges against Li Ruihuan. It had little success. There was no way to substantiate the claims and the officials in Tianjin remained loyal to Li. The team returned to the capital after just a few weeks' effort. Jiang could only hope to persuade other Politburo members on different grounds. Accordingly, a meeting of the PBSC was scheduled for October 17 where the issue of Li Ruihuan would be discussed openly for the first time.

---

14. There were two additional if marginal benefits for Jiang. It allowed him to take center stage at the National Day celebrations on September 30, where Premier Zhu was forced to read an ode to his reign; and it ensured that he was not treated like a lame duck when he visited the US in late October.

Li was well prepared for the meeting. Indeed, it appears that he decided beforehand to retire. The accumulated weight of slander and rumor—plus perhaps his own belief in the need for a thorough renewal of the leadership—had affected his decision. He may have felt that he could not win a direct confrontation with Jiang.

Despite the importance of the issue, the atmosphere as the meeting opened was relaxed.[15] Jiang broached the issue of succession as soon as formal proceedings began. He described the broad process of transition from the old to the new leadership. He said that a "complete transition" was "important, necessary, and urgent." General interjections of approval were voiced by Li Peng, Li Lanqing, and Li Ruihuan himself. After about twenty minutes, Jiang turned to the issue of Li Ruihuan, saying:

> Comrade Ruihuan, I know that on the issues of cadre renewal and the succession from old to young you have taken the clearest stand. You and I both came to the center to work thirteen years ago. According to Xiaoping's saying [about the three generations of leadership], we are both part of the same generation. Comrade Jintao still cannot compare with the experience and skills of you or me. He is a newcomer. But the back waves of the Yangtze River push the front waves ahead of them. You have always totally supported Jintao's work. The best way we can support Jintao is to free him from constraints and allow him to march into battle unfettered. If you and I are still on stage when Comrade Jintao takes over, it would obviously not be helpful for him to jump boldly into his work.

---

15. Our account of this meeting is drawn from Zong Hairen, "Li Ruihuan tuixiu neiqing" (Inside Information about Li Ruihuan's Retirement), *Xinbao*, December 17, 18, 19, and 20, 2002. Zong says that his information on the meeting comes from reliable sources close enough to provide the level of detail described, but not from official minutes.

At this point Li cut Jiang off, saying:

> Comrade Zemin, I know what you're getting at. I certainly do not crave power. I am not infatuated with politics, nor am I skilled at scheming. Although my physical and emotional health are good and my mind still works well, I have long been prepared to retire. I had long waited for you to put forth your views, hoping you would summon me for a heart-to-heart talk. But until now you have never requested to talk to me, much less to have a heart-to-heart talk with me. On this, I am not pleased with your performance as Party general secretary. I feel you have not done a good job. Now you raise this question at a Standing Committee meeting, so obviously it is a well-prepared tactic.

Such an open censure of a fellow Politburo member at a formal meeting is rare. Jiang attempted to defend himself, but Li would not give him the floor, continuing with another bombshell:

> I can openly say to everyone, I will not join the new Central Committee [and hence Politburo]. My responsibilities will end with the completion of my term [as chairman of the CPPCC] next spring. I would also like to say to everyone: since this summer, rumors and slanders about me have circulated everywhere. The more time goes by the worse they become. Without a doubt it is because some people want to blacken my image. Some people do not wish me to continue in office. Still, wisdom is knowing yourself. I am not that skilled. I cannot run the whole world. After Mao and Deng died, China continued to develop. I trust that under Comrade Jintao and following the reform path of Comrade Xiaoping, the future of China will be even better than today.

After this surprise declaration, the room fell into silence. The first to speak was Li Peng. Li Ruihuan's intention to stand down, he said, was commendable and should be accepted by the Standing Committee. As for the spreading of rumors, this was a serious matter and should be investigated. Li Peng appeared to play his role here as Jiang's comrade in conspiracy, offering praise that made Li Ruihuan's decision easier for others to accept.

After that meeting, Li Ruihuan was a fallen leader. At the Party congress, he avoided most of the sessions, making only one speech in a meeting with Tianjin delegates, where he emphasized the importance of the Party representing the majority of the people (rather than the elites favored by Jiang) and warned cadres against losing touch with the people. He took time out to attend an exhibition of modern Chinese paintings, and left Beijing the day the congress closed to watch a tennis tournament in Shanghai.

In the months of the transition, Li took himself out of the CPPCC's work completely, leaving it to the vice chairmen of the body. Yet he did not lose a chance in these final days to make his points again and again. Meeting with editors of the CPPCC News on January 16, he urged journalists nationwide to "report the truth," hinting that "truth" should not be a euphemism for Party propaganda. "We're not talking about only certain truths, but the whole truth and the fundamental truth."[16]

Li also made a point of holding meetings with Hu Jintao and Wen Jiabao in his final months, urging them to grasp the nettle of political reform. In one talk, he praised Hu's decision to have the official press carry reports each time the Politburo met, a reform Hu launched shortly after taking over as general secretary in November.

The ouster of Li Ruihuan was the last and arguably the greatest of Jiang's victories in purging rivals to his authority since coming

---

16. Xinhua Online News, January 17, 2003.

to power in 1989 (see Chapter 6). It left Hu Jintao more vulnerable to the machinations of ambitious colleagues on the new PBSC. More important, it was a significant blow for advocates of political reform.

The Final Three. The last three men to be selected members of the new PBSC were promoted as a direct result of the purge of Li Ruihuan. Once Li had agreed to retire, there were only six designated members for the new PBSC. Traditionally the body has had an odd number of members to avoid split votes, so it was necessary to consider adding another person. Within the existing Politburo, there were three members who would not be retiring and who might be considered for the vacant slot—Wu Guanzheng, Jia Qinglin, and Huang Ju.[17]

At the same October 17 meeting at which he declared his intention to step down, Li Ruihuan recommended Wu Guanzheng for the vacancy. Although Wu has been portrayed in Western press accounts as a harsh ruler who suppressed the Falungong as Party secretary in Shandong, internal Party reviews praised him for his scientific decision-making, which means consultation with experts and in Chinese terms is considered a democratic thing to do. He is considered open-minded and approachable. Li's suggestion was immediately endorsed at the meeting by three other PBSC members—Zhu Rongji, Hu Jintao, and Wei Jianxing—and was passed unanimously.

If only Wu had been promoted, however, not only would Jia Qinglin and Huang Ju have been conspicuously left behind, but it would have been an obvious slap in the face for their patron, Jiang Zemin. Li Peng spoke again, saying that the exclusion of Jia and Huang from the new PBSC seemed unfair since they were the Party secretaries of the major cities of Beijing and Shanghai respectively,

---

17. Politburo alternate member Wu Yi was not considered for PBSC status although her fellow alternate, Zeng Qinghong, had already been assured a position on the PBSC.

where notable progress had been made under their leadership. Jiang Zemin chimed in to express agreement, saying:

> In order to preserve unity, I propose that we expand the PBSC to nine people from seven in order to include Comrades Qinglin and Huang Ju. I hope everyone will consider this. Most of all we should hear the views of Comrade Jintao. His views are more important than any of ours.

By handing the floor to Hu Jintao, Jiang prevented Li Ruihuan and Zhu Rongji from speaking in opposition to the proposal. Both men were known to view Jia and Huang as spineless representatives of Jiang. Li Ruihuan knew that their presence on the expanded PBSC would saddle Hu Jintao with an unwieldy body and less control than he would like. Zhu had his own concerns. He had spent much time as premier trying to slim down the bureaucracy. Moreover, he had worked assiduously to crack the huge smuggling racket in Fujian province and must have been loath to see one of the top suspects in that case, former Fujian Party chief Jia, promoted to the PBSC.

Hu seemed surprised by the proposal to expand the PBSC to nine, but he regained his composure and spoke in favor of it, presumably mindful of the need to defer to Jiang to the end. With his support expressed, there was no point in Li Ruihuan or Zhu Rongji voicing opposition.

On the afternoon of October 21, Jiang's secretary, Jia Ting'an, phoned the Xinhua News Agency, instructing it to send a dispatch announcing new appointments the following afternoon. On October 22, Xinhua issued a release announcing that new Party chiefs had been appointed in Beijing, Shanghai, and Chongqing. While the incumbent in Chongqing was to be given "another post," Jia and Huang "are transferred to posts at the central authorities," it said without further explanation.

This sudden announcement ensured that Jia's and Huang's nomination to the PBSC could not be sidetracked while Jiang was visiting the US and Mexico from October 22 to 29. However, it had a negative impact in political circles in Beijing. It was tantamount to circumventing the congress and announcing two new PBSC members ahead of time. Many retired Party elders felt that it broke all conventions. They saw it as a classic example of Jiang Zemin's paranoia about losing control. The liberal elder Wan Li, a Li Ruihuan supporter, commented, "It's a sign of his pettiness (*xiaoren zhi xin*)."

These last-minute changes meant that the Party and state assignments previously worked out for the new PBSC required some reconfiguration. Certain assignments remained fixed: Hu Jintao as Party general secretary, Wen Jiabao as premier, Zeng Qinghong as head of the Party secretariat and point man for personnel and organization, and Luo Gan as security chief. These four are the key figures of the new leadership, even though their formal ranks are one, three, five, and nine respectively.

Known as a stickler for corruption-free government, Wu Guanzheng was given the secretaryship of the Party's anti-corruption body, the CDIC, even though this had traditionally been held by the internal security czar, in this case Luo. By spinning off the responsibility to a separate PBSC member, albeit a weak one, the change opened the possibility of a more neutral handling of corruption cases.

Li Ruihuan's purge meant that the chairmanship of the National People's Congress was open. Wu Bangguo was promoted to that position with the support of outgoing NPC chairman Li Peng. The appointment gave him a higher formal ranking in the PBSC than Wen—his one-time rival for the premiership. This was small consolation, however, for the loss of real power to the reformist Wen. Wu's new assignment, in turn, opened a vacancy in the relatively powerless position as chairman of the CPPCC, the consultative body for non-Party figures that is supposed to help legitimate CCP rule. The Politburo handed that position to Jia Qinglin.

Greater contention occurred over the more important position of executive vice-premier. Jiang had originally planned to give this position to Li Changchun. Zhu and Wen supported the plan, which enjoyed wide consensus, since Li was seen as no more than a weak ally of Jiang's and had done important work on handling economic and financial issues in several locations in his career (see Chapter 4).

But with the elevation of Huang Ju, a more loyal supporter of his, Jiang's allegiances changed. Jiang urged that Huang be promoted to the position. He also encouraged the Shanghai municipal Party committee and government to issue a joint letter to Hu Jintao asking that Huang be appointed as executive vice-premier to ensure that the Party center remained supportive of Shanghai. Li Changchun, seeing the trend of events, told Hu that the demands of his work overseeing Party propaganda and ideology were so great that he would rather not be considered for a State Council post. Huang was confirmed as executive vice-premier by the NPC in March 2003. In Zong Hairen's view, the result is that Wen Jiabao is the weakest premier in PRC history, hemmed in by a deputy with a powerful patron, a local power base, and a conservative approach to economic reform.

Jiang Zemin and the military succession. The full retirement of Jiang Zemin was the most controversial issue of the succession. Jiang had been promoted to the top posts of the Party, state, and military after Tiananmen to make possible the complete retirement of Deng Xiaoping. Now many felt it was his turn to step down from all three. But would he?

From the beginning, Jiang's retirement from his Party and state positions was not in doubt. In 1997, as part of the successful attempt to get rid of a PBSC colleague, Qiao Shi, Jiang had promised to retire in 2002 (see Chapter 6). Then seventy-one, he accepted the principle that no one aged seventy or older should be appointed to the Politburo; but he made himself a one-time exception, promising that he would retire at the next Party congress. Between 1997 and 2002, Jiang on several occasions repeated his promise to step down from the Politburo—and thus as general secretary—in 2002, both informally and in internal meetings.[18] The liberal Li Ruihuan expressed the views of other Politburo members in making clear the case for Jiang's retirement. According to Li:

> Implementing the transition from old to new and introducing a corps of younger cadres is the greatest historical mission of the 16th Party Congress. If we don't implement the transition from old to new, we can't hold the congress. The state leaders of the big countries in the world, like the United States, Russia, and Britain, are only in their forties and fifties. Hu Jintao is up to the job.

Li also said:

> Hu Jintao has all the qualifications to serve as the leader of the new generation, and at sixty [in December 2002] he will by no means be too young. We should exercise the political boldness of Comrade [Deng] Xiaoping [who appointed] people like Li Peng, Qiao Shi, [Tian] Jiyun, and [Hu] Qili as secretaries in the Party Secretariat or vice-premiers when they were fifty-five or fifty-six. With ten years' experience what need is there for him [Hu] to wait?

In the summer of 2002 the Western press reported rumors circulating

---

18. This information from Zong Hairen confirms rumors that surfaced frequently in the overseas press. For example, the pro-Beijing *Jingbao* (Mirror) in Hong Kong reported that Jiang repeated the promise at a Party plenum in 1998 and again at the Beidaihe meeting of 2001; "Jiang Zemin zaitan shiliuda quanmian jiaoban" (Jiang Zemin Again Talks about the Complete Succession at the 16th Congress), *Jingbao*, October 2001. Zong says that the promise appeared at least five times in documents circulated by the Central Committee, one of which in 1999 was distributed as far down as the county level (*xian tuan ji*).

in China that Jiang intended to tear up the consensus and remain on the PBSC as general secretary.[19] To be sure, from 1999 onward, people close to Jiang, among them Shanghai Party secretary Huang Ju and his Beijing counterpart Jia Qinglin, had occasionally floated the idea of Jiang staying on as general secretary. Ideological campaigns launched by Jiang's supporters in 1998 and 2000 treated him as if he were an indispensable authority comparable to Mao and Deng, who had made themselves exceptions to every rule and had intervened in government until infirmity made it impossible for them to speak.

But it is unlikely that Jiang seriously considered trying to keep his post as general secretary. His authority and legacy might have been irreparably damaged by the power struggle that would have resulted from such a move. Among the senior leaders only Hu Jintao, who had the most to lose but was wary of getting on the wrong side of Jiang, responded positively to claims that Jiang was a theorist on the level of the Party's greats. Aside from some provincial Party secretaries loyal to Jiang, no other high official expressed support for that idea, not even his closest aide, Zeng Qinghong. Nor could Jiang remain as state president, having served in that position since 1993. The national constitution limits the state president to two five-year terms.

If Jiang's retirement from the top Party and state posts was unavoidable, the same was not true of his chairmanship of the military commission. There are no rules governing the succession to this post. Mao held it until he died. Deng gave it up two years after his retirement in 1987 from all other high posts, and after having used the position as the base from which to intervene in Party politics during the 1989 Tiananmen crisis.

---

19. E.g., Erik Eckholm, "China's President May Be Reluctant to Cede Power," *The New York Times*, July 13, 2002; Charles Hutzler, "A Twist in China's Succession Script," *The Wall Street Journal*, July 2, 2002; John Pomfret, "Chinese Leader Throws a Curve: Jiang's Reluctance to Retire Could Spark Power Struggle," *The Washington Post*, July 21, 2002.

According to the earliest consensus in the Politburo, Jiang would hand over the chairmanships of both the Party and state military commissions (two formal titles for the same post) when the latter changed hands in March 2003. Some of Jiang's supporters lobbied for him to remain, however, arguing that his experience was needed at a time of large-scale change. In 2001, the three senior generals who ran the military commission under Jiang floated a series of trial balloons citing the need for "stability in the army and the country" and implying that he should continue as military chairman. In January 2001, at a conference on political work—i.e., ideological training—within the military, the head of the PLA General Political Department, Yu Yongbo, stated that Jiang Zemin's remaining in the post of chairman of the military commission was crucial for the stability of the army and the nation. At an enlarged meeting[20] of the General Staff Department Party Committee in January 2002, Chief of General Staff Fu Quanyou called upon all members of the Party organization in the military "at all times and under all circumstances consciously to maintain a high level of unity in ideology, politics, and action with the Party Center and the Central Military Commission with Comrade Jiang Zemin as the core." In the coded language of Chinese communism, the phrase "at all times and under all circumstances" signaled loyalty to Jiang Zemin. A deputy chief of staff, Xiong Guangkai, appealed directly to Jiang to stay on.

On their own, these appeals were not enough to change the Politburo consensus. The military's political influence was much reduced from what it had been in 1989, and there was no military representative on the PBSC. All of Jiang's fellow members of the PBSC who were seventy or older—Li Peng, Zhu Rongji, Wei Jianxing, and Li Lanqing—continued to make clear through informal channels, such as

---

20. An enlarged meeting is one attended by invited guests who are not members of the committee.

comments to their staffs, that they intended to retire completely. This implied that in their view there was no crisis that required upsetting established expectations and allowing Jiang to retain the CMC post. Retired Party elders, including Wan Li, Qiao Shi, Song Ping, and Liu Huaqing, all voiced the opinion that Jiang should relinquish the military position.

Li Ruihuan, who at that time expected to remain on the PBSC, was outspoken on the issue. Li was more than just a critic of Jiang. He was also an advocate of more transparent and predictable succession arrangements at all levels. Li had expressed the hope that Jiang would formally outline his plans for a complete retirement at a meeting of the Politburo well before the congress. When Jiang failed to do so, Li voiced his concern. He said that the new generation was sufficiently experienced and the nation's political, economic, and international situations sufficiently stable to allow a full and orderly transition. He pointed out that Hu Jintao's three years as vice-chair of the CMC gave him far more military experience than Jiang had had when he was thrust into the chairmanship five months after Tiananmen.

As the question of Jiang's future dragged into September, opinion in the Politburo remained against him. Jiang then made a preemptive and surprising move. In late September, he formally proposed to the Politburo that the twin military chairs change hands at the 16th Party Congress in November rather than as planned in March 2003. Although his proposal seemed designed to show modesty and a confidence in Hu Jintao, he must have calculated that the request would not be accepted since it would thrust Hu into the sensitive position four months early, creating worry at home and abroad. The proposal enhanced Jiang's political capital in the final weeks of bargaining before the 16th congress by drawing attention to his importance for a smooth transition. The message was amplified by the appeals it elicited from his allies in the military not to step down early.

As expected, the Politburo rejected the suggestion. It decided that the handover of the CMC in March 2003 would take place as planned. The informal Politburo retirement age of seventy required CMC vice-chairs Zhang Wannian and Chi Haotian to stand aside at the November 2002 Party congress, along with the other over-seventy members of the CMC.[21] The congress elected as CMC vice-chairs the two new military members of the Politburo, Generals Cao Gangchuan and Guo Boxiong, who had entered the commission as regular members in 1998 and 1999.[22]

In the months after the Party congress, Jiang began to hint that he intended to retain the military post past March 2003. He insisted that he remain atop the hierarchy in protocol lists of China's leaders, despite

---

21. When plans still called for Jiang to step down as CMC chair, some thought was given to asking one older, more experienced officer to stay on as a CMC member to act as a protective presence ("imperial guardian") while Hu Jintao worked to consolidate his authority, but this proposal ran into difficulties. The two older candidates for promotion from longtime regular CMC members to vice-chairman were Generals Fu Quanyou and Yu Yongbo. Both had spoken in favor of Jiang Zemin's continuing control of the CMC, meaning that their continuation in office would not have been welcome to Hu. Also, such veterans were considered unable to keep up with the demands of rapid technological change in military affairs. Finally, Fu and Yu were both over seventy. If one stayed on the CMC, he would outrank younger members and would have to take one of the military seats on the Politburo, breaching the age limit on Politburo appointments. In the summer of 2002, the PBSC rejected this plan for Fu and Yu and also rejected promoting CMC member Xiong Guangkai to minister of defense. Some consideration was given to allowing the pair to "retire to the second line," Fu as a vice-chairman of the NPC and Yu as a vice-chairman of the CPPCC. But this met with strong resistance within the broader Party membership, not only because of their advanced age but because of the belief that it was inappropriate for military figures to hold senior positions in the two parliamentary bodies. Fu and Yu therefore retired at the 16th congress. Xiong retained his status as an alternate member of the Central Committee, although in voting he fell from the 37th least popular to the 10th least popular member.

22. The degree of consensus on the military succession was reflected in the accuracy of outside media reporting on the issue in advance of the 16th congress. The three PLA candidates for Politburo membership as new CMC vice-chairmen were accurately reported months in advance in Luo Bing, "Xinjie hexincang mingdan yichu" (The New Core-Level Name List is

having stepped down from Party's top position. His hand was now strengthened since the new PBSC was stacked more heavily in his favor than the previous one.

Some military officers made public statements that they would "resolutely obey the commands of the Party center [now led by Hu Jintao], the Central Military Commission, and Jiang Zemin," phrasing that implied a split leadership for the indefinite future. At a private meeting with Jiang and Hu Jintao, General Yu Yongbo stated baldly, "I'm a resolute supporter of Jiang. People say I am doing this for personal gain. But I plan to completely retire. So there is no question of personal gain. Jiang's remaining will ensure stability in the army and the nation." While the new members of the CMC appointed at the 16th congress were not followers of Jiang, they did not want to open a split between themselves and the outgoing military brass. Therefore, the official position of the new CMC uniformed leadership was that Jiang should remain as chairman.

A week after the congress, Jiang told a visiting delegation of retired US defense and national security officials that he would remain in the position for several years, "at the request of my comrades."[23] The claim was duly reported in the Western media, presumably as Jiang intended.[24] Washington was sufficiently convinced that Jiang would

---

Released), *Zhengming* (Hong Kong), May 2002, pp. 6–8. Although Cao is considered to be the informal senior military member of the Politburo, his formal rank on the body is below that of Guo. The reason is that Cao is the oldest member of the new Politburo at sixty-six, and joined the body at the same time as a civilian, Li Tieying, ten months his junior, was politely forced into retirement. This indicates that Cao will have only one five-year term on the Politburo. Moreover, it signifies the elimination of the formal rank of standing CMC vice-chairman.

23. The meeting was reported by *Xinhua*, November 22, 2002, although excluding mention of Jiang's claim, which comes from Zong Hairen.

24. Susan V. Lawrence, "Jiang will retain his post as Chinese military head," *Asian Wall Street Journal*, November 28, 2002, p. A1.

remain that in December 2002 it sent in the name of President George W. Bush a message of congratulation on his reelection as Party CMC chairman at the 16th congress. The message was reported by the official Xinhua News Agency on December 12, which said Bush had written that he "looked forward to further cooperation with Jiang during his tenure as CMC chairman." Focused on the war on terrorism, Washington had no interest in pressuring Jiang to retire. This support strengthened Jiang's hand.

In a last-ditch attempt to dislodge Jiang, the new Politburo circulated a draft plan for all top state positions in early January. The suggested chairman for the CMC was given as Hu Jintao, in accordance with prior expectations. In private comments that were widely circulated within Zhongnanhai, military elders Liu Huaqing and Zhang Zhen, along with Party elders Wan Li, Qiao Shi, and Song Ping, all called for Jiang to step down. Li Ruihuan, who remained CPPCC chairman until March 2003, added to the pressure, telling a meeting of the body's standing committee in late January that Jiang should "vacate the position to allow younger comrades to play a bigger role." In a separate talk to Party elders and former colleagues, he recalled, "Once Comrade Xiaoping decided to retire [as CMC chairman in 1989], no matter how many people asked him to remain, some even crying and begging, he went ahead without hesitation. It's useless to say anything now. Whether you say retire or don't retire, the decision is in the hands of that person [Jiang]. If he decides to retire, he can certainly do it."

However, the other powerful retiring elder, Li Peng, did not join the chorus calling for Jiang's retirement. This was critical. As a person with seniority equal to Jiang's, Li Peng could have insisted on being given a post of equal rank—probably state president—as the price for allowing Jiang to remain. Li had originally wanted Jiang to step down. But after the 16th congress, he changed his mind. He may have feared that Hu would not be fully committed to preventing a reconsideration of the Tiananmen verdict. Jiang returned the favor by supporting the election of several of Li's protégés to posts in the NPC and CPPCC, including Li Tieying, He Chunlin, and Li Guixian.

International security tensions did not seriously enter the debate. One potential crisis flared briefly in August 2002, when the president of Taiwan, Chen Shui-bian, said he would urge the Taiwanese legislature to consider passing a law to govern the holding of a referendum on the island's future status. Since Beijing considered holding a referendum tantamount to declaring independence (regardless of the referendum's outcome), the statement raised the possibility that China might go to war over Taiwan in the near future. But Chen quickly moderated his rhetoric under pressure from Washington, and Beijing was given Washington's assurance that it did not support Chen on the issue. Nor did the international crisis over the US invasion of Iraq in early 2003 or renewed tensions over North Korea's nuclear program enter the discussions over Jiang's role, a reminder that the issue was about personalities, not policies.

Hu Jintao now saw that forcing Jiang out would create more problems than it would solve. In his spring festival visits to elders Wan Li, Qiao Shi, and Song Ping, he sought their support for retaining Jiang in office, but in the interests of Hu himself.[25] He also formally proposed to the new PBSC that Jiang remain, saying this was in the "greater interests" of the Party, state, and military.

By the time the NPC opened in early March, Jiang had secured approval to remain as military commission chair. The extension of his term did not pass without a mild protest: in secret voting, 8 percent of the 2,985 NPC delegates voted against him or abstained.

It is unclear how far Jiang will seek to extend his powers and when

---

25. Hu even went to the trouble of visiting the bedridden elder Song Renqiong. Owing to his ill health, Song misunderstood Hu's words, thinking it was Li Peng who intended to remain in office. Song commented: "Tell Li Peng to keep working hard."

he will step down.[26] Although he has been elected to a five-year term as CMC chair, Jiang may see his power wane, even in the absence of a direct challenge, to the extent that Hu Jintao is able to consolidate his authority. This factor or encroaching age may lead Jiang to leave his post before its term is up.

The military's role in domestic politics—and hence the potential power of the military commission chair to influence events beyond the sphere of military policy narrowly construed—is no longer what it was in Deng Xiaoping's time. Dealing with civil unrest is the responsibility of a separate force called the People's Armed Police that is larger and better trained than it was at the time of Tiananmen and which answers chiefly to the civilian authorities. Even in matters of foreign and security policy, and policy toward Taiwan, where the military has a crucial and legitimate voice, its role has been cut back since 1997 in favor of "leading small groups" on foreign and Taiwan affairs located in the central Party apparatus.

Indeed, there were signs that the professional military itself was dissatisfied with Jiang's continuation in office. The resulting split leadership on national security affairs could make it difficult for the military to know where to place its loyalties in a situation of political crisis. "Having two centers will result in problems," the PLA's main newspaper, the PLA Daily, quoted two military delegates to the NPC as saying.[27]

---

26. Some press reports in the Beijing-controlled press in Hong Kong said that Jiang retained the right to be consulted on important matters and to read Politburo reports. They also said that he would hand over the CMC position to Hu before the 17th congress. See Tang Wencheng, "Zhonggong xin lingdao jiti ruhe fuxin?" (How Will the New CCP Leadership Rule?), *Jingbao* (Mirror Magazine), January 2003, pp. 24–26. Another report in the same magazine said that Jiang wanted to lead China's "cultural and ideological revival." See Leng Mo, "Jiang Zemin zhizede zhuanbian" (Jiang Zemin's Changed Role), *Jingbao* (Mirror), January 2003, pp. 27–29.

27. Wang Wenjie, "A Report on Efforts by Military Delegates to Study President Jiang's Important Speech to the PLA Delegation," *Jiefangjun bao* (PLA Daily), March 11, 2003, p. 5.

Nor does Jiang have the unique personal authority that Deng Xiaoping commanded, the support that Deng enjoyed from a group of like-minded elders, or the wide-ranging political authority granted to Deng and two other colleagues by a secret 1987 Politburo resolution that gave three senior retiring Party Elders the right to intervene in Politburo decisions. While Jiang will no doubt be asked to provide his views of military needs and security questions, he may not be able to control policy even on tense security issues like Taiwan or North Korea, much less on nonmilitary issues like economic and political reform or ideology. That is why, despite Jiang's incomplete retirement, it is fair to call the leadership transition a qualified success.

Fractured unity. For the first time in its own history—and one of the few times in the history of any Communist state—the Chinese Communist Party at the 16th Congress brought about an orderly solution to the most difficult problem that faces an authoritarian regime, succession. It promoted a cadre of dedicated, competent leaders, who command authority in the bureaucracy and who share broad views about China's future. Most of the credit goes to Deng Xiaoping, who from beyond the grave managed this innovation in the functioning of Communist systems by initiating the twenty-year process of cultivating younger officials that came to fruition in 2002–2003. In some sense, everyone in the new leadership is a child of Deng's reforms. Jiang Zemin's success in partially derailing the consensus suggests, however, that the succession procedures, although much improved, remain fragile.

The new leadership is more balanced among factions and interests than any preceding ruling constellation. The group of Politburo members sponsored by Jiang Zemin is the largest, but is not in a position to dominate. Li Peng and Zhu Rongji each have a key follower in a powerful position. Hu Jintao and Zeng Qinghong both have strong power bases. Lacking a dominant figure, the new leadership needs to work by consensus if it can, even though its members are divided both by personal ambition and to some extent by policy preferences. The expansion of the PBSC from seven members to nine will make reaching consensus more difficult. The new group thus begins in a state of fractured unity, held tenuously together by the complex balance of forces that created it. Hu Jintao will need to consolidate his authority, as Jiang did after he came to power, or risk seeing it undermined by the elite instability that normally disrupts authoritarian regimes.

3

THE POLITICIANS

THREE MEMBERS OF the new Politburo Standing Committee—Hu Jintao, Zeng Qinghong, and Wen Jiabao—are most suited by position and temperament to contend for influence: Hu Jintao because he holds the top posts in the Party and state, Zeng Qinghong because he has the strongest network of political allies and contacts and the most political skill, and Wen Jiabao because as premier he controls the day-to-day affairs of the state apparatus. All three have broad specific responsibilities to deal with many issues because of their positions (formal and informal) in the new leadership; and each has a distinctive set of policy preferences. The three of them, however, should not be seen as rivals—at least not at the start. Their relations range from friendly to respectful and their policy goals and personal ambitions are potentially compatible. Whether they will be able to cooperate will determine how stable Chinese politics remains for the next five years.

Hu Jintao, age sixty, serves as general secretary of the Chinese Communist Party, state president of the People's Republic of China, and vice-chairman of the Central Military Commission. Affable and cautious, Hu Jintao is the consummate Chinese Communist organization man. He has always gone where he was assigned and done what he was told to do. The Party duly rewarded his loyalty with its highest offices.

In his early career Hu moved smoothly from hydropower engineer to Party functionary. Then he served as Party secretary in two of China's poorest provinces, Guizhou and Tibet, before being unexpectedly appointed to the Politburo Standing Committee as its youngest member, at the age of forty-nine, in 1992. Hu now holds control over the Party and the state, although his lack of immediate control over the military means he is no strongman. He can take control of China's destiny only if he forms alliances with some of his colleagues and rivals in the Politburo Standing Committee. But this challenge may fit his personality. Always immaculate, composed, and controlled, Hu's idea of leadership is not to impose a new vision but to consult widely and create consensus.

Hu Jintao's ancestors were tea merchants from the central province of Anhui who migrated to Taizhou, a town in Jiangsu not far from Jiang Zemin's home town of Yangzhou. The family of Hu Jintao's father did business mainly in Shanghai, where Hu Jintao was born in December 1942. After the death of his mother he and his two younger sisters moved back to Taizhou to live with their grandparents. There Hu Jintao attended elementary and middle school. (The Hu clan temple in Anhui is a national historical site, with excellently preserved Ming dynasty architecture and decorations. Hu Jintao has never visited it.)

In 1959, Hu passed the entrance exam for China's elite technical institution, Qinghua University. He completed his bachelor's degree in 1964 in hydropower engineering, and then stayed on to serve as a political instructor[1] and do postgraduate research. In 1964 he was admitted to the Chinese Communist Party.

At the height of the Great Proletarian Cultural Revolution in 1968, Hu Jintao responded to Chairman Mao's call to "go where the fatherland needs you" and volunteered for service in the remote, arid north-

---

1. *Zhengzhi fudaoyuan*—a person in charge of the ideological training and mobilization of students.

western province of Gansu. Soon he was managing Party affairs for the local branch of the Ministry of Water Resources and Electric Power (Shuidianbu, now defunct). He worked for the ministry between 1968 and 1974, when Li Peng was managing Party affairs for the ministry's Beijing municipal electric power bureau, but the two never had any direct contact. Like Li and Jiang Zemin in the older generation and many in his own generation, Hu thus made an early career transition from technician to Party technocrat.[2] From 1974 on, Hu served on the staff of the Gansu provincial construction commission.

In 1980, when Deng Xiaoping called on senior officials to promote cadres who were "more revolutionary, younger, more knowledgeable, and more specialized," Gansu's first Party secretary, Song Ping, reached down into the provincial cadre ranks and promoted Hu Jintao to the position of deputy head of the construction commission, over the heads of a number of more senior cadres. Two years later Hu was named secretary of the provincial branch of the Communist Youth League (CYL). Song Ping then recommended to the central Party authorities that they invite Hu to study at the Central Party School in Beijing with other talented young cadres. There Hu met Luo Gan, later to be his colleague in the central organs in the 1990s and on the Politburo from 1997 on.

Hu was elected second secretary of the Communist Youth League in 1982 and first secretary in 1984.[3] At this point his modesty, industry, and obedience to instructions turned temporarily into a disadvantage. The then Party leader Hu Yaobang was a strong reformer who

---

2. See Gilley, *Tiger on the Brink*, p. 61, and Li Cheng, *China's Leaders: The New Generation* (Rowman and Littlefield, 2001).

3. As Hu's final promotion neared in 2002, stories that he was a member of a student dance team at university in the 1960s and that he "occasionally danced solo at parties" while serving in the Youth League in the 1980s were deleted from his official biography. See Susan V. Lawrence, "It Ain't Over Till It's Over," *Far Eastern Economic Review*, August 8, 2002.

preferred people who showed originality and were willing to take risks. Even though Hu Jintao came out of the CYL, where the senior Hu had also made his early career, Hu Yaobang passed over Hu Jintao for further promotion in Beijing, sending him instead to China's poorest province, Guizhou, as Party secretary.[4]

Hu Jintao accepted the assignment willingly and from 1985 to 1988 performed it dutifully. He acted like a model local leader, visiting all of Guizhou's eighty-six county-level administrative units, living modestly, and listening patiently to the local people. But after three years in the post he left no impact on the province's economy, and the local cadres took note of the fact that he did not move his family to the province.

In June 1988 the Party secretary in Tibet collapsed from altitude sickness and had to resign. To fill the job quickly, the new head of the Party, Zhao Ziyang, who had succeeded Hu Yaobang, proposed Hu Jintao, who was seen as suitable because he was young and adaptable and had already worked in two backward provinces. Zhao certainly did not think that he was laying the basis for Hu Jintao's subsequent promotion, any more than Hu Yaobang had in assigning him to Guizhou. But Hu's old patron Song Ping—by then working in Beijing as a member of the PBSC and supervising high-level Party transfers and promotions as head of the Organization Department—perhaps saw the situation more clearly. He supported the appointment as an opportunity for Hu Jintao to demonstrate his abilities. The Politburo approved the transfer.

The Tibet assignment promptly turned into a nightmare. On December 10, 1988, just as Hu Jintao was completing the handover of

---

4. According to a semi-official biography written by two journalists of the Beijing-run newspaper in Hong Kong *Dagong bao* (Ta Kung Pao News) Hu Jintao was considerably closer to Hu Yaobang than his official dossier reveals, a fact possibly downplayed because of Hu Yaobang's removal as Party general secretary in 1987 for tolerating student protesters. See Ma Ling and Li Ming, *Hu Jintao* (Hong Kong: Ming Pao Press, 2002).

duties in Guizhou, Lhasa was rocked by riots which left one lama dead and thirteen people injured. The death on January 28, 1989, of the Panchen Lama, who was much revered in Tibet, set off a series of street disorders in Lhasa that lasted through the first three months of that year. Hu Jintao was poorly prepared to handle the crisis. He was the first Party secretary to serve in Tibet who lacked a military background. Since he had just arrived, he had no trusted assistants, local networks, or ties with the military garrison. Finally on March 7, on Beijing's orders, Hu's subordinate, the local government chairman, declared martial law in Lhasa, thus bringing the unrest under control. Although no one suspected it at the time, this act set a precedent for the use of martial law in Beijing just two and a half months later.

According to *Disidai*, Hu told a friend at this time that he felt pessimistic about his future. It seemed that he had reached a dead end in his career and would never rise beyond the level of provincial Party secretary. As in Guizhou, he made no lasting impact on Tibet. He found it difficult to get used to the altitude and spent an average of five months of the year in Beijing. At least this gave him an opportunity to stay in frequent touch with his patron, Song Ping, who was at the height of his influence.

There is no evidence that Hu faked his problems with Tibet's altitude, and there were many examples of earlier officials who had been affected by the climate there. But the time spent with his patron in Beijing was to prove critical to his sudden 1992 elevation to the Politburo Standing Committee, which took place thanks to Song Ping's skillful packaging of Hu's career as an exemplar of Party loyalty (see Chapter 2). Hu's PBSC membership was renewed in 1997. At the next meeting of the National People's Congress in 1998 his position as heir apparent was confirmed with the award of the state vice-presidency, and the following year he received the vice-chairmanship of the Central Military Commission.

Hu never exercised any real power, however, during either his first or his second term in the PBSC. In the Party apparatus, Hu held three important posts relating to Party personnel matters, which gave the impression that he had substantial influence over high-level appointments when in fact he did not. He was a secretary in the CCP Secretariat with responsibility for promotions and appointments.[5] He was also head of the Central Party School, where up-and-coming young cadres are trained, and deputy chairman of an important body called the Central Organizational Committee, which draws up the organization charts for the national-level Party and state bureaucracies and decides how many cadres can be assigned at what ranks to each office.[6] These positions would seem to have put Hu in a position to create a power base through appointments and promotions at levels below the Politburo. He did manage to promote a score or so of cadres who had served with him in the Communist Youth League. Most of them, however, hold posts in central ministries or the provinces doing propaganda, ideological, or administrative work, and have little experience in economic management, which is an increasingly crucial qualification for real influence. Only two close associates of Hu's—Wang Zhaoguo, an NPC deputy chairman and the Party Propaganda Department head Liu Yunshan—were promoted to the Politburo in 2002.

Real authority over appointments under Jiang Zemin was controlled by Jiang's trusted subordinate Zeng Qinghong, operating from his post as deputy director and then director of the Party Central Office and reporting directly to Jiang. Zeng's power over personnel matters was formally recognized when he joined the Politburo and the

---

5. The CCP Secretariat (*shujichu*) is the power center for Party affairs. Its business is run by seven to nine secretaries (*shuji*) who are high-ranking Party officials.

6. Not to be confused with the Organization Department. This was the *Zhongyang jigou bianzhi weiyuanhui*. As deputy chair of this committee, Hu would normally be expected to run its work and report to the chair (Li Peng from 1993 to 1998 and Zhu Rongji from 1998 to 2003).

Secretariat in 1997 and became head of the Organization Department in 1999.

Hu Jintao's state vice-presidency after 1998 was even emptier. Jiang never made Hu acting president while he was out of the country. The only time Hu substituted for Jiang in a presidential role was in May 1999, when Jiang wanted to avoid the political risk of addressing the nation on television to call for calm after the US bombing of the Chinese embassy in Belgrade. Among a globe-trotting leadership, Hu was noteworthy for the infrequency and low profile of his foreign trips, until the final years of his vice-presidency, when he visited Russia and Western Europe (2001) and the United States (2002). Jiang did not even ask him to be one of the hosts at the October 2001 Asia-Pacific Economic Cooperation meeting of heads of state in Shanghai, although the lower-ranking Zeng Qinghong was much in evidence there.

In the third branch of power, the military, Hu, as vice-chairman of the Central Military Commission, was confined to symbolic duties, such as speaking at a meeting which conferred posthumous military honors on Wang Wei, the Chinese pilot whose fighter jet collided with an American surveillance plane over the South China Sea and crashed in April 2001. Hu's other major responsibility involved a conflict between civilian and military leaders: he chaired the group set up by the PBSC in 1999 to oversee the military's divestiture of its business empire, ordered the previous year by Jiang.[7]

What Hu did accomplish during his decade as heir apparent was to retain that status by staying out of the limelight, except when called upon to promote Jiang Zemin's ideological movements or to second Jiang in undermining Premier Zhu Rongji. Rather than chafing against this role, Hu Jintao cultivated it. He rarely granted interviews

---

7. For more on this see James Mulvenon, "PLA Divestiture and Civil-Military Relations: Implications for the Sixteenth Party Congress Leadership," www.chinaleadershipmonitor.org, Winter 2002.

even to Chinese journalists, much less to the international press. He showed deference to all his colleagues, even those well beneath him in protocol rank. He made a special point of listening carefully to Li Peng at meetings and of taking notes when Li spoke. As deputy chair of the Central Organizational Committee he simply passed along proposals from Zeng Qinghong (who was only an alternate Politburo member) concerning Party offices and from Luo Gan concerning state offices, without questioning any of them. In doing so he was aware that Zeng was doing Jiang Zemin's bidding and Luo that of Li Peng, and that if he was to get along with the two senior leaders he would have to get along with their closest aides.

To the extent that Hu developed a distinctive profile in his second term in the PBSC, it was as a booster of Jiang Zemin, the man with the most control over his political future. After late 1998, when Zeng Qinghong on behalf of Jiang launched the unpopular Three Stresses campaign to "stress study, stress politics, and stress healthy trends," Hu gave frequent public speeches to promote it. In 2001, he took the lead in publicizing Jiang's theory of the Three Represents—that the Party should represent advanced productive forces, advanced culture, and the broad masses of people, in other words the interests of new elite groups. He personally organized a team of fourteen high-level cadres to give lectures on the theory around the country. Hu often referred to Jiang as if he were a major Marxist theorist on the level of Mao Zedong or Deng Xiaoping. In these ways he helped build a rationale for adding Jiang's theories to the Party constitution at the 16th Party Congress. This deference must have made Jiang more confident that if he handed over power to Hu, his image would be treated kindly by the new leadership.

While Hu Jintao accomplished the feat of survival, he came to office with the weakest power base of any new Chinese leader except Mao's short-term successor Hua Guofeng. The elders who chose him are out of the picture (Deng died in 1997 and Hu's patron Song Ping is retired). In a decade as designated successor, he was unable to build a strong faction in the shadow of Jiang's overwhelming power, whose main beneficiary instead was Zeng Qinghong. Two of his strong supporters, the Fifth Generation candidate and Henan Party secretary Li Keqiang and the liberal elder Li Ruihuan, failed to make it onto the new Politburo. Hu has made no mark on policy and established no field of authority in which he speaks with special credibility.

Hu is, nonetheless, widely accepted and even liked in upper Party circles for being patient and modest, a good listener and a consensus-builder. He is considered in Chinese Communist terms "democratic" in work style: sincere and open, uninterested in empty show, thoughtful, modest, and sympathetic. The most common evaluation of him by superiors and colleagues is "good at unifying comrades" (*shanyu tuanjie tongzhi*). A man who concentrates on details, Hu seeks solutions for problems straightforwardly and in established channels, and tends to worry as much over small problems as big ones. He is a rule-keeper rather than a rule-bender, a balancer rather than a visionary.

Despite his Shanghai smoothness and executive-suite appearance, Hu has little foreign experience. Nonetheless, through extensive briefings and participation in policymaking discussions, his foreign policy knowledge is sophisticated and his views are nuanced. He knows first-hand the problems of backwardness and poverty in the Chinese interior, but lacks experience with macroeconomic management. He will need to rely on others to help him keep China's economy strong and find ways to reduce the growing gap in wealth between the coast and the interior.

Close analysis of his statements suggests that he has some strong policy views, but these are in line with the policies of the Jiang Zemin years rather than creative or original. (His views are discussed in Chapters 7 and 8.) In the months after his appointment as Party general secretary, Hu made a point of emphasizing the need to close China's yawning income gap and to pay more attention to the plight of the poor, especially farmers and laid-off workers. He also introduced some modest enhancements of political openness by allowing the official media to report details of Politburo meetings.

Just before the March 2003 handover of state posts, a group of liberal elders wrote to Hu Jintao and incoming premier Wen Jiabao congratulating them for their new open, populist style and urging further reforms, such as more independent courts and freer media.[8] Weeks later, Hu and Wen fired the minister of health and the mayor of Beijing for their responsibility in covering up the spread of the new epidemic disease SARS (Severe Acute Respiratory Syndrome) and embarked on a more open information policy about the spread of the disease and the government's actions to cope with it.

These actions and events made clear Hu's and Wen's symbolic separation from Jiang Zemin's style of leadership. They did not signal an intent to weaken the Party's role. Indeed in some ways the SARS crisis created an opportunity to reassert central power over ministerial and provincial bureaucracies and over China's fractious, geographically mobile public.

Whatever his long-term intentions, Hu's first imperative in his early months and even years in office is to consolidate power. His best hope for both survival and influence lies in maintaining good working relations with his colleagues, something for which his personality suits him. Fortunately for him, the very weakness of his initial power base makes him acceptable to his major rivals.

Zeng Qinghong, age sixty-three, is the fifth-ranked member of the Politburo Standing Committee, vice-president of the People's Republic of China, and the senior member of the Party Secretariat, with special responsibility for personnel and organizational matters.

---

8. Supplied to Radio Free Asia by Zong Hairen, the open letter was broadcast in three segments on March 15, 16, and 17, 2003.

Severe-looking, with a sharp nose, and a bit heavy, Zeng Qinghong has a somewhat intimidating presence which is leavened by a liking for informal windbreakers and a hidden sense of humor. He is another engineer in the top leadership, a one-time student of automatic control systems. Although he is ranked only number five and is little known either to foreigners or to Chinese outside the top echelon of the Party, he is the leader with the boldest ideas and the greatest potential to steer China in new directions. He has told friends that he would be willing to reverse the official condemnation of the 1989 democracy movement, hold competitive elections at the county level, allow the existence of independent political parties, and give permission for non-Party-controlled newspapers.

Zeng might be called an "ideological omnivore"[9]—he feeds freely on whatever theory or idea seems to him the most practical way to make China a strong and respected nation. He is the only member of the new PBSC with the political vision and resources to challenge Hu Jintao for dominance either behind the scenes or, if a crisis occurs, for official position.

Zeng rose to high office on the coattails of Jiang Zemin. The son of a revolutionary elder, he used his superior connections and his impressive skills as a tactician to conceive and carry out the three political maneuvers by which Jiang consolidated his power in the 1990s (see Chapter 6). In the new power structure he will control Party personnel matters through his position in the Party Secretariat and head of the Central Party School, which will place him in a good position to reinforce his faction for the future. He is wide-ranging in his political dealings, seeing power rather than ideology or opinion as the dividing line between himself and others. For anyone in the new leadership Zeng could be a welcome ally or a dreaded enemy.

---

9. The term "ideological omnivore" was used in the former USSR by conservative critics of Mikhail Gorbachev's reforms of the mid- to late-1980s.

In the early 1930s Zeng's father, Zeng Shan, was chairman of China's first experiment with communism, the Jiangxi provincial soviet. His mother, Deng Liujin, was one of the few women survivors of the Long March. Zeng Qinghong was born in 1939 and grew up in Jiangxi province in the care of his grandmother and aunts, whose husbands had all been killed in Kuomintang extermination campaigns against the Communists and their supporters. He went to school in Shanghai and Beijing, and studied automatic control systems at the Beijing Institute of Engineering, graduating in 1963. He joined the CCP at the age of twenty-one in 1960. Thanks to his high-ranking parents' connections with senior PLA officers, from the mid-1960s to the mid-1970s Zeng was able to get a series of technical jobs in military-run research institutes. Since the PLA was the one reasonably safe haven during the Cultural Revolution, Zeng was largely insulated from its turmoil. For no more than a year, he was subject to the mandatory program by which urban youths were "sent down" to the countryside.

It was Zeng's mother who helped him make the shift from engineer to apparatchik. In 1979, she approached a fellow Party elder, Yu Qiuli, a former colleague of Zeng Shan then serving as a Politburo member and head of the State Planning Commission. Yu hired her son as his personal secretary. When Yu took over the PLA's General Political Department in 1982, Zeng followed his mentor back to the barracks. But with Yu's permission he left after a few months, telling friends that military service was no longer a valuable credential for a political career in the era of Deng Xiaoping. With Yu's help, and benefiting from Deng's program to promote young technocrats, he took a series of successively higher-ranking jobs in the Ministry of Petroleum Industry (now defunct), of which Yu had been the founding minister.

But Zeng felt that his prospects would be still better in Shanghai, China's largest city. In 1984 he was able to transfer there with the help of two former subordinates of his father, Chen Guodong and Wang Daohan, who were respectively Shanghai Party secretary and mayor.

At forty-five, Zeng became deputy director of the Shanghai municipal Party committee's Organization Department, and rose to director within a year. During the next nearly two decades, he expanded his control, first in Shanghai and then at the national level, over this crucial sector of the Party bureaucracy, which controls cadres' careers.

It was in Shanghai that Zeng first exhibited his willingness to experiment with administrative and political reforms; in doing so he was following a tendency being encouraged by the Party's then General Secretary Hu Yaobang. He launched an internally circulated newspaper, *Organizational and Personnel Information News* (*Zuzhi renshi xinxi bao*),[10] which became a principal voice of the political reform movement of the mid-1980s. The paper often published extracts of the reformist internal speeches of central leaders.

Zeng's ability to think outside conventional boundaries and also his tendency to cultivate people by attending to their needs was shown by his handling in 1985 of the case of Qi Benyu, an official of the Cultural Revolution era whom Mao had turned on and put in prison. Qi was released after eighteen years in a Beijing prison and sent back to Shanghai to live out the rest of his life. Zeng argued that since the cost of living was higher in Shanghai than in Beijing, Qi should get a higher salary and a larger apartment than was standard for prisoners of his rank who were released to live in Beijing. That small act of generosity toward a political untouchable won Zeng respect as a person not constrained by the ideological divisions of the past.

Jiang Zemin became the city's Party chief in 1987 and took an immediate interest in Zeng, who by then had risen to the rank of deputy secretary of the municipal Party committee, overseeing the organization and propaganda departments. Jiang had closer relationships with

---

10. "Organizational"news refers to news about CCP personnel policies; "personnel" news refers to news about government personnel policies. Both kinds of work are supervised by the Party Organization Department.

two other deputy secretaries, Huang Ju and Wu Bangguo, whose careers he subsequently promoted. But when he left Shanghai for Beijing to serve as general secretary after the 1989 Tiananmen protests, he asked permission to bring only Zeng with him.

As a new leader appointed over the heads of several others more senior and powerful than he was (especially PBSC members Li Peng, Qiao Shi, and Yao Yilin), Jiang knew that he needed an aide who had personal connections throughout the hierarchy and especially with the Party Elders. Jiang's request to bring Zeng with him was approved by Li Peng in his capacity as the then senior member of the Standing Committee. It was also approved by number-six-ranking Elder Yang Shangkun in his capacity as Deng Xiaoping's representative. Zeng was given a post as deputy head of the Party's Central Office, but his main job was working for Jiang Zemin. By engineering the fall of rivals to Jiang's authority three times during the 1990s, he became indispensable to Jiang. As Jiang consolidated his power Zeng's influence also increased.

It was widely rumored that Zeng did not advance quickly into the Central Committee and Politburo despite Jiang's support because of the opposition of officials who resented him.[11] In fact, Zeng preferred the quiet exercise of real power and was in no hurry to raise his official profile. In 1992, while serving as deputy director and heir apparent to the directorship of the Central Office (which he took over in 1993), Zeng did not press for a seat on the Central Committee, even though that meant that he soon became the only head of the Central Office in the Party's history who was not a Central Committee member. In 1997, he joined the Politburo as an alternate member—a triple jump, skipping the normal prior stages of candidate and full Central Committee membership. This rank was just high enough to make him

---

11. See, for example, Agence France-Presse, "Zeng Qinghong, Jiang's Right-Hand Man, Is Foiled Again," September 26, 2001.

eligible to take over the Party's Organization Department from its outgoing director, Zhang Quanjing, when he retired in 1999.

Although Zeng was formally subordinate to Hu Jintao, who had nominal responsibility for personnel affairs in the Party Secretariat, he exercised actual control over the fate of senior cadres throughout the 1990s because he spoke for Jiang Zemin. Zeng made personnel decisions and Hu could only approve them. Thus Hu Jintao's role as designated successor afforded him little opportunity (or temptation) to build a personal power base.

In the late 1990s Zeng was instrumental in promoting two policies that aimed to establish Jiang Zemin's legacy, one a campaign for internal reform of the Party, the other a fundamental revision of Party ideology. The Three Stresses campaign was aimed at instilling greater discipline, especially among provincial leaders who often disobeyed central directives. Despite considerable opposition from influential Party circles, the campaign was promoted nationwide. The study materials that were distributed gave as much prominence to Jiang Zemin's writings as to those of Mao Zedong and Deng Xiaoping.

Perhaps most important in the long run, the campaign created dossiers on all officials at the ministry and provincial levels, providing details on their political and ideological "problems," what they had written about these problems in their "self-examinations," what they had said in the mandatory "heart-to-heart talks" with the teams sent out from Party Central to run the campaign, and what was said about them by their subordinates. All these records flowed into Zeng Qinghong's office in Zhongnanhai, where they became a further resource for his control of the careers of officials at the level below him.[12]

The second task Zeng carried out on Jiang's behalf was to manage the shift in Party ideology announced in 2000 and inscribed in the Party's constitution in 2002, the Three Represents, which called upon

---

12. See also Zong, *Zhu Rongji zai 1999*, pp. 138–176.

the Party no longer to think of itself as representing only its traditional Marxist constituencies, the workers and peasants. It was now to represent "the development demands of China's advanced social productive forces, the forward trend of China's advanced culture, and the basic interests of the broadest number of China's people." These were code words for making the Party a more urban, bourgeois regime, akin to the old Soviet idea of the "state of the whole people," a concept the Chinese Communist Party had bitterly criticized as revisionist during the 1960s. The shift was further consolidated in Jiang Zemin's invitation to private entrepreneurs to join the Party in a speech on the Party's eightieth anniversary on July 1, 2001. Zeng was the chief drafter of this speech.

Again these activities put Zeng in a more powerful position than the higher-ranking Hu Jintao. Zeng launched the Three Stresses campaign and Hu served as the campaign's chief promoter. Zeng developed the Three Represents idea and Hu again distinguished himself only as a supporter. Hu was aware that Zeng would join the PBSC at the 16th Party Congress and that he would represent a strong faction in the Fourth Generation. Hu was careful throughout the 1990s to pay heed to Zeng's suggestions, and often asked Zeng to say a few words at the end of any meeting over which he presided.

With the 16th Party Congress looming, starting in 2000 Jiang made a point of getting Zeng more public attention and openly praising him on several occasions, such as at the meeting of the heads of state of the Asia-Pacific Economic Cooperation organization in Shanghai in October 2001. In 2002, Jiang dispatched Zeng on state visits to Japan, Switzerland, and Austria.

Alone among Jiang Zemin's followers, Zeng did not support Jiang's decision to stay on as chairman of the Central Military Commission. He argued to Jiang that his interest lay in retiring—that staying on would mobilize opposition among other elders, damage Jiang's historical image, and hobble the Party with an ambiguous leadership structure. All of this would damage the Party's authority, especially in the West, making it look as if it were not self-confident or united enough to carry out a normal transfer of power.[13] Zeng had his own interests at stake as well. If Jiang remained influential during Zeng's first term in the PBSC, he would have only his second term left in which to make his own mark.

Barring a major slip by Hu Jintao, it would be difficult for Zeng to replace Hu, because emerging norms of Chinese Communist politics make Hu the leadership core of his generation. Hu's special skill is not making mistakes. Moreover, Hu has many supporters in the Party who would not support an attempt to remove him.

But replacing Hu should not be necessary for Zeng. Rather, he will seek to influence Hu's programs, especially on political issues. Zeng has strong potential support as the leading member of the Jiang faction, which includes new PBSC members Wu Bangguo, Li Changchun, Jia Qinglin, and Huang Ju (see Chapter 4) and several state ministers. Second, he enjoys the dominant position in the power network of sons (and a few daughters) of retired and deceased senior Party officials— the so-called "princelings faction" (*taizidang*). Zeng looked after their careers during his years as head of the Organization Department, and no other identifiable group of officials compares with them in political potential. The leading members of this faction now include Xi Jinping and Bo Xilai (both discussed in Chapter 5), and the offspring of Deng Xiaoping, Jiang Zemin, Chen Yun, and Liu Shaoqi.

Zeng's career has been lived in Jiang's shadow. But he has his own vision of the future, one less constrained by Party tradition than that

---

13. A reflection of this thinking in the CCP can be seen in the following line from the pro-*Beijing Jingbao* (Mirror) in Hong Kong: "Because some anti-China forces and Western media have tried to use the problems in China's transition to damage the stability of China's top level succession, the top levels of the CCP are even more determined to disregard this outside interference and maintain the political stability of the succession." Xin Rong, "Jiang Zemin tiqian tuichu shiliuda lilun kuangjia" (Jiang Zemin Sets Forth the Theoretical Framework for the 16th Congress in Advance), *Jingbao*, July 2002.

of his patron. Among the three politicians in China's new leadership, he is the one whose future actions are least predictable and most worthy of attention.

Wen Jiabao, age sixty-one, is the third-ranking member of the Politburo Standing Committee. He serves as premier of the State Council.

Mild-looking and conservatively dressed, Wen Jiabao is a master of survival from inner Party political disasters, with an uncanny ability to get along with everybody in top power circles. He is remembered in the West, if at all, for a dramatic appearance in Tiananmen Square at the height of the 1989 protests, accompanying Party General Secretary Zhao Ziyang on his tearful visit to the student leaders just before his fall from power. Despite his association with the deposed Zhao, Wen survived after Tiananmen and prospered in his sensitive, inner-Party work in Zhongnanhai because of his scrupulous fairness and attention to detail on behalf of a series of new, more conservative bosses. He later worked in the State Council, assisting Zhu Rongji in tackling China's toughest economic problems. Wen's skill as an economic manager is not in doubt, nor is his ability to work within the institutional and personal complexities of Party Central. What is unclear is whether he will be more successful than Zhu, his predecessor and mentor, in getting resistant bureaucracies to carry out reformist economic programs.

Wen is committed to privatizing failing state-owned enterprises, except for those in strategic sectors such as arms production and energy, and to continuing Zhu Rongji's policy of integrating China with the world economy. He is an expert on China's rural economy, and will likely pursue policies to reduce rural taxes and improve farm incomes. Another of his concerns is to construct a social welfare system, and especially to find money for unemployment insurance, a national pension plan for urban residents, and disability insurance. He is more sensitive to environmental concerns than other Chinese economic policymakers past or present. These policies will be liked in the West. But he does not favor a Western-style competitive political system. He prefers a Singapore-style neo-authoritarian system, in which elections are tightly controlled and the courts defer to the government in order to control potential social disorder.

Wen studied geomechanics—methods of exploring and developing underground resources—at the Beijing Geology Institute and was then assigned to work in Gansu province in 1968. He stayed there until 1982, mostly in a geoprospecting team reporting to the provincial geology bureau. Gansu was also where Hu Jintao worked during virtually the same period in the electrical power sector, but there is no mention in the investigation reports of any contact between the two men.

Like other members of his generation, Wen Jiabao's career took off in response to Deng Xiaoping's Four Transformations policy—to make the cadre corps younger and more professional. In response to this policy, the province's first Party secretary, Song Ping (also Hu Jintao's patron), arranged for Wen's accelerated promotion to deputy head of the provincial geology bureau. This led to Wen's accompanying the minister of geology and mineral resources, Sun Daguang, on a ten-day trip through the province in 1981. Sun was so impressed by Wen's knowledge of the province's resources and his vision for how to manage them that, with Song Ping's approval, he had Wen transferred to his ministry in Beijing the following year as head of its policy research office and a member of its Party cell.[14] Around this time the central Party Organization Department was conducting a talent search among Four Transformations cadres for people who could be selected for further promotion. Its full-scale investigation of Wen gave him the highest possible marks, and his name was duly entered on the list of candidates for elevation to ministerial rank.

---

14. A Party cell or "fraction" (*dangzu*) is a small group of the highest-ranking Party members inside a non-Party organization such as a ministry. It decides on all politically important matters.

In 1984 the Politburo decided to appoint a relatively young official, Wang Zhaoguo, to head the Party's Central Office, and to appoint one outstanding candidate from the Organization Department's list of potential young ministry-level cadres to serve as Wang's deputy. The Central Office is the nerve center in charge of coordinating and managing the daily paperwork of the Party leadership, including the Politburo and the Secretariat. It also manages the Central Guards Bureau, which is responsible for the security of Zhongnanhai and the top leaders. While not a policymaking body, its wide administrative responsibilities make it an influential organ and its staff are privy to all the Party's secrets. After poring over its list of possible candidates and conducting additional investigations, the Organization Department recommended two young cadres, Wen Jiabao and Wu Bangguo, who was then working in Shanghai. Wen got the assignment when Wu's superiors in Shanghai said that they had their own plans for him there.

Thus began a tumultuous eight-year stint in the Central Office during which Wen worked under three consecutive general secretaries and faced the most challenging episodes of his career. Within a year, Wen's boss Wang Zhaoguo was promoted to the Secretariat and Wen found himself in charge of the Central Office. All these personnel moves were part of an effort by then General Secretary Hu Yaobang to water down the influence of hard-liners in the central leadership. Hu, however, soon became a victim of the struggle. He was dismissed from office after student protests in late 1986 gave Party conservatives a chance to charge him with ideological laxity, though he remained on the Politburo.

Wen might have lost his position as well, but he demonstrated his talent for survival. At an inner Party meeting to criticize Hu Yaobang in early 1987, Wen performed an impressive ritual of self-criticism while avoiding any attack on his fallen boss. Left-wingers and liberals alike appreciated his willingness to take responsibility for his own actions without, as the Chinese saying goes, "casting stones on someone who has fallen down the well."

The conflict between liberals and hard-liners intensified under the newly appointed general secretary, Zhao Ziyang. Wen quickly became involved in formulating Zhao's wide-ranging political reform plans, which were announced at the 13th Party Congress in November 1987. Wen's involvement in the Zhao camp was highlighted at the congress by his promotion to the position of alternate member of the Secretariat. Again, the unassuming Wen found himself caught up in a high-stakes political battle. During 1988 the leadership split widened. The death of the deposed General Secretary Hu Yaobang in mid-April 1989 sparked a round of student protests that intensified and resulted in the Tiananmen hunger strike.

Over the next four weeks, Wen, as head of the Central Office, was responsible for coordinating affairs for Zhao Ziyang, the embattled head of the Party. He slept only two or three hours a night, amid tense meetings and fevered report-writing. With Zhao's fall from power when martial law was declared on May 20, Wen's office was cut off from all important information, which was redirected to State Council secretary Luo Gan, the close associate of Premier Li Peng.

After the June 4 crackdown, three full members of the Secretariat —Hu Qili, Rui Xingwen, and Yan Mingfu—were dismissed for siding with Zhao. As in 1987, Wen's position was precarious. But again he survived, by making a full account of his actions in the enlarged Politburo and Central Committee plenum meetings that followed the crackdown, while avoiding direct attacks on the deposed Zhao. That humble, honest attitude won praise from Elder Yang Shangkun and even from Li Peng, both of whom excused Wen's pro-Zhao behavior during the crisis as a case of doing one's job. He survived as director of the Central Office, now with the task of serving the third general secretary in five years, Jiang Zemin.

When Jiang arrived in Beijing at the height of the Tiananmen protests to be briefed in preparation for his accession to the general secretaryship, Wen met him at the airport and accompanied him to meetings with the Elders. Jiang was grateful for the way Wen handled his living arrangements and other details of his move to the capital. He was aware of his own political weakness in Beijing and decided to leave Wen in place because of his reputation for loyal service and his knowledge of how to get things done. Wen's survival strengthened an emerging Party understanding that service positions, even sensitive ones, are apolitical, and their occupants are not to be lightly switched with every change in higher policymaking offices.

Wen proved his worth by helping Jiang Zemin manage relations with Li Peng in the period from 1989 to 1992. Jiang had been promoted over Li's head, and the two men were locked in a battle for supremacy. Wen spent considerable time dealing with Li Peng through his opposite number in the State Council general office, Luo Gan. Yet Wen did not become identified as a Jiang partisan. He managed Central Office affairs without being perceived as taking sides, just as he had done for the previous two general secretaries.

A delicate problem was how to treat Zeng Qinghong, whom Jiang had placed in Wen's Central Office as a deputy director. It was obvious that Jiang would want Zeng to succeed Wen as director of the office after the 14th Party Congress in 1992. That meant that Wen had to give Zeng some say, while not upsetting the senior-ranking incumbent deputy, Xu Ruixin, a former personal assistant to the highly influential state president, Yang Shangkun. To offend either Zeng or Xu would be to offend their powerful patrons. Wen's solution was to leave Xu undisturbed in his key position as head of the office's secretarial bureau, which handled the flow of paperwork, while assigning Zeng to handle the office's personnel issues, a less important task which left Zeng time for projects assigned to him by Jiang Zemin. To compensate for Zeng's relatively minor duties, Wen accorded him higher protocol rank than Xu in the office, on the grounds that Zeng was a few years older and had been given the personal rank of vice-minister slightly earlier. In this way both men were treated with respect and both of their patrons were satisfied.

The tension between the two deputies' patrons sharpened in the months prior to the 14th Party Congress. Jiang Zemin was then lobbying Deng Xiaoping for Yang Shangkun's removal from the presidency (see Chapter 6). Wen again practiced the higher politics of not playing politics. Disregarding the impending purge of Xu Ruixin's patron, he followed standard procedure and assigned Xu, as head of the Central Office's secretarial bureau, to lead the secretarial bureau within the temporary congress secretariat. Not long after this, Yang Shangkun and his cousin, General Yang Baibing, were purged for their suspected challenge to Deng Xiaoping's authority, and Xu was transferred. He served the remaining years of his career as a vice-minister of civil affairs.

In 1993 Jiang Zemin carried out his plan to promote Zeng to direct the Central Office. Having served his transitional purpose, Wen might now have been sent into semiretirement. But he had performed so well that Jiang had other plans for him. Jiang had already upgraded him to full member of the Secretariat and alternate member of the Politburo. Now Jiang wanted to appoint Wen a vice-premier with special responsibility for agriculture.

Here Wen's career hit a temporary snag, because two other factions coveted the same vice-premiership. Premier Li Peng wanted it for his ally Jiang Chunyun, the Party chief of Shandong province. Liberal elders Wan Li and Tian Jiyun wanted the position for their favorite, State Councilor Chen Junsheng. The three factions engaged in spirited negotiations in the months after the 14th Party Congress but could not reach agreement. As a result, the agriculture portfolio was handed to incumbent vice-premier Zhu Rongji, who was appointed head of a newly created Leading Group on Agriculture.

Wen had to settle for the job of assisting Zhu as deputy of this group. He served in this position from 1993 to 1995. During these years, he also made himself useful by informally helping newly appointed PBSC member Hu Jintao understand the workings of Zhongnanhai, something for which Hu remains grateful.

After 1995, Wen was again deprived of a desirable position. He lost his modest assignment in agricultural affairs when Li Peng finally succeeded in promoting Jiang Chunyun to vice-premier in charge of agriculture, an appointment that gained a record-low 64 percent of the votes from NPC delegates. From 1995 to 1997, Wen was still a member of the Secretariat and an alternate Politburo member, but he was not very busy.

It took until the 15th Party Congress in 1997 for Wen's career to gain new impetus. Several factors were at work. Most important was Jiang Chunyun's political collapse as a result of the exposure of a large-scale corruption scandal in his former province of Shandong shortly after he left there.[15] Jiang Chunyun was forced out of the vice-premiership after one term, just as Li Peng was retiring as premier. That allowed Jiang Zemin to renew Wen's nomination for vice-premier. It helped that the incoming premier was Zhu Rongji, who had been impressed with Wen during their work together in the Leading Group on Agriculture. Wen was promoted to full Politburo membership at the 15th Party Congress and elevated to vice-premier at the next NPC meeting in 1998.

Once he was installed as vice-premier, Wen's career was back on track. Zhu Rongji gave him direct responsibility for rural affairs and the environment, including agriculture, poverty relief, flood control, and reforestation. He shared responsibility for development planning and financial affairs. No fewer than ten ministerial-level bodies and eight cabinet-level organizations came under his authority.[16] He managed to visit most parts of the country on inspection tours and became

---

15. A corruption scandal involving bribes of $320,000 uncovered in the resort city of Tai'an in 1995 led to the execution of the city's police chief and the jailing of five other top officials, including the city's Party secretary Hu Jianxue. Hu was considered to be a protégé of Jiang Chunyun.

16. See Zong, *Zhu Rongji zai 1999*, p. 179.

one of the most knowledgeable senior leaders on rural issues. He took charge of drafting the country's ten-year plan for reducing rural poverty. He also took advantage of his partial responsibility for financial affairs to master the economic and financial portfolios, winning Zhu's trust. He was further rewarded by being included in the Party's top-level bodies for overseeing banking and economic policy, first as secretary-general of the Central Financial and Economics Leading Group and later as head of the Central Financial Working Committee, created during the 1997–1998 Asian financial crisis.

Wen also helped manage the Western Development Strategy—plans for investing central government money to develop resources in Xinjiang and to link that remote region more closely to the rest of China. He supervised flood relief efforts, and became an expert in environmental protection and the problems of sustainable development.

All this was wonderful training for future promotion to the premiership, which Zhu Rongji had in mind for Wen. Wen made a reputation as a quick study of complex economic issues and an unwavering proponent of state enterprise reform and global economic integration. In evaluating Wen for his investigation report, Zhu Rongji described him in the terse four- and six-character phrases typical of inner-Party evaluations as follows:

> [A leader] at the head of the charge, dares to take responsibility, a careful thinker, a clear speaker; good at getting the big picture, quick-moving; doesn't panic when nearing the battlefield, quiet and calm; treats even minor affairs seriously, sees the situation in overview. Good at uncovering problems, good at adjusting relationships.

Wen, however, is no clone of Zhu. Zhu is impatient, outspoken, and brutally critical of subordinates. Wen is an introvert; he gives careful thought to problems, buries his head in his work, and prefers a more consensual style of administration. He avoids the media and does not seek out opportunities to rub shoulders with the global elite, in contrast with Zhu, whose international contacts made many in China believe that he fawned over things foreign. Unlike Zhu and indeed most Chinese leaders of both the Third and the Fourth Generations, Wen has a thorough knowledge of and sincere concern for rural China. All this may make Wen a less familiar and welcome figure than Zhu among global business and political leaders, but he will be more popular and better able to build coalitions among Chinese officials. In a political system where grand plans can be subverted by silent noncooperation, these qualities may enable Wen to push reform further than Zhu was able to do. Zhu, for example, failed in his goal to rid the state sector of enterprises that consistently showed losses.

No less important has been his continued ability to avoid making enemies. Wen gets along well with Hu Jintao, which makes it likely that there will be no rivalry between the two, in contrast to the relations between Jiang Zemin and the two premiers who served with him, Li Peng and Zhu Rongji. Wen also enjoys the respect of Zeng Qinghong, who admires political survivors. Even Luo Gan, the flagbearer of Li Peng's conservatism, has no conflicts with Wen. Wen's main challenge will come from his vice-premiers, especially Executive Vice Premier Huang Ju, who is in charge of fiscal and financial matters, and the vice-premier in charge of state investments in industry and infrastructure, Zeng Peiyan. Both are cronies of Jiang Zemin and can be expected to try to soften the impact of reform on large state enterprises, state banks, and industrial ministries.

4

THE MANAGERS

MANAGERS ARE AS necessary to government as visionaries and manipulators. The new senior Chinese leadership has six of them, all with impressive credentials and reputations for competence. Although none has the ambition or the power base to displace Hu Jintao at the pinnacle of power, or to gain dominance over policy as a whole, each will have great authority in his own sphere of work, as well as a strong voice in collective decisions. Among them, these technocrats will oversee the economy, legislation, the legal system, Party discipline, and domestic security. Their daily decisions will have both immediate and long-lasting effects on the lives of the Chinese people.

Wu Bangguo, age sixty-one, is the second-ranking member of the PBSC; he serves as chairman of the Standing Committee of the National People's Congress.

A straight-backed man with a thin face, Wu Bangguo is known for his common touch. A Party investigation report once described him as "having a high level of political ideology, creative in his work, effective in whatever he does, with a democratic work style, easily approachable, especially good at unifying comrades, hardworking and simple, and placing high demands on himself." As chairman of the National People's Congress Standing Committee, Wu will be the chief officer of the NPC. The National People's Congress is China's increasingly assertive legislature. It is elected every five years by members of the provincial-level people's congresses and has a membership of about three thousand, including both Communist Party and non-Party members. The NPC meets only once a year for a few weeks, and spends most of its time in subgroups studying and expressing its support for government policy. It approves preselected candidates for state posts and adopts laws that have been vetted by a permanent Legislative Affairs Committee and other NPC organs. It also has the right on paper to initiate legislation, and must approve any legislation suggested by other agencies, so it has the potential to serve as a base from which to launch reforms of domestic politics and administration. Wu, however, has given no indication that he has bold ideas for change, and his quiet personal style makes it doubtful that he will seek to exploit the power potentially inherent in his new job. He will participate in collective decisions as a PBSC member and will probably work to keep the NPC functioning as a cooperative element in the Party-dominated regime.

Wu was born in Anhui province and graduated in 1967 from Qinghua University with a specialty in electron vacuum tubes from the department of radio electronics. He began his career as a worker in an electron tube factory in Shanghai, and rose through various production, technical, and administrative posts in the city's electronics and telecommunications industries until 1982. At that point Wu's career changed, as had those of Hu Jintao, Wen Jiabao, Luo Gan, and others of the Fourth Generation, in response to Deng Xiaoping's order for the Four Transformations of cadres.

The Shanghai Party secretary, Chen Guodong, and the Organization Department chief, Hu Lijiao, conducted a citywide talent hunt in response to Deng's order. They discovered in Wu a prime example of a young cadre who came from humble origins, maintained a modest lifestyle, was a Party member (since 1964), had a college degree, was productive at work, and was popular with colleagues. Wu became Shanghai's youngest nominee to the 1982 12th Central Committee, as an alternate member. The next year he became Party secretary of Shanghai's science and technology commission and a member of the municipal Party committee's standing committee. These appointments signaled his shift from work focused on production to Party work.

Wu's advance to a national-level position might have taken place the following year when Beijing began casting around for a young cadre to fill a vacant position in Zhongnanhai's Central Office (see the biography of Wen Jiabao in Chapter 3). But he had just joined the Shanghai Party committee, and its leaders wanted him to stay. That Wen got the job instead of Wu may help explain why Wen and not Wu became premier in 2003. Wu remained in Shanghai for another decade. He became a deputy Party secretary in 1985, and in 1991 took over as Party secretary at the recommendation of Zhu Rongji, who was bound for Beijing.

The Party's investigation report notes that Wu's style of life did not change when he first rose to relatively high rank in Shanghai. His family continued to live in its old apartment, and on hot summer nights Wu would put out a plastic stool and sit chatting with neighbors, wearing an undershirt and short pants, the Shanghai male uniform for such occasions.

Although he had worked closely with Jiang for only a year and a half when the latter was Shanghai Party secretary in the late 1980s, in that short time Wu's attention to detail and deference to Jiang's wishes made him a protégé. That in turn won him entry to the Politburo in 1992 when Jiang as the new general secretary had his first chance to promote some of his own people. This was followed by Wu's transfer to Beijing as a member of the Party Secretariat in 1994 and his appointment to a vice-premier position the following year.

Still, Wu was only Jiang's second choice for vice-premier. Jiang's inner-Party evaluation of Wu at that time praised him in these terms:

"A straightforward way of acting, serious about his duties, fulfills every assignment, down-to-earth work style." But Jiang added that he "lacks boldness and creativity." Jiang had a higher regard for Shanghai mayor Huang Ju, a tireless cheerleader for Jiang. But Huang's transfer to Beijing was blocked by other senior leaders, so Jiang got the approval of the Politburo and the then still influential Elders to promote Wu.

Some call Wu a member of the "Shanghai gang" (*Shanghai bang*), meaning the Jiang Zemin faction.[1] It is true that Wu is one of over a score of Shanghai officials whom Jiang transferred to important positions in Beijing. But once in Beijing, Wu did not act as a Jiang partisan. When he worked in the State Council under Li Peng from 1995 to 1998 he served Li loyally. When Wu later found himself in the middle of a struggle over state enterprise reform between Jiang Zemin and Zhu Rongji, he maintained neutrality rather than doing Jiang's exclusive bidding.

Wu's portfolio as vice-premier under Li Peng from 1995 to 1998 included industry and transport. Although Zhu Rongji, as executive vice-premier, had primary responsibility for economic matters, Li Peng used to go around him and make inquiries directly to Wu about matters within Wu's portfolio. Wu managed this difficult situation by routing his replies to Li through Zhu's office, keeping Zhu informed while not slighting Li.

When Zhu became premier in early 1998, Wu retained his position as vice-premier while his portfolio of responsibilities expanded to include all the economic and industry-related ministries, as well as national defense industry, labor, and welfare. The thankless task of reforming state industries fell primarily to him in these years. It would have been hard for anyone given this responsibility to establish a record of outstanding achievement: there were too many obstacles to turning

---

1. See, for example, Cheng Li, "The 'Shanghai Gang': Force for Stability or Cause for Conflict?" www.chinaleadershipmonitor.org, August 2002.

these technologically backward, overstaffed enterprises into profitable, modern firms. (Wu nonetheless claimed considerable success, as shown by remarks we translate in Chapter 7.) Constant outbreaks of worker protest and frequent interventions by Party ideologues worried about the political implications of privatization meant that efforts to bring about reform were gridlocked by political considerations.

In any case, Wu was not the man for the job. In contrast to his harsh-mannered boss, Zhu Rongji, Wu was known for being softhearted, unable to say no. Provincial officials developed a habit of going over the heads of their direct superiors in the central government to plead with Wu for delays in carrying out enterprise reform measures or for the approval of already-rejected major construction projects.

Another frustrating responsibility of Wu's during these years was the safety of production workers. During his term as vice-premier China continued to suffer from the world's worst safety record in mining and industry, although the failures in this field cannot be blamed on lack of exhortation by the central government. A third unfortunate assignment was one that he was given because Li Peng trusted him. At Li's suggestion, Zhu Rongji assigned Wu the oversight of the massive and controversial Three Gorges Dam project in Hubei. The project is on schedule but has drawn constant foreign criticism for environmental damage and abuse of human rights in the course of resettling people from the areas that will be flooded by the dam.

Those hard days are behind Wu now that he has moved into the chairmanship of the National People's Congress. That body is Party-dominated, but also includes many non-Party delegates, and offers a channel for grassroots issues to be vetted at a high level. Wu Bangguo's affable manner should make him a more effective representative of the Party to non-Party constituencies and to the public than his im-mediate predecessor, Li Peng. The post of NPC chair carries number two protocol rank in the Party, in deference to the NPC's constitu-tional position as the repository of popular sovereignty. But Wu's personality is less forceful and his power base less developed than those of such previous incumbents of the post as Li Peng and Qiao Shi. In the collective deliberations of the PBSC, Wu, who spent his entire career in the state-owned industry sector, will probably be a voice for caution in economic and political reform.

Luo Gan, age sixty-seven, is the ninth-ranking member of the PBSC and secretary of the Central Politics and Law Committee. He will be in charge of internal security and police matters.

The oldest member of the new leadership, Luo Gan is a large man who emanates a feeling of energy. He keeps fit, swimming and playing tennis regularly. Trained in East Germany as a specialist in metallurgical pressure processing and machine casting, he holds the prestigious rank of senior engineer (*gaoji gongchengshi*), akin to full professor. He has a severe expression, wide wire-rimmed glasses, and pursed lips, and is known as decisive, stubborn, and not easily approachable. Luo is hard-working and hard-driving at the office. In private, he indulges a taste acquired in Europe for wine, whiskey, cognac, tobacco, and foreign movies.

As chief of Chinese internal security since 1997, Luo has supervised fierce repression not only of members of organized crime, drug smugglers, and the like, but also of political dissidents, participants in independent religious groups including unauthorized Christian groups and Falungong, and opponents of Chinese rule in Xinjiang. He has presided over an unprecedented increase in the use of the death penalty. Yet some of his other policy priorities converge with those of international human rights advocates. He has tried to reduce corruption and abuse in the Chinese court and prison systems by increasing funding for both. He has warned the courts not to make mistakes in imposing the death penalty. And he has initiated reform of China's anachronistic household registration system, which until recently tied rural residents administratively to the land.

Luo is sensitive about his negative image in the West, and cultivated a modest friendship with the former US ambassador to Beijing, James Sasser, as part of his effort to dispel that image. Yet as China's chief domestic spymaster, he views relations with the West as a matter of détente rather than partnership. He is the temple guardian for the legacy of Li Peng, ready to direct his fearful gaze at anyone who would seek to revise the verdict on the 1989 Tiananmen crackdown in which Li played a crucial part. He will be the chief obstacle to political reforms under the new leadership, and is the most likely figure to be purged if a power struggle over political reform emerges before his term of office expires in 2007.

Although he has exercised great influence since 1988, few in China or abroad have written at any length on Luo.[2] He was born in Shandong and studied steel processing in Beijing before being sent to East Germany for training in 1954. He remained there for eight years, first learning German at Karl Marx University in Leipzig, then undertaking factory training and academic studies in metallurgy in Leipzig and Freiburg. It was during his stay in Germany that he gained admission to the Chinese Communist Party. On his return to China in 1962, Luo was assigned to the First Ministry of Machine-Building, which ran China's car and truck industry. He served in its research institutes for eighteen years. This coincided with time spent in the same ministry by Jiang Zemin, but the two never came into contact. Similarly, they both

---

2. Luo is barely mentioned in most standard treatments of the Fourth Generation. See Li Cheng, *China's Leaders*. A rare example of a portrait is provided in Xin Di, "'Nenggan wushi' de Luo Gan" (Luo Gan: The 'Capable and Practical' Leader), *Guangjiaojing* (Wide Angle Magazine, Hong Kong), May 1999, pp. 44–45. There is a short biography by Dong Pang, "Mishubang pingbu qingyunde dianfan Luo Gan" (Luo Gan: The Classic Example of a Secretary Faction Member Who Rose Through the Ranks) in *Zhonggong disidai mengren* (The Hot Prospects of the Fourth Generation), edited by Xiao Chong (Hong Kong: Xiafeier Press, 1998). See also "Luo Gan: Zhongguo diyi gancai" (Luo Gan: China's First Talent) in *Zhonggong disidai*, edited by Lin Hua, pp. 20–21.

later served at different levels in the import-export management bureaucracy without having any relationship. Luo nonetheless likes to highlight these career overlaps with the claim that Jiang is his "old leader."

Like others of the Fourth Generation, Luo's leap from technician to cadre came in the early 1980s as a result of Deng Xiaoping's Four Transformations movement. In 1981 he was promoted to be vice-governor of the province of Henan, where he was working, and the following year, at age forty-six, he was appointed deputy provincial Party secretary.[3] The Party Center then decided in 1983 to promote a group of promising young cadres to ministerial rank and give them new assignments. Luo was one of the beneficiaries of this policy; others included Zhu Rongji, Wen Jiabao, and Wu Bangguo. Luo was brought to Beijing to serve as vice-chairman of the official All-China Federation of Trade Unions, where he remained until 1988.

The fateful relationship that would remake his career developed in late 1987 when the new acting premier, Li Peng, was revamping the State Council with conservative technocrats like himself.[4] One of Li Peng's trusted allies from their days studying in the Soviet Union, the director of the State Economic Reform Commission, Li Tieying, recommended Luo. As a conservative from the heavy-industry sector trained in the socialist bloc, Luo shared many traits with both Li Tieying and Li Peng. After interviewing Luo three times, Li took him on as minister of labor.

In assuming control of the cabinet, Li Peng had retained the body's chief administrator, Chen Junsheng, even though Chen was an appointee of the liberal former premier Zhao Ziyang. Li wanted his

---

3. His title was provincial Party secretary but since there was also a first secretary, his rank was equivalent to a deputy secretary.

4. Li Peng became acting premier in 1987 after the premier, Zhao Ziyang, was transferred to the post of Party general secretary to take the place of Hu Yaobang, who had been dismissed. Li was confirmed as premier at the National People's Congress meeting in 1988 and served two terms until 1998.

own man in the job, but did not want to appear to clean house precipitously, which would have been considered a misstep in the atmosphere of meritocracy and collective leadership that the Party leaders were cultivating. But fortune favored Li's designs. At the annual beachside leadership retreat in Beidaihe in August 1988, Chen suffered a brain hemorrhage while working around the clock on proposals for price reforms that were then being furiously debated among the senior leaders. He was sent on leave to convalesce. After consulting Li Tieying and the executive vice-premier, Yao Yilin, among others, Li Peng chose Luo Gan to fill the vacancy. Li paid a polite personal visit to Chen Junsheng to urge him to resign for his own health.

The post of secretary-general of the State Council is parallel to that of director of the Party Central Office, which Wen Jiabao held at the time. While the responsibility of the director of the Party Central Office is wider than that of the secretary-general of the State Council (as would be expected given the preeminence of the Party in China's political system), both officials are primarily concerned with staffing and coordinating the work of their respective policymaking bodies.

Taking over the position was a challenge for Luo, who had virtually no experience with economic affairs, which dominate the State Council's work. It was widely noted that the conservative "Soviet faction" under Li Peng was running the government and blocking the rapid economic reform plans promoted by Zhao Ziyang and his followers. Yet Luo could, from his own training and experience, provide little ideological ammunition for the premier on economic affairs.

Li Peng instead assigned Luo to coordinate political, legal, and personnel matters. In his role as the cabinet's coordinator on internal security issues, he was in a position inferior to the Party person handling these issues, PBSC member Qiao Shi. But it was nonetheless a fortuitous entrée to a path that would lead higher.

When the Tiananmen Square demonstrations erupted in April 1989, Luo's portfolio suddenly became the most important one held by a member of the cabinet staff. In the tense weeks of the demonstrations and hunger strike leading up to the military killings of citizens in parts of Beijing, Luo was Li Peng's assiduous lieutenant, seeing to it personally that every one of the premier's orders was carried out. Luo even cleared a building inside Zhongnanhai once inhabited by Mao Zedong—the famous "swimming pool" complex—for Li and his wife to occupy when the protests made travel around Beijing difficult and dangerous. On the night of June 3, as the military moved into the square and killings started around the city, Luo Gan remained at Li Peng's side, keeping him abreast of the latest developments as reported directly to him by the military, security, and intelligence agencies. On the afternoon of June 5, with the cleanup operation in full swing throughout the capital, Luo presided over a meeting to brief heads of Party and government departments—officials kept mostly in the dark through the previous weeks. Typical of Luo's thoroughness was his post-crackdown order to Chinese embassies abroad to collect videotapes of the demonstrations from foreign television programs. Images gleaned from the tapes helped security agencies track down and arrest demonstrators who had scattered throughout the country.

These events created a personal bond between Li Peng and Luo Gan. Luo formed the habit of ending almost all of his long work days by going to Li Peng's temporary Zhongnanhai residence for a swim, followed by a long talk with Li and his wife. Even after Li left the premiership and moved out of Zhongnanhai and Luo achieved still higher office, he continued to make personal calls on the Li family about once a week.

After Tiananmen, with Zhao Ziyang purged and discredited, Li Peng was able gradually to replace pro-Zhao vice-premiers, ministers, and cabinet administrative staff. In 1993, Li promoted Luo to the position of state councilor, with responsibilities for organizational and personnel arrangements in government departments. Luo retained his key position as State Council secretary-general.

At this time Li extended his protégé's influence over internal security affairs. The Party committee in charge of this sector is called the Central Politics and Law Committee (CPLC). Established after the Cultural Revolution, the CPLC coordinates the work of the police, intelligence, justice, prison, and prosecutorial arms of the government. Qiao Shi had become the CPLC secretary when he joined the Politburo in 1985, an assignment which helped him move up to the PBSC in 1987. Qiao was relatively liberal, having refused to side with the hard-liners when the PBSC was called upon to vote on martial law during the Tiananmen crisis.[5] He had nonetheless survived the Tiananmen events politically and retained control of the CPLC. In 1992, he handed over its secretaryship to an ally, Ren Jianxin, while retaining oversight of this sector on the PBSC.

Luo Gan had achieved some influence over the CPLC agencies during Tiananmen, far more than a State Council staff member has in normal times. The opportunity to extend that control came in 1993 when the position of CPLC deputy secretary became vacant. Li Peng nominated Luo to fill it. In 1997, when Qiao Shi was removed from the PBSC, Luo was promoted to membership in the Politburo and the Secretariat. This put him in position to replace Ren Jianxin as CPLC secretary since he now outranked Ren, who was only a Secretariat member. Despite an effort by Jiang Zemin to derail the appointment (see Chapter 2), Luo took over the CPLC.

With Li Peng's shift from premier to chairman of the NPC in early 1998, it appeared doubtful that Luo would remain a state councilor in the new cabinet of reformist Premier Zhu Rongji. Zhu expressed a desire to be rid of Luo. But Li Peng, now joined by Jiang Zemin, who shared some of Li Peng's conservative economic ideas, convinced Zhu to allow Luo to stay. Luo continued to supervise the security agencies. Added to his positions as CPLC secretary and Politburo member, this made him a strong candidate for PBSC membership in 2002.

---

5. See *The Tiananmen Papers*, p. 192.

In the ten years that Luo has served near or at the top of the security system, he has developed a distinctive mix of policies, combining coercive repression and rationalizing reforms. He has had a major impact on loosening the limits on internal migration that have discriminated against rural dwellers since the 1950s, and he has overseen an increase in funding and a strong drive for improved attention to rules and professional conduct in the judiciary and the police (see Chapter 7).

At the same time, Luo has used the Chinese state's vast coercive powers with an intensity that is in some ways unprecedented even in the PRC's history. He headed the Leading Small Group to Deal with Falungong that was set up after that religious organization's April 25, 1999, demonstration in front of Zhongnanhai. Under his leadership the Party classified Falungong as an "evil cult" and conducted an all-out propaganda and police campaign that appears to have come close to eliminating the group within China.

In 1997 Luo redirected an ongoing "strike-hard" (*yanda*) anti-crime campaign in order to intensify arrests and convictions of political and religious dissidents. During the campaign, according to the Party's statistics, more than 60,000 alleged criminals were killed by police and the courts in the four-year period between 1998 and 2001, a far higher number than even the highest Western estimates (see Chapter 7). Luo has also given determined leadership to the Party's fight against separatism among the Uighurs, a Muslim group in the strategic northwestern region of Xinjiang (see Chapter 8).

Luo's job also involved him occasionally in relations with the West, where he exhibited practical attitudes devoid of hostility. In 1999, when American planes bombed the Chinese embassy in Belgrade, anti-American sentiment ran high in the Chinese leadership. Luo's patron Li Peng called the bombing "an insult and challenge to the Chinese people" that showed that the US was China's "enemy."[6] Luo

---

6. Zong, *Zhu Rongji zai 1999*, pp. 74–75.

made several secret trips to observe the embassy neighborhood in Beijing to make sure that it was adequately protected and that the US ambassador, James Sasser, was safe. After the September 11, 2001, terrorist incidents in New York and Washington, Luo spoke in the Politburo in favor of intelligence-sharing with the Americans to help them prosecute the war in Afghanistan.

Luo, then, is a complicated figure, a resolute law-and-order man who has shown an interest in making the extremely punitive control system more fair and effective. He pays attention to criticisms from the West, at least when they make sense within his own frame of reference, but he is willing to do whatever he thinks necessary regardless of international opinion when he thinks the Party's rule is challenged. He is not a personable man, but his colleagues respect his dedication and capacity for work. The most sentimental part of his makeup may be his loyalty to Li Peng, which—together with his own involvement in the 1989 crackdown—dictates that he will oppose any proposal to reverse the verdict on Tiananmen. If the new leadership remains cautious on political reforms or wider social liberalization, Luo may thrive. But he would be vulnerable if the leadership moves to embrace the kind of liberal reforms that were aborted as a result of the Tiananmen events.

Li Changchun, age fifty-nine, is the eighth-ranking member of the PBSC, supervising the Party's work in propaganda and ideology.

Li Changchun is an experienced and forceful economic reformer who has left his mark on three of China's most dynamic provinces. Energetic, creative, and decisive, he enjoys mixing with people, and is considered approachable and good at motivating subordinates. Like his patron Jiang Zemin, Li likes to appear in public and to see his name in the newspapers. But in contrast to Jiang, Li has been a bold reformer, pushing for considerable changes wherever he has governed. He handled several highly publicized bankruptcies of state-backed financial groups in Guangdong in such a way as to help protect China from the contagion of the Asian financial crisis. He also pioneered efforts to make it easier for poor people to sue government. Taking risks, he has sometimes suffered setbacks. His stewardship of two of China's most important provinces, Liaoning and Guangdong, was marred by corruption scandals that brought down followers of his, although without implicating him.

Li's early career moved faster than that of the more cautious Hu Jintao, but the conservative backlash after 1989 propelled Hu's career ahead of Li's. Li nonetheless has risen very near the top. At age fifty-nine, he still has over a decade of active political life ahead of him.

Li Changchun was born into a modest family in Jilin city in Jilin province, on the frigid plains of northeastern China. He studied automation in the department of electrical engineering at Harbin Industrial University, then was assigned to work in an electrical circuits factory in the large northeastern industrial city of Shenyang during the Cultural Revolution. In 1980, when Deng Xiaoping called for the promotion of young and educated cadres, Li was named deputy Party secretary and deputy bureau chief in the city's bureau of mechanical and electrical industries, and then rose rapidly to vice-mayor. In 1982 he was selected as an alternate member of the Party Central Committee—the youngest member at age thirty-eight, and thus ahead in his career of other promising young cadres who were also chosen as Central Committee alternates at the time, including Hu Jintao, Wu Bangguo, and Luo Gan.

After serving for three years as Shenyang's mayor and Party chief, in 1986 Li was elevated to acting governor, and then governor and deputy Party secretary, of Liaoning province, of which Shenyang is the capital. This made Li the youngest provincial governor at the time. During his years leading the city and then the province, Li tackled the problem of inefficient state-owned enterprises (SOEs), which dominate the economy of this rust-belt province. Conservatives believed that closing SOEs would throw too many people out of work and threaten state dominance of the economy. Li drew on his own experience working in SOEs to argue that perverse incentives made some of them unreformable: the worse they were managed, the more likely the state was to bail them out. A new idea at the time for breaking this logic was to force some SOEs into bankruptcy. The threat of bankruptcy was supposed to make SOE managers and workers perform better. As mayor of Shenyang, Li offered the city as an experimental site for trying out the provisions of the national draft bankruptcy law. (It is a common practice in China to try out a law in a particular place for a period of time before adopting it.) He drew press adulation around the country when he actually forced the first SOE in China into bankruptcy in 1985.

Even after the fall of Hu Yaobang in 1987 brought a mood of conservatism to Beijing, Li continued to push SOE reform in Liaoning, ordering the "separation of Party and enterprise"—a pullback of Party organizations in factories from interfering in economic decisions by factory managers. Li also encouraged sending students and managers from the province overseas to study, especially in fields related to foreign trade and investment.

Li won praise at the time. But his relationship with some of the high-flying cadres in the provincial capital would come back to haunt him. In 2001, Li's former subordinate in Shenyang and successor as mayor, Mu Suixin, and other officials whom Li had promoted there were accused of stealing tens of millions of yuan in public funds. Mu was sentenced to death with a two-year postponement of execution (he later died in jail). Li was never personally implicated. The Party's Central Disciplinary Inspection Commission, which exposed the incident, blamed it on the bad character of the criminals rather than on Li Changchun's management of the province's affairs. Nonetheless, perhaps not coincidentally, the incident put a blot on Li's record just at the time when Jiang Zemin was trying to promote his candidacy for premier in the 2002 succession.

From 1990 to 1998, Li was assigned to the large and predominantly rural central province of Henan, first as governor and then as Party secretary. This added valuable diversity to his experience as an economic manager. But his work there was not very successful. Incomes of the province's rural residents stagnated, an AIDS epidemic began as a result of the unhygienic collection of blood plasma (see Chapter 7), and population control measures were not enforced.

During his years in Henan, Li formed a political alliance with Jiang Zemin. In the 1980s, when he and Jiang were administering competing provinces—Liaoning and Shanghai, both strongholds of traditional state-owned industry—Li had earned Jiang's disapproval by demanding special policy concessions for Liaoning, similar to those that the central government had granted Shanghai to enable it to modernize its economy. (Li's request was overruled by Deng Xiaoping.) In the 1990s, however, the two men's situations were different. Li was trying to advance his career and Jiang Zemin was laboring to consolidate power in Beijing. Jiang began to see Li as a mirror image of himself, and as a more promising successor than Hu Jintao. Jiang called Li in for private conversations every time Li was in Beijing. In 1997, Jiang personally ensured that Li was promoted to the Politburo.

The following year, Jiang sent Li to take over as Party secretary of the booming southern province of Guangdong, in a bold and ultimately successful effort to take over the province from an independent group of locally born leaders referred to as the "Guangdong gang." Li relished the assignment, shaking up the leaderships of cities in the province that he deemed to be too entrenched. Moreover, a crisis in Guangdong's hyperactive, risk-prone financial institutions gave Li a providential opportunity to weaken the power of local elites. The Guangdong International Trust and Investment Corporation (GITIC) and the Guangdong Enterprises (Holdings) Group (GDE) were two large financial conglomerates with roots among the families of local Party mandarins. When the Asian financial crisis struck in 1997–1998,

GITIC owed creditors about $4.5 billion, while GDE owed $6 billion. Much of their debt was unsecured and often not even, as required, reported to the central government's foreign exchange administration. The newly arrived Li Changchun set up a group of specialists under former central bank deputy governor Wang Qishan to evaluate the situation. In late 1998, with the determined backing of Zhu Rongji in Beijing, he forced GITIC into bankruptcy and GDE into a restructuring in which creditors had a leading part. When foreign creditors protested that bankrupting GITIC would damage China's sovereign credit, Li countered convincingly that if they assumed that the Chinese government would back up a private financial institution merely because of the personal connections of its executives, then they had failed to exercise due diligence. The provincial government did, however, make good GDE's debts because it was a provincial government agency. Li's bold actions did no long-run damage to Guangdong's or China's credit ratings. Li also borrowed $4.6 billion from a special central government fund to close hundreds of shaky credit unions and credit cooperatives in the province.

Another of Li's achievements in Guangdong was to pioneer the development of a legal aid system that funded suits by poor people against government agencies (see Chapter 7).

Li's work in Guangdong thus strengthened his image as a decisive leader and a reformer. It also broadened his experience in a new type of setting, an outward-looking exporting and financial center in contrast to the industrial and agricultural heartland provinces in which he had served before. Politically, Li turned Guangdong from a kingdom that Jiang Zemin could not control to one of Jiang's favorite bases—so much so that Jiang selected Guangdong as the place from which to launch his Three Represents campaign in 2000. Li reciprocated by praising Jiang's idea as an important contribution to Marxist theory, which he mentioned in the same breath as the theories of Mao and Deng. It was around this time that Jiang formed the wish to see Li succeed Zhu Rongji as premier,[7] although Zhu was busy preparing the way for Wen Jiabao to inherit that position.

Li made sure to pay frequent visits to Guangdong's two resident Party elders, Ye Xuanping and Ren Zhongyi, men widely respected in China for their part in resisting the excesses of the Cultural Revolution. He also went out of his way to be a good host whenever Li Peng and his wife, Zhu Lin, came to the province. Li Peng gradually became a supporter.

However, Li Changchun's prospects for becoming premier were damaged by several last-minute developments which appeared to reflect initiatives of Jiang Zemin's and Li Peng's ill-wishers. One was the case of Shenyang mayor Mu Suixin, mentioned earlier. Second, Li came in for direct censure from Zhu Rongji over a $500 million export rebate fraud scandal that was uncovered in the Guangdong coastal city of Shantou in 2000. (Export rebates cover a wide range of reimbursements to exporters for various taxes they have paid in the production and sale of their goods, including duties on imported materials, domestic value-added taxes, and export taxes.) The racket began when export rebate rates in China were increased in late 1999. In the first half of 2000, reported exports from Shantou shot up by 83 percent as the racket processed fake export receipts. In August Zhu set up a three-hundred-person special investigation team that bypassed Li Changchun and other Guangdong leaders as well as Shantou's corrupt paramilitary command. In the crackdown that followed, nineteen people were executed and another thirty jailed for life. Zhu made a point of personally criticizing Li Changchun at Politburo and other meetings for failing to detect and control the scam.

Third, Li was widely criticized in Beijing political circles for having

---

7. Jiang's wish to see Li become premier has previously been reported. See, for example, Lu Fei, "Li Changchun zhengzhi hangqing jixu kanzhang" (Li Changchun's Political Prospects Continue to Look Good), in *Shiliuda qiaweizhan*, edited by Xiao Chong, pp. 216–221.

promoted the career in Guangdong of one of Jiang Zemin's female friends, Huang Liman. Huang was considered incompetent. Moreover, her husband and sister had business interests in Shenzhen, the special economic zone near Hong Kong, where Li recommended her to serve as Party secretary. Li had done this to please Jiang, but Jiang's enemies in Beijing used his compliance with Jiang's wishes as a count against him.

Jiang nonetheless was intent on securing Li's promotion to PBSC status. That goal was achieved when Jiang blocked the promotion of a Fifth Generation cadre to the seventh PBSC seat (see Chapter 2). But Li's chance to obtain the important economic reform post of executive deputy premier in the State Council was blocked by the last-minute elevation of Huang Ju to the PBSC. Jiang preferred Huang to Li for the cabinet post, given Huang's longer and clearer record of loyalty to him. As a result, Li ended up as the sole member of the PBSC without a specific post in the cabinet or Party bureaucracy, and was charged with supervising the Party organs that deal with propaganda and ideology.

Li's career forms an instructive contrast to Hu Jintao's. Li had major achievements in three of China's most important provinces; Hu accomplished little in two of China's most backward provinces. Hu's career outpaced Li's because he took fewer risks and made fewer enemies. Li has more expertise in more of the complex economic and financial issues that face China than any other member of the new PBSC except Wen Jiabao. He has a forceful, winning personality and the courage to promote sweeping reforms. In the current PBSC's five-year term of office he is likely to help loosen the Party's tight control over information and encourage the growth of a more independent role for the media. He is young enough to serve a second term in the PBSC, when he might become still more influential.

Jia Qinglin, age sixty-three, is the fourth-ranking member of the PBSC and chairman of the Chinese People's Political Consultative Conference.

Jia Qinglin, the strongly built, square-faced offspring of a worker family, was raised in the northern heavy-industrial province of Hebei and trained as an engineer. He served as a government and Party leader for over a decade in the coastal province of Fujian. Jiang Zemin moved Jia to Beijing in 1996, where he served as Party secretary and a Politburo member before his elevation to the Standing Committee. Jia's reputation was marred by a major corruption scandal that broke in Fujian after he left, although he was never prosecuted for what many suspect was his involvement.

Jia's career has depended heavily on Jiang Zemin's support. He is expected to defend Jiang's policies and reputation as a member of the new leadership. He lacks an agenda of his own, and the independent power base or broad popularity that would enable him to promote one. Although he will participate in collective decisions as a PBSC member, his assignment as head of the Chinese People's Political Consultative Conference—a consultative body consisting mostly of "democratic personages" who are not Communist Party members—puts him out of the direct line of policymaking.

Starting in middle school in the 1950s, Jia Qinglin studied industrial enterprise planning and the design and manufacture of electric appliances. He became a Communist Party member while still in college, and graduated in 1962 from the Hebei Engineering Institute. For over twenty years, until 1985, Jia worked in various posts under the First Ministry of Machine Building, the ministry in charge of building cars and heavy vehicles like trucks, tractors, and earthmovers in the Mao-era command economy.

It was in the First Ministry that Jia formed his connection with Jiang Zemin. During the late 1970s and early 1980s, Jiang's patron Wang Daohan served as minister, and Jiang as deputy head and then head of the ministry's foreign affairs bureau. Jia's job as manager of the ministry's import-export arm (the China National Machinery and Equipment Import and Export Corporation) in 1978–1983 put him in frequent contact with Jiang. When Deng Xiaoping demanded the promotion of younger and more professionally trained officials, the ministry selected Jia as one of its "keypoint cultivation" cadres and in 1983 sent him to run the Taiyuan Heavy Machinery Factory in Shanxi province as both manager and Party secretary.

In 1985, the Organization Department transferred Jia to Fujian. Under the province's liberal Party secretary Xiang Nan, Jia ran the provincial Party organization department and the local Party school, along with other tasks of "Party work." When Jiang Zemin was promoted from Shanghai to head the Party in Beijing, one of his first moves was to arrange for Jia's elevation to provincial governor in Fujian, a step that was carried out in 1991. In 1993, Jiang arranged Jia's further promotion to provincial Party secretary. The outgoing secretary, Chen Guangyi, pleaded with Jiang not to be transferred to Beijing, saying he preferred to remain in Fujian as head of the provincial people's congress. But to remove any competition to his protégé, Jiang refused the request. Chen became head of China's government bureau in charge of state-owned airlines, and Jia took over not only the Party secretaryship but also the chairmanship of the people's congress.

Holding concentrated power did not enable Jia to perform with particular distinction in Fujian. He told the local cadres that he favored "ceaselessly liberating thought, carrying out practical, determined struggle, fully relying on the masses, and thoroughly transforming work styles"—a platform of typically Jiang-style generality. In contrast to Xi Jinping, who was serving as Fuzhou mayor at the time (see Chapter 5), Jia's dossier does not record concrete achievements in improving people's lives or promoting economic growth.

What marked his administration, and damaged his personal reputation, was a $6.4 billion smuggling scandal that was uncovered in the port city of Xiamen in 1999, after he had been transferred to Beijing. Zhu Rongji called this the biggest smuggling case in the history of the PRC and vowed to get to the bottom of it. The smuggling allegedly centered on a man named Lai Changxing and his company, the Yuanhua Group, which had bribed members of the local customs administration and military command in order to import black-market automobiles, gasoline, cigarettes, and a wide range of other controlled commodities without government permits. Lai was a personal friend of Jia and of Jia's wife Lin Youfang, who as general manager of the provincial government's foreign trade corporation was involved in matters involving import and export. Jia's involvement was thus widely suspected, but has not been proven. Jiang Zemin stifled discussion of Jia's role by inquiring frequently into the Central Disciplinary Inspection Commission's investigation, and by paying a conspicuous symbolic visit to the Beijing municipal government (Jia's unit) to express his support for its work. In Fujian the new governor, Xi Jinping, oversaw the purge of dozens of officials associated with the case but saw to it that Jia was not implicated, thus protecting his own status as one of the most promising of the younger fifth generation of leaders.

Ironically, Jia's career had meanwhile benefited from Jiang Zemin's energetic prosecution of the 1995 corruption case against Beijing Party secretary Chen Xitong (see Chapter 5). Chen's political demise cleared the way for Jia's promotion to Beijing. Jiang brought Jia to Beijing in 1996 as deputy Party secretary and in due course had him promoted to mayor and then Party secretary. In this way the important Beijing Party apparatus was turned from a stronghold of Li Peng into a base of support for Jiang and his followers.

Jia's performance in Beijing was no more remarkable than his work in Fujian. Where the ambitious Chen Xitong had burnished his public image with construction and environmental protection projects, the more compliant Jia Qinglin was not as good at wringing budgetary allocations out of the central authorities. In the personalized culture of Zhongnanhai, Jia was blamed for a 1998 incident in which his secretary and two other young cadres were killed when an official car they had taken on vacation went off the road in Shanxi. Other officials believed that if Jia had set a high personal standard of rectitude, his assistant would not have been vacationing in an official car and driving recklessly. But because of Jia's close ties to Jiang Zemin the incident was hushed up.

Beijing remains a stronghold for the pro-Jiang faction under the new Beijing Party secretary, Liu Qi, a subordinate of Jia's who has succeeded him now that Jia has moved to the CPPCC. In any future power struggle involving Jiang's reputation or influence, Jia Qinglin and his colleague Huang Ju are likely to be the strongest advocates of the pro-Jiang position. However, Jia is the most politically vulnerable member of the new leadership. The Yuanhua smuggling case remains open, partly because Lai Changxing, the man alleged to have been chiefly responsible, fled to Canada and has so far successfully resisted extradition. The Central Disciplinary Inspection Commission's team in charge of the case remains active; indeed, the official who ran the investigation, He Yong, was promoted at the 16th Party Congress to the important post of one of seven secretaries of the Party Secretariat and deputy secretary of the Central Disciplinary Inspection Commission under PBSC member Wu Guanzheng. The discipline commission will continue to investigate the case, not only because of its enormous scale, but because it affords an opportunity for Hu Jintao and his allies to chip away at the power base of one of Jiang Zemin's main followers. If the discipline commission makes headway in the case, and especially if China manages to extradite Lai Changxing from Canada, Jia could become the first political casualty in the new leadership.

Huang Ju, age sixty-four, is the sixth-ranking member of the PBSC and executive deputy premier of the State Council.

Huang Ju is a youthful-looking, articulate Shanghai native who, like so many of his colleagues, is a Qinghua-trained engineer. He is the only member of the new leadership to have worked his entire career in one place. His experience is also relatively narrow, encompassing only state-owned industry and municipal Party affairs. Nonetheless, Huang is a favorite of Jiang Zemin and models himself on Jiang in appearance and political style. This relation to Jiang has brought him to the center of power, but will be a liability as he seeks to establish his own influence within the new leadership.

Always a good student, Huang studied electrical machinery manufacturing at Qinghua University in the late 1950s and early 1960s, then worked for twenty years as a technician and Party official in a series of state-owned Shanghai factories, especially the Zhonghua Metallurgical Plant, where as a young technical cadre he passed safely through the Cultural Revolution. In 1983 he was selected for special promotion under Deng Xiaoping's rejuvenation program for the cadre corps, and was given a seat on the muncipal Party standing committee as the member in charge of Party work in the industrial sector.

The patrons behind Huang's promotion were Shanghai Party secretary Chen Guodong and Organization Department director Hu Lijiao, who also fostered the careers of Wu Bangguo and Zeng Qinghong. When Jiang became mayor of Shanghai in 1985, Huang advanced to deputy secretary of the Party committee and soon thereafter to vice-mayor. Jiang liked Huang's energy, his instinct for publicity, and his attentiveness to orders, and relied on him to manage urban planning and construction and Shanghai's fiscal relations with levels of government above and below Shanghai. Nonetheless, as recounted in Chapter 3, when Jiang moved to Beijing in 1989 he elected to take Zeng Qinghong with him rather than Huang Ju.

Huang remained in Shanghai. He rose to mayor in 1991, when Zhu Rongji was transferred to Beijing, and to Party secretary in 1994, when Wu Bangguo followed Zhu to the capital. Along with the Party secretary post, Huang received a seat in the Politburo. But Jiang's attempts in 1997 to get Huang promoted to a job in the central government were unsuccessful. An Organization Department report criticized

Huang for distancing himself from old friends when he acceded to high office, in contrast to Wu Bangguo, who had been known for his accessibility. When Wu and Huang were both serving in Shanghai, Wu as Party secretary and Huang as mayor, Wu ordered the media not to cover his activities, but the papers and TV were full of reports of Huang's doings, which many cadres viewed as inappropriate since the Party secretary outranks the mayor. Another criticism of Huang was that while Wu had not interfered in his decisions as mayor, when Huang became Party secretary he interfered constantly in the decisions of his successor, Xu Kuangdi. The unfortunate Xu was transferred to Beijing in early 2002 to serve as director of the Chinese Academy of Engineering and subsequently became a concurrent vice-chair of the CPPCC.

Like his mentor Jiang, Huang has been good at "following the line of upper-level officials" (see Chapter 6). He checked all his major Shanghai decisions with Jiang, and inherited Jiang's role of attending to Elders Chen Yun and Li Xiannian and their wives when the couples wintered in Shanghai.

As executive deputy premier, Huang will be a spokesman for continuity of the Jiang Zemin line, in particular preferring the interests of such advanced cities as Shanghai and of state enterprises over the needs of the more backward, rural interior. He is likely to make life more complicated for his direct superior, Wen Jiabao, who would have had an easier time implementing his reform programs if Jiang Zemin had continued to back his original choice for executive deputy premier, Li Changchun.

Wu Guanzheng, age sixty-four, is the seventh-ranking member of the PBSC and Secretary of the Central Disciplinary Inspection Commission.

A muscular, weathered, taciturn man of peasant background, Wu Guanzheng is an accomplished local administrator who in his earlier posts developed a relatively open style of governing that reminded many Chinese of Li Ruihuan. Although Wu is not a political crony of

Li's, he emulates Li's populist style and straight way of talking. Wu, however, lays less stress on common sense and more on the importance of expert advice to administrative decision-making.

It was Li Ruihuan who insisted on Wu's elevation to the PBSC as part of the price for his own retirement. The agency Wu will run, the Central Disciplinary Inspection Commission, is charged with investigating cadres at all levels who are accused of corruption or abuse of power. Because the commission is a Party rather than a state unit, it operates flexibly, and has the potential either to politicize anti-corruption investigations or not. Although ranking only seventh in the PBSC, Wu will enjoy considerable bargaining power with other leaders, whose associates are potential targets of corruption investigations, and at critical junctures he may be able to use this influence to promote political reform.

Like most of his colleagues, Wu is an engineer, trained in the early 1960s in thermal measurement and automatic control in Qinghua University's Power Department. He joined the CCP as an undergraduate in 1962. After postgraduate study he was assigned to a large state-owned chemical factory in the central industrial city of Wuhan. From 1975 to 1982 he served in a series of posts in the city government's science and technology administration.

Wu's career accelerated in 1982 in conjunction with Deng Xiaoping's campaign to promote younger and more technically proficient cadres. Wu was elected as an alternate member of the 12th Central Committee, along with Hu Jintao, Luo Gan, Wu Bangguo, and Li Changchun. Less than a year later he was appointed mayor of Wuhan.

Wuhan is a major industrial city and provincial capital of more than seven million people in central China. It consists of three towns divided by three rivers that flow together there. When Wu arrived, the towns were linked by a single bridge and fleets of ferries. According to his Party dossier, Wu rode the buses and ferries incognito for twenty days, then embarked on measures to speed traffic and alleviate congestion. He purchased new boats, enforced traffic rules, and set up staggered work hours to relieve congestion. He assigned university experts as advisers to local factories. He created a policy advisory group of about one hundred professors and engineers to give advice on economic development. One of his most celebrated innovations was to invite a retired West German engineer named Werner Gerich to run the city-owned Wuhan Diesel Engine Factory, which had been losing money. He gave the new manager carte blanche to fire excess workers, change product lines, reorganize production, and generally implement Western profit-making principles.[8] This was a bold move in 1984, when state enterprise reform was still in the talking stage nationally. Fully backed by Wu, in two years Gerich turned the stagnant plant into a money-making enterprise, earning Wu Guanzheng kudos not only for vision and daring, but for his ability to establish a relation of trust with a foreigner.

In 1986 Wu was transferred to his native province of Jiangxi to become governor and, nine years later, Party secretary. Here again he established an advisory group of specialists, the Jiangxi Provincial Government Policy Advisory Commission, composed of ninety-three technicians and professors, many of them non-CCP members. Wu announced that he would not make any major decision in economic policy without having his advisers review at least two competing policy options. He invited these experts to speak at meetings of the provincial government's top decision-making bodies.

At a time when national policymaking under Deng Xiaoping was politicized and personalized, and most local leaders followed orders from above, Wu's actions in Wuhan and Jiangxi suggested several innovative principles of administration: among them, that economic decisions should be separated from ideological debates, that decision-

---

8. This experiment and others are described in Dorothy J. Solinger, "Wuhan: Inland City on the Move," *China Business Review*, March/April 1985, pp. 27–30.

making should be carried out in a relatively open way with various points of view represented, and that China should bring its policy-making procedures into convergence with those of the supposedly scientific West. Wu was thus a strong reformist. But when the atmosphere turned conservative in 1989 he did not get into political trouble. This was partly because he did not suggest any direct weakening of the Party's power, partly because of the support of conservative Beijing leader Yao Yilin, who hailed from the same province where Wu was born and was now working, and partly because he seemed to be obtaining successful results in one of China's poorest provinces.

In 1997 Wu was promoted to run one of the country's largest, richest provinces, Shandong, as Party secretary, and was elected to the Politburo. Here again he established a nonpartisan expert advisory group. The investigation report on Wu reports approvingly that he also imposed a system of target management on the provincial Party committee, requiring each provincial Party agency to set goals for its work in the context of the provincial development plan and then to manage its activities around the achievement of these targets.

In the Chinese context, Wu's cultivation of experts is seen not only as "scientific" but as populist, because it means consulting the kinds of people who have no say in other jurisdictions around the country and who may speak for the interests of unrepresented groups. It is a misnomer to characterize his practice of having experts testify as a system of public hearings, as some have done, because the meetings were not public. Still, the experts exerted more influence under Wu than they did elsewhere in China. Wu's peasant background, his plain personal style, his simple traveling arrangements when he took trips to the grass roots, and the fact that his relatives have not become rich, all added to his image of a leader close to the people.

Hu Jintao has an affinity for Wu. Both graduated from Qinghua, both were elected Central Committee alternates in 1982, both served as provincial Party secretaries, both are publicity-shy. Although they have never worked in the same unit, they have met often at meetings and they like one another. Wu's position as head of the Central Disciplinary Inspection Commission could make him a potent ally as Hu moves to consolidate his power.

In the absence of Li Ruihuan, Wu and Li Changchun are the two members of the PBSC with the strongest political reform credentials. They lack the seniority or political resources to promote political reform on their own, but if political winds drive Hu Jintao and Zeng Qinghong in the direction of reform, the four of them would not lack for ideas or support in the Party apparatus and could prove a potent combination.

5

SUPPORTING CAST:
YOUTH, WOMEN, AND ELDERS

SINCE POWER IS closely held within the Politburo Standing Committee, the influence of those outside this select group might seem insignificant. Yet as the Party attempts to institutionalize its rule and as the state rises in importance compared to the Party, the broader political elite are becoming more involved in day-to-day decisions. In filling out our knowledge of the new leadership, four groups in particular are important. The regular Politburo members participate in crucial decisions, even if only in a subsidiary role. Both leading members of the Fifth Generation and female members of the new political elite are worth understanding because they point to the possibilities for reinvigoration and gender equality in elite Chinese politics. Finally, the omnipresent Party Elders are important because of their lingering influence and the potential for their intervention in a crisis situation.

The Politburo. Below the nine top men of the Politburo Standing Committee are the fifteen regular members and one alternate member of the Politburo. This group will collectively join in the decisions that guide China for the next five years, while individually holding the key posts in the Party, state, and military. In normal times, with power concentrated heavily at the top, the regular Politburo members remain, for the most part, in the background of PRC political life. They are a quiet part of the inner-Party consensus-building process on major issues. Some individuals may become more important as time passes. In the event of a political crisis, some could rise quickly as did Jiang Zemin and Li Ruihuan—both Politburo members backed by Elders— in 1989.

TABLE 2

REGULAR (NON-STANDING COMMITTEE) MEMBERS OF THE
16TH POLITBURO (AGES AS OF MARCH 2003)*

1. Wang Lequan, 58 (Xinjiang Party secretary)
2. Wang Zhaoguo, 61 (standing vice-chairman, NPC)
3. Hui Liangyu, 58 (vice-premier in charge of rural issues, environment, and minorities)
4. Liu Qi, 60 (Beijing Party secretary)
5. Liu Yunshan, 55 (director of the Party Propaganda Department)
6. Wu Yi, 64 (vice-premier in charge of foreign trade)
7. Zhang Lichang, 63 (Tianjin Party secretary)
8. Zhang Dejiang, 56 (Guangdong Party secretary)
9. Chen Liangyu, 56 (Shanghai Party secretary)
10. Zhou Yongkang, 60 (minister of public security)
11. Yu Zhengsheng, 57 (Hubei Party secretary)
12. He Guoqiang, 59 (director of the Party Organization Department)
13. Guo Boxiong, 60 (vice-chairman, Central Military Commission)
14. Cao Gangchuan, 67 (minister of national defense, state councilor, and vice-chairman, Central Military Commission)
15. Zeng Peiyan, 64 (vice-premier in charge of planning and infrastructure)
Alternate: Wang Gang, 60 (director of the Party Central Office)

*Names listed in stroke-count order.

The new Politburo members resemble the PBSC in age, educational backgrounds, patronage connections, and long, successful bureaucratic careers. Most of these officials are in their late fifties and early sixties. There are no carryovers from the previous body, except for Wu Yi, the only female member, who was an alternate in the preceding Politburo.

Orderly, deliberative processes governed the selection of the regular members of the Politburo as they did the selection of most of the Standing Committee. All of them have proven themselves as administrators and policymakers over several decades. All were evaluated by the Organization Department and approved for promotion by the outgoing Politburo. Several of the new members have joined the body mainly in recognition of their excellent work in ministerial-level positions at the central or provincial level (Wu Yi in foreign trade, Zhang Dejiang in Zhejiang province). Yet factional considerations were strong in the making of other decisions. Hui Liangyu, for example, a stolid member of the Hui minority with only a post-secondary education who will be in charge of agriculture as vice-premier, was favored by both Jiang and incoming premier Wen Jiabao. Four of the fifteen members (Zeng Peiyan, Hui Liangyu, Chen Liangyu, and Cao Gangchuan) are closely associated with Jiang Zemin. Two, Yu Zhengsheng and Zhou Yongkang, are allies of Zeng Qinghong.

The new supreme leader, Hu Jintao, can count on only two members of the new Politburo (Wang Zhaoguo and Liu Yunshan) to represent his Communist Youth League–based faction. Hu might have had another supporter, Fujian Party secretary Song Defu. But in the summer of 2000, Jiang told a Politburo meeting that since Hu would already have two factional allies in the Politburo, adding another would be inappropriate, a rare explicit reference to factional alliances. "As to whether he [Song] should be promoted to a member of the Political Bureau, we should take the overall situation into consideration. Jintao, Zhaoguo, and Liu Yunshan will all enter the Political Bureau. Should we take this into consideration?" Jiang said, implying the affirmative answer to his own question.

Zhang Lichang, the Party secretary of Tianjin, was one of the younger cadres given accelerated promotions during Deng's 1980 invigoration campaign who rose to Politburo status. He was made an alternate member of the Central Committee in 1982. His failure to make it all the way to the PBSC owes to the fact that Tianjin had the bad luck to be closely associated with Li Ruihuan, the major rival to Jiang Zemin after 1989. Zhang was mayor there from 1993 until being made Party chief in 1997. As a Li ally, Zhang was never considered for PBSC promotion at the 16th congress.

The new minister of public security, Zhou Yongkang, once worked with Zeng Qinghong in the state petroleum ministry. Zhou was given glowing reports in the investigation reports for the 16th congress despite having served only brief stints as minister of land and resources and then Party chief of Sichuan province. In addition to being appointed minister of public security, he has joined Luo Gan's Central Politics and Law Committee as deputy secretary, putting him in a position to take over the internal security portfolio when Luo retires in 2007. This serves as an indication that the internal security portfolio will fall into Zeng Qinghong's hands after 2007.

Another interesting figure is alternate member Wang Gang, who is director of the Party's Central Office. He has some fresh ideas for reform in several areas (see Chapters 7 and 8). The two military members, Cao Gangchuan and Guo Boxiong (described in Chapter 8), are on the body in order to coordinate civil and military functions.

The Fifth Generation. Some observers doubt that the Chinese Communist Party will still exist in ten years, but the positioning of a Fifth Generation to take power in 2012 shows that it intends to survive. As described in Chapter 2, the careful selection process to promote cadres under fifty resulted in the emergence of Xi Jinping and Li Keqiang as the most promising members of the Fifth Generation. There was a chance, ultimately foiled, that one of them might gain Politburo or even PBSC status. Another cadre close to their age, Bo

Xilai, was also considered for the Politburo and will be a competitor for power.[1]

Xi Jinping, age forty-nine, is a large man with the build of a football player, a no-nonsense person who plays down his prestigious origins as the son of a well-known Party official. He avoids the media spotlight and for a provincial leader spends an unusual amount of time on the road visiting rural areas and factories. Xi's career so far has been scandal-free, unlike the careers of his two competitors. His wife, Peng Liyuan, is a beautiful and popular folk singer attached to the PLA General Political Department's song and dance troupe, who has managed to be discreet about her private life despite the publicity she receives from her work.[2] Xi was widely liked by a broad cross-section of the old PBSC, including Zhu Rongji, Li Peng, and Li Ruihuan. Even though Xi was one of the provincial leaders least enthusiastic about the Three Stresses campaign, Jiang Zemin also supported his rise. His greatest asset may be his lack of a clear ideological position, which allows hard-line and liberal officials alike to support him.

Xi Jinping is the son of Xi Zhongxun (1913–2002), one of the founders of the Communist guerrilla armies of north China. When Mao and his troops fled to northwest China on the Long March in the mid-1930s, it was Xi Zhongxun who welcomed them to their new base area in and around Yan'an. Xi was briefly jailed during an inner-Party factional struggle at that time, but was soon released and

---

1. While all three men ended up as just regular Central Committee members, their ideas and experiences are important reflections of life in the provinces and of the views of the Central Committee elite, which some scholars believe are increasingly salient in Chinese politics. See for example Susan Shirk, "The Succession Game," in *The 16th CCP Congress and Leadership Transition in China*, Woodrow Wilson International Center for Scholars, Asia Program Special Report, September 2002. Also Li Cheng and Lynn White, "The Sixteenth Central Committee of the Chinese Communist Party: Hu Gets What?," *Asian Survey*, Vol. 43, No. 4 (July/August 2003), pp. 553–597.

2. Biographical material on Peng Liyuan is available at www.chinatv-net.com/all/compere/gx-pengliyuan/ply.htm.

went on to a series of high offices in the revolutionary movement and the new Communist regime. Xi Jinping was born into the privileged environment of high Beijing officialdom in 1953, when his father was chief secretary to the cabinet.

Xi learned the cruelty of Mao's politics at a young age. His father was purged a second time in 1962, accused by Mao of involvement in an anti-Party plot.[3] Xi Jinping was only nine years old. His father was sent to work in a factory in central China, tortured during the Cultural Revolution, and then placed under house arrest in Beijing for another ten years, until 1977. Young Xi and his brothers and sisters not only had to fend for themselves, but also faced discrimination as the offspring of a member of the anti-Party "black gang." At sixteen, Xi Jinping was sent to live as a peasant in an agricultural commune in the same poverty-stricken northwestern province of Shaanxi where his father had once been a guerrilla leader.[4]

---

3. Mao accused Xi Zhongxun of sponsoring publication of a novel about his old superior in the 1930s, Liu Zhidan, as a way of trying to rehabilitate the reputation of another former colleague who had been purged in the mid-1950s, Gao Gang. For details about the novel, Xi's role, and the political controversy surrounding it, see Roderick MacFarquhar, *The Origins of the Cultural Revolution, Vol. 3: The Coming of the Cataclysm, 1961–1966* (Columbia University Press, 1997), pp. 293–296. It was in this connection that Mao uttered one of his more famous sentences: "Using novels to carry out anti-Party activities is a great discovery." Mao's purge of Xi in 1962 was a precursor of the Cultural Revolution, which he launched in 1966.

4. In a 1992 interview with *The Washington Post*, Xi recalled being locked up "three or four times" in 1968 as a result of his father's plight. In Shaanxi, he had to attend daily "struggle" sessions, where he was often forced to read out denunciations of his father. "Even if you don't understand, you are forced to understand. It makes you mature earlier," he told the newspaper. See Lena H. Sun, "Post for a 'Princeling,'" *The Washington Post*, June 8, 1992, p. 12. One report issued in China said that Xi actually ran away from his assigned farm in August 1969 but was arrested in Beijing by police and sent back to the farm the following year. It said that he endured a year of cruel treatment before his conditions were improved as a result of his "good attitude." See "Xi Jinping: Zai xiwangde tianyeshang chicheng" (Xi Jinping: Galloping on the Field of Hope), in *Zhonggong disidai*, edited by Lin Hua, pp. 94–96.

His size and strength (he is nearly six feet tall) helped him to survive the grueling life of the countryside and the cruel treatment of Red Guards. He won wrestling matches with the farmers and was renowned for his ability to carry a shoulder pole of twin 110-pound buckets of wheat for several miles across mountain paths. The peasants liked him (his father's local reputation must have helped in this), nominated him for Party membership in 1974, and then elected him as Party branch secretary in the production brigade (equivalent to a village). In 1975, the local government recommended Xi for admission to Beijing's Qinghua University as a "worker-peasant-soldier student." (College admissions in those days were based on political recommendations, not examinations.) These experiences established his self-confidence and demonstrated his ability to make his way without his father's help.

By the time Xi graduated as a chemical engineer in 1979, his father was back in power as governor of Guangdong province. The child of the black gang was now once again a red princeling. Through his mother's intercession, Xi found jobs in the administrative offices of the State Council and the Central Military Commission. But he was impatient with the influence-mongering and court flattery of Beijing and asked for a transfer back to the countryside. In 1982 the State Council office sent[5] him to serve as a deputy Party secretary and then Party secretary of Zhengding county in Hebei province, a hotbed of leftism that had spurned many of the market-oriented reforms being promoted by Beijing.

Dispatching such a young cadre to such a responsible post at the county level was another example of Deng Xiaoping's policy of cultivating a younger and more technocratic cadre corps. In Zhengding Xi gained a reputation as hard-working and practical. He built a theme park based on the Chinese pre-modern novel *Journey to the West* that

---

5. The term is *paiqian*, or "seconded." Xi was still an official of the State Council, serving in a local post as a form of training.

proved a boon to the local economy, and he came to be called by the nickname "God of Wealth."[6] The province's Party leaders reported that Xi was "liberated in his thinking, deeply in touch with reality, hard-working and thrifty, and good at rallying others."

In 1985 Xi was assigned to the southeastern coastal province of Fujian, opposite Taiwan, where he worked for the next seventeen years. His first assignment was as executive deputy mayor and Party standing committee member in the picturesque port city of Xiamen. The transfer there took place when the previous deputy mayor, An Li, another scion of a highly placed family, was recalled for incompetence. The city authorities shrewdly asked Beijing to send another vice-mayor who had connections in Beijing. Xi's father, by then serving on the Politburo, and the elder Xi's friend, General Secretary Hu Yaobang, decided to send young Xi to fill the vacancy. Again, Xi's superiors' evaluation of his work was laudatory: "modest, full of ideas, hard-working, unpretentious; insists on eating meals in the city government cafeteria, washes his own clothes, refuses excessive banqueting, has warm relations with Party committee and city government staff."

Xi's career was well-enough launched that it was not affected by his father's fall from power a third time in January 1987. When Party conservatives attacked Hu Yaobang for his lenient attitude toward student protests, Xi Zhongxun was the only Politburo member who defended him. Both Hu and Xi were demoted, Xi into semiretirement as an NPC vice-chairman.[7] Young Xi, however, was promoted in 1988

---

6. A serialized television drama which ran in China from 1985 to 1986 called *Xinxing* (New Star) was reportedly based on the example of Xi Jinping while working in Zhengding. See "Xi Jinping" in *Zhonggong disidai*, edited by Lin Hua, pp. 94–96.

7. Xi served in this post for five years, then retired. After a long bout with Alzheimer's disease, he died on May 24, 2002. His death was the lead story in the next day's *People's Daily*, and the paper devoted almost the whole of its back page to his eulogy. The entire PBSC appeared at his funeral on May 30, 2002.

by his superiors in Fujian to the rank of Party secretary in Ningde prefecture, in part because Hu Yaobang's former ally Wang Zhaoguo had been sent to Fujian as governor the same year. At thirty-five, Xi was the youngest person in the province to hold such a high rank. He performed well, contributing to the economic development of the backward region in which he was working. After two years he was promoted again, to serve as Party secretary of the provincial capital, Fuzhou. After five years there, in 1995 he joined the provincial-level leadership as a deputy Party secretary.

Xi Jinping was by now rare among cadres of his age and rank in having served at almost every level of administration (village, county, city, prefecture, province) and in a wide range of environments (the agricultural interior, the mountainous, poor part of Fujian, an export-oriented coastal city, and the provincial capital). He had won praise in each assignment. In 1997, the Organization Department in Beijing decided to prepare the way for his possible promotion to the central level by giving him an alternate membership in the new Central Committee. Because he was not nationally known, the Party congress failed to elect him to one of the 150 alternate seats. But the Organization Department was determined that he should have a seat. Xi was written in as an "over-quota supplemental" (*ewai zengbu*) alternate member of the new Central Committee, giving the 15th Central Committee an odd number of alternates, which was unusual.

In 2000, Xi was appointed governor of Fujian. He cultivated the image of one who cuts through red tape and gets things done, which he did in matters ranging from urban beautification to public housing. In one project in 2000, he resettled, over a period of four months, 43,000 people from wooden shanties into new concrete tower blocks in Fuzhou; these had been the last group of people living in such conditions in the city. The investigation report noted that not a single person protested against the plan, an indication of Xi's ability to elicit popular support among people affected by his programs.

While in Ningde prefecture, Xi had taken an interest in resettling fishermen who still lived on their boats because they had never been allocated state housing. There were about 17,000 such people in 1997. Upon taking over as Fujian governor, Xi returned to the issue and vowed to resolve it once and for all. By the end of 2000, all 17,000 had been resettled in rent-free new houses. When Xi visited the new residential area in Ningde in late 2001 he commented, "Had it not been for the ten years [of the Cultural Revolution], you should have been resettled long ago. We in the CCP should not fail to meet our obligations!"

As governor, according to his Party dossier, he introduced reforms that reduced by half the number of approvals required for any investment project, domestic or foreign-funded. He cut in half the number of levels in the provincial civil service hierarchy, in response to a national campaign that had been started by Zhu Rongji in 1998 but implemented only patchily around the country.

During Xi's governorship private enterprise accounted for two thirds of the Fujian economy. Much of his activity was directed at making the province an attractive place for investors from Taiwan, which is directly across the Taiwan Strait and where a version of Fujian dialect is widely spoken. To this end, he urged his subordinates to practice "limited government" and to take an attitude of "public service." His lectures hectoring provincial cadres for laziness, careerism, and caution were said to compare with those of Zhu Rongji when he was mayor of Shanghai, both in their confrontational tone and in producing results. "Many of our civil servants still think they are running a planned economy. Whenever there's a problem they seek to add more staff and introduce more government structures," he said at one meeting. On another occasion, he accused provincial officials of spending all their time chasing promotions and engaging in alliance-building: "These people may manage to secure better jobs now and again. But as our efforts [to improve government efficiency] build up steam, they will fall by the wayside."

Weeks before the 16th Party Congress, Xi was transferred to Zhejiang, where he was appointed Party secretary. This was a lateral transfer, but Zhejiang is considered a more important province than Fujian. Service there will broaden Xi's experience and help him consolidate his credentials as a Fifth Generation successor. The previous incumbent, Zheng Dejiang, joined the Politburo at the 16th congress, breaking a long tradition according to which those sent to the comfortable southern coastal province became too immersed in the local culture to be suitable for further promotion or simply lost their political ambitions. If Xi performs well, he can hope to join the Politburo at the 17th Party Congress in 2007.

Another promising young leader is Bo Xilai. Bo shares much of Xi Jinping's experience, but his biography is also different in important ways. His father is Bo Yibo, the elder on whom Deng Xiaoping relied to manage Party personnel affairs through the 1980s and 1990s. The younger Bo and Xi both suffered when their fathers were dismissed from office during the Cultural Revolution. In 1968, when he was eighteen, Bo was sent to work in a Beijing factory that made tools for repairing machinery. But Bo's father came back to power in 1978 and has remained influential ever since, although he is no longer in good health. Like Xi Jinping, Bo Xilai received a prestigious education, at Beijing University, but he is unusual among the new leadership in not having studied engineering. Instead, he majored in world history and later took a graduate degree in journalism. Bo, like Xi, was assigned to work in Zhongnanhai after college and, like Xi, soon asked for a transfer to the provinces. Bo went to the northeastern industrial province of Liaoning in 1984 as a deputy Party secretary in a rural county administratively attached to Dalian, a city of some two and a half million people.

From there, he was transferred to the Party committee of the Dalian economic zone, and then to the city's Party committee. He became deputy Party secretary and mayor of Dalian in 1993. Bo was chosen by Jiang Zemin as the new Liaoning governor in 2001, four years after Bo and his father helped Jiang force his rival Qiao Shi into retirement. Like Xi, Bo made his career in the provinces, in the process casting off the shadow of his father. Both men, as a result, resent suggestions that they reached their positions because of their pedigrees.

As a person, Bo is different from Xi. He is more factional in his political ties, having nailed his flag to Jiang Zemin's mast long ago, and more prone to media displays. On one occasion, Bo as Liaoning governor took 6,800 people from his province to the open city of Shenzhen for a trade fair and investment conference, a swaggering move that few provincial governors would dare to make. Bo defended the act by pointing to the number of new business contracts signed as a result. He argues that courting media attention is part of his responsibility to communicate with the people:

> As a mayor or governor, you're working for the people, so you should let the people know what you're doing. It's important to use the media for this purpose. When I was in Dalian, every department of city government was dealing with reforms that involved changing old ideas and reconciling diverse interests. That required us to win over the majority of people's support for each reform. In addition, the people are the boss. We have to tell them what we're up to. That means the problem of "media exposure" [of a leader] is unavoidable.

As mayor of Dalian, Bo was known to pay little attention to the city's Party secretary, his superior in the political hierarchy. Bo made major decisions in the name of the city government without passing them before the Party committee for discussion and approval. Bo held that the management of the city was his business. He wanted to make the city an international fashion and trade center. "We have to think of the city as a state asset. If we don't manage this asset well and only think about enterprises in the city rather than the city itself then it will lose value and become useless," he told subordinates on one occasion. Bo managed Dalian well, boosting revenues and paying off debt while starting successful infrastructure and urban beautification projects. When he was promoted to governor of Liaoning, Bo's aides in Dalian organized street committees to bring out hundreds of retired workers, middle school teachers, and students to give him a noisy send-off. Critics said it reminded them of how Bo and two of his brothers used to mobilize fellow students for "struggle sessions" against the staff at their elite middle school in Beijing at the start of the Cultural Revolution.

Additional criticisms have dogged Bo's career. His wife, Kai Lai, is accused of trading on family connections to promote her law firm. She has opened branches in Beijing, Shenyang, Shanghai, Shenzhen, and foreign countries including the US and Japan. She has also promoted her business in the press. A saying in Dalian has it that "Bo Xilai relied on his father to make his career, Kai Lai relied on her husband to make her business." Bo Xilai courted wider rebuke by his heavy-handed attempts to control reports on his wife by local journalists.

Bo has been a key promoter of Jiang Zemin's policies and image. He angered locals by erecting a huge billboard of Jiang in downtown Dalian in 1997, when no other city in the country had done such a thing. Bo then failed to win election as a delegate to the 15th Party Congress in 1997 from fellow Party members in Dalian. This seemed an unusually pointed snub. Jiang arranged for him to come anyway as a "specially invited delegate." But at the congress Bo failed to win election to the Central Committee, even as an alternate member.

Despite these handicaps, in the future Bo may well advance in Party status, and eventually achieve Politburo membership. For now, as a result of the Politburo's October 2002 decision not to advance any of the younger leaders to Politburo status, he remains governor of Liaoning.

The third of the cadres around the age of fifty who are leading candidates for future Politburo membership is Li Keqiang, the most promising cadre in his age group to emerge from the traditionally influential Communist Youth League. The CYL is the Party's most important adjunct organization. Despite the decline of its influence, connections formed there are still valuable for future advancement. Hu Jintao, who served in the league headquarters for a few years, has used his time in the PBSC to foster the careers of a score or so of officials from the league who share his views and are thought to be loyal to him. The only member of the CYL faction in the Politburo now besides Hu himself is Wang Zhaoguo. Hu Jintao has thus placed his Fifth Generation hopes on Li even though Li's mediocre performance as governor and then party secretary of Henan produced doubts about his potential among other members of the top leadership.

Li's personality and managerial style are similar to Hu Jintao's. Both are open-minded, good listeners, careful, cooperative, affable in relations with colleagues and subordinates, and unimaginative. As CYL secretary, Li carried out the traditional functions of the league (political propaganda and ideological training among young people in schools, factories, and the military) but developed no new programs despite the ferment in the society around him.

While Xi Jinping and Bo Xilai are the sons of top Party leaders, Li is a commoner from one of China's poorest provinces. While Xi and Bo had the help of family connections to gain higher positions, Li worked his way through the CYL on his own merits. Xi and Bo are more familiar with local conditions, having spent most of their careers in the provinces, while Li has worked mostly in Beijing. Xi and Bo are adept managers, while Li's latter-day career as a provincial governor has been marked by tragedies that many in Beijing view as signs of weakness as a leader.

Born in Anhui province in 1955, Li Keqiang answered Mao's appeal to educated youths to learn from the peasants by "going down" to Fengyang county, the province's legendary poor area, in 1974. He became Party secretary of his commune in 1976. After the Cultural Revolution, he studied law at Beijing University as part of the first class admitted under reestablished entrance examinations. (He later earned a doctorate in economics at Beijing University through part-time study.) At the university, Li became a student leader, heading the Party-run students' association and winning commendation from the university's Party cell as one who "earnestly implements the Party line, principles and policies; maintains unanimity with the Party on ideology and politics; [and is] morally and intellectually superior as a student."

After graduation in 1982, Li was assigned to the CYL, whose first secretary, Wang Zhaoguo, recommended that he be put in charge of nationwide university student affairs and made an alternate member of the CYL secretariat. Within a month of that appointment, Wang was transferred to the Party Central Office and replaced at the CYL by the young Hu Jintao, who served as first secretary from 1983 to 1985. With Hu's departure and another round of leadership changes in the CYL, Li rose to full membership in the CYL secretariat and became head of the national youth and children's associations.

By 1992, Li was slated to become CYL first secretary. But to the surprise of Party leaders he failed to win election as an alternate Central Committee member at the 14th Party Congress (a fate that would befall Xi Jinping and Bo Xilai at the 15th Party Congress five years later). That was an obstacle to his taking over the CYL first secretaryship, since by tradition that post was filled by at least a Central Committee alternate member.

The Politburo convened a special meeting to consider the case. It was agreed that Li's failure did not reflect his personal qualities but rather a failure of the congress secretariat to make clear to delegates that the Party Center intended to appoint him CYL secretary, which would have prompted delegates to ensure that he was elected. The Politburo decided to make Li the CYL first secretary despite his lack of rank, and this was formally confirmed in May 1993.

For the second time, Li came under the direct leadership of Hu Jintao, now elevated to the PBSC and in overall charge of the CYL along with the official trade union and the women's association. Li was praised for keeping the CYL strictly in line with Party policy on all issues. He made some improvements in matters like internal selection procedures and consolidation of weak branches. But the CYL's influence over young people declined under his leadership. Some provincial CYL leaders were critical of Li's approach, saying that it failed to reflect the creativity and daring that characterize youth. Internal critics said that the CYL spent more time making demands and issuing orders to young people than listening to their demands and seeking to earn their trust.

Li was up for consideration as a future Fifth Generation leader in 1997, along with Xi Jinping. He was elected a Central Committee member at that year's 15th Party Congress. Another necessary credential for advancement was experience working in local government. That came in 1998, when, with Hu Jintao's support, he was made governor of populous Henan province (93 million people). The assignment was a challenge, giving Li the opportunity to expand his experience and prove himself for further promotion. The investigation reports on his work, however, were mixed.

Li was most in his element doing the kind of mobilization work that had been the staple of life at CYL headquarters. His conduct of Jiang Zemin's Three Stresses campaign was considered one of the most effective in the country. Under his direction, the provincial Party committee convened no fewer than 114 meetings to discuss the campaign, and investigation groups visiting from the Party Center were able to interview two hundred cadres and provincial citizens. The Xinhua News Agency's classified internal report for Party leaders entitled "Proofs on Domestic Situation"[8] (*Guonei dongtai qingyang*)

---

8. This intelligence periodical is called a "proof," but its contents are not later printed in final form.

carried an enthusiastic article on how Li and his colleague, Henan Party Secretary Ma Zhongchen, personally traveled around the province exhorting cadres to take the campaign seriously.[9] Hu Jintao himself made a personal visit to help Li push the campaign.

Li was again given glowing coverage in the Party press in 2001–2002 when he sent 43,000 cadres from the provincial, city, and county levels to 10,000 poor villages to put Jiang Zemin's theory of the Three Represents into practice by solving local problems: among them were repairing bridges and roads, installing water and electricity systems, fixing unsafe schools, and finding money for children whose families could not afford tuition. The example of can-do cadre teams from the higher levels was supposed to set a model for local cadres who had been unable to solve such problems.

Before launching this campaign, Li made a special visit to Party elder Song Ping (Hu Jintao's patron) in Beijing to seek his views and support. Song himself had launched similar projects of "rural socialist education" for cadres nationwide in the post-Tiananmen chill of 1990, and earlier in the "socialist education movement" of the 1960s. The post-Tiananmen campaign had been called off after criticism from patriarch Deng Xiaoping. Song enthusiastically endorsed Li's similar concept.

Despite his politically correct campaigns, Li's term in Henan was plagued by disasters that, while not his fault, highlighted the weakness of his responses. First, the province suffered from a crime wave, including a series of armed bank robberies in the capital city of Zhengzhou. It ranked officially as the third-least-safe province in the country and the fifth-worst for solving criminal cases. The root of the problem was the weak economy—poverty was a cause of crime, while inadequate funding contributed to inadequate police work. But

---

9. Normally the Three Stresses campaign would have been spearheaded by the provincial Party secretary rather than the governor, but Ma Zhongchen was not an enthusiast of the campaign, and Li Keqiang took the lead.

observers both in Beijing and in the province held Li responsible. In fact, a group of prestigious local retired officials and educators sent Li a letter urging him to take control by launching a propaganda campaign to educate people on the wrongfulness and futility of trying to solve their economic difficulties through crime.

Second, there was a series of tragic fires. Among other incidents in 2000, 74 lives were lost in a fire at an illegal pornographic theater in the city of Jiaozuo, and 309 in a fire at a shopping mall in Luoyang. In each case Li rushed to the scene and ordered an investigation. However, had the same incidents occurred a year later he would have been punished under a leadership responsibility system introduced in 2001 by the State Council to prevent disasters. As it was, his reputation suffered since his responses were considered slow and ineffectual.

Henan was also the site of a large-scale cotton supply scam which, embarrassingly for Li, was exposed on national television when he happened to be in Beijing. The scandal involved farmers and middlemen trading in cotton in violation of the government monopoly and selling low-quality, adulterated, and discarded cotton to state acquisitions stations, causing financial losses to the state. Li returned to the province to lead the investigation, but he suffered further humiliation when Zhu Rongji's State Council sent its own team of investigators to override his.

Most revealing of his administrative inadequacies was his ineffective, even cruel, response to the AIDS crisis which was affecting the province when he got there (see Chapter 7). Although the unhygienic blood collection practices that led to the crisis mostly took place prior to his arrival, Li was blamed for failing to control the problem and for blocking attempts to draw attention to it.[10]

---

10. For a media report which concentrated on the political failures of the AIDS crisis in Henan and named both Li Changchun and Li Keqiang, see "China's AIDS Scandal," *Asian Wall Street Journal*, August 15, 2002.

These incidents led many in Beijing to conclude that Li, as an administrator, too often found himself in a passive position, responding to events after they had gotten out of control. While he faithfully carries out policies, he is seen as lacking the energy that people look for in leaders. Even though he did not advance to the Politburo in this round, he may nevertheless emerge as a strong rival to Xi Jinping for leadership if the Fifth Generation comes to power.[11]

Women Leaders. Women account for just 5 of the 198 members of the Central Committee chosen at the 16th congress and 22 of the 158 alternate members. Just one of these women, the sharp-minded and energetic Wu Yi, made it into the Politburo, and none into the PBSC.

Despite its revolutionary aims, Communist China has always lagged in the political advancement of women. In the Mao era, all those who reached high positions were the wives of senior Party members, notably Mao's actress wife Jiang Qing; Ye Qun, the wife of Mao's ill-fated designated successor Lin Biao; and Zhou Enlai's wife, Deng Yingchao.

During the reform era a good many self-made women have risen in business and society. But women have remained largely shut out of high office. Women are classified with ethnic minorities, intellectuals, and youth as groups for whom quotas have been established for lower-level positions. It is an internal rule that every provincial leadership, for example, must have at least one woman as a deputy governor or deputy Party secretary. But at the Central Committee and Politburo levels there are no guidelines. There has never been a woman in the PBSC and few have reached as high as the Politburo.

Questions of gender representation were not explicitly considered in the deliberations preceding the 16th Party Congress. Perhaps as a result, the 16th congress marked a setback for women's roles in the

---

11. There were several outside reports that Li was the leading candidate for Fifth Generation core. See, for example, Wu Jiaxiang, *Jiaoli shiliuda*, p. 201.

political elite since there had been eight full members of the previous Central Committee (although only seventeen alternate members). Nonetheless, Wu Yi's elevation to full Politburo status makes her the first woman to hold that rank since 1985 and arguably the first ever to have reached it on the basis of merit.

Wu, age sixty-four, is the best-known female politician in China. Widely liked and admired, with a fine sense of humor and a reputation for dressing smartly in the style of Western businesswomen, Wu is remembered in the West for her polite but tough negotiating behavior as China's foreign trade minister between 1993 and 1998.

Wu is a child of Mao's revolution; as a fervent youth she chose petroleum engineering as her field of study in the late 1950s. She worked as manager of a refinery in Gansu province after graduation, and then returned to manage refineries in Beijing. In 1983, she was sent as part of a team from Beijing to conduct "Party rectification work," i.e., attempts to improve the performance of Party officials, in Hunan province, where she impressed the provincial Party secretary, Mao Zhiyong. His praise called her to the attention of the Organization Department, which made her a Central Committee alternate member in 1987. The following year she was promoted to vice-mayor of Beijing in charge of industry and trade. She won a reputation for being demanding but not abusive with subordinates. She was transferred to the foreign trade ministry in 1991, becoming minister in 1993.

Since 1998, Wu has overseen foreign trade policy as a state councilor and had a large part in formulating China's negotiating position on entering the World Trade Organization. As those talks heated up in 1999 she told one Politburo meeting that the government should be ready to revoke some concessions already made to the US and to carry out a national poll to assess public opinion on the acceptable costs of joining the WTO. Despite her hard-nosed position, she was always a strong backer of Premier Zhu Rongji and his efforts to achieve China's entry into the trade body.

Wu became an alternate Politburo member in 1997, and her pro-motion to full membership at the 16th Party Congress was one of the Politburo's least controversial decisions. Because of her excellent reputation as an administrator, Premier Wen Jiabao temporarily appointed her acting minister of health during Beijing's SARS crisis in the spring of 2003, but her long-run portfolio as vice-premier will center on foreign trade and women's issues.

Among the new female members of the Central Committee is Liu Yandong, who was a deputy director of the Party's United Front Work Department from 1991 to 2002. The department handles the Party's relations with non-Party groups like intellectuals, religious leaders, and the eight authorized non-Communist political parties. Liu was promoted to become the department's first female director following the 16th congress, a position where she will have a part in cultivating ties with political and civil groups in Taiwan. Zong Hairen comments that she is among the most admired up-and-coming female politicians in China. She also serves as a vice-chairman of the Chinese People's Political Consultative Conference, where she coordinates rela-tions between the Party and the officially sanctioned democratic par-ties, religious groups, union, and youth and women's organizations. Liu, fifty-seven, is the daughter of a Long March veteran of the Party, Liu Ruilong. She was born in 1945 on the eastern shores of the river flowing through the Party's Yan'an redoubt, hence her given name "Yan East" (Yandong). Another beneficiary of Deng Xiaoping's cadre reinvigoration campaign, Liu was promoted to the Communist Youth League Secretariat in 1982, forming an early allegiance to Hu Jintao. In 1991 she was transferred to the United Front Work Department under another ex-CYL colleague, Wang Zhaoguo. Wang recommended her to take over as standing deputy director in 1997, laying the basis for her promotion to director in 2002.

The advance of Wu and Liu on merit may signal a welcome change for women in politics in China. Wu Yi never married. When she became a vice-mayor of Beijing, a rumor spread that she was the lover of President Yang Shangkun. The gossip prompted her to remark, "Why is it in China that any time a woman reaches a high position, people start to speculate about who her [male] mentor is? No one can believe you have come to office on your own merits." The explanation, of course, is that with the brilliant exception of Wu, male patronage has previously been the only way to the top for women in Communist China.

Yet that may be changing. Jiang Zemin's favorite female politicians, Chen Zhili and Huang Liman (for more on them see Chapter 6), both faced opposition to advancement at the 16th congress. Chen Zhili, the minister of education from 1998 to 2003, was a candidate to join the Politburo but was dropped from the running early in the deliberations and became a state councilor instead. Huang, who became the Party secretary of the southern city of Shenzhen in 1998, was hoping to join the Central Committee but barely scraped onto the list of alternate members, receiving the third-fewest votes.

This is a reminder that Jiang, despite his preponderant influence, could not unilaterally place anyone on the Politburo or even the Central Committee if they lacked wider support. Their setbacks, along with the promotion of Wu Yi and Liu Yandong, may signal the decline of the long tradition of female politicians rising in politics on the strength of a close personal relationship to a powerful male.

Elders. The role of the elders (*yuanlao*) is a barometer of institutionalization in post-Mao politics. There were no elders in the Mao period—high officials either died in office or were purged. But elders became important politically during the Tiananmen crisis in 1989, when Deng Xiaoping and seven other retired officials took decision-making power out of the hands of the Politburo Standing Committee, purged two of its members, decided on martial law, ordered the military crackdown on the demonstrators, and appointed Jiang Zemin to take power. This episode, however, was made possible by two unique conditions. First, Deng had been given the right to intervene by a secret 1987 Politburo resolution that has never been subsequently renewed.[12] Second, his power was undergirded by his control of the military in his capacity as chair of the Central Military Commission —a post that in 1989 reverted to its more normal status as a position held concurrently by the serving general secretary.

The composition of the elders changed in the 1990s. Deng Xiaoping and his contemporaries died (Deng in 1997, Yang Shangkun in 1998). The liberals Wan Li and Qiao Shi, the hard-liner Song Ping, and the military man Liu Huaqing retired from office one after another. They joined three others already in retirement, former vice-president Rong Yiren,[13] the last surviving Deng-era Elder Bo Yibo, and former Politburo member Song Renqiong. This new group of seven top elders refrained from imposing their views on serving officials. Nor did they have an opening to do so, since by the mid-1990s Jiang Zemin had consolidated his power and there was no paralysis in decision-making in which the elders could have intervened (see Chapter 6).[14]

Today, the top elders, whose order of rank according to protocol is determined by the highest office they held before retirement, are as follows: Li Peng, Wan Li, Qiao Shi, Zhu Rongji, Li Ruihuan, Song Ping, Liu Huaqing, Wei Jianxing, Li Lanqing, Rong Yiren, Bo Yibo, and Song Renqiong. Jiang Zemin will join this list as number one if and when he steps down as chair of the Central Military Commission. (Former Party General Secretary Zhao Ziyang is not listed among Party elders because he was formally removed from office in 1989 rather than being allowed to retire.) There is also a wider group of

12. *The Tiananmen Papers*, p. 102, n. 1.

13. A non-CCP member nonetheless granted elder protocol status by the CCP because he had served as PRC vice-president.

14. See Zong, *Zhu Rongji zai 1999*, for evidence on how the elders behaved during that year.

elders that includes all former Politburo members, NPC vice-chairmen, vice-premiers, state councilors, CPPCC vice-chairmen, and former CMC members. Elders who held the rank of central leaders before retirement receive "class-one guard service" (*yiji baowei daiyu*), which includes bodyguard service from the Central Guards Bureau, top-level housing, secretarial service, and personal transport. They also have access to classified documents and they can expect to be politely consulted by leaders in office. They might, in a crisis, be called to attend "enlarged" meetings of the Politburo or PBSC where they could weigh in on major policy decisions. Their ability to exert real power, in short, is ill-defined and will depend on events.[15]

On the one hand, the norm of an institutionalized succession process carries the corollary that those who retire should withdraw from politics. This precedent has been adhered to by those out of power since the mid-1990s. Retirement now means what it says. As noted, the new elders lack direct powers to intervene of the sort that Deng Xiaoping held in 1989. On the other hand, if the balance of power within the Fourth Generation should become unstable, a power struggle among PBSC members could draw the elders in. Another possibility is that the issue of political liberalization might arise in such a way as to prompt responses by elders who are conservative, such as Li Peng and Song Ping, or those such as Li Ruihuan, Wan Li, and Qiao Shi, who are relatively liberal. Elders might also exert indirect influence through their followers in office.

---

15. No student of Chinese politics should assume that an obscure elder far down in the Party hierarchy is necessarily insignificant. A reminder of that lesson came in early 2000 when Ren Zhongyi, a former Guangdong Party secretary, published an article in the relatively open-minded newspaper *Nanfang zhoumo* (Southern Weekend) that called on the Party to introduce political reforms to give genuine power to the National People's Congress and eliminate "personality cults and dictators." The article was quickly reprinted in newspapers across the country. Ren Zhongyi, "Zaitan jianchi sixiang jiben yuanze" (Revisiting Upholding the Four Cardinal Principles), in *Nanfang zhoumo*, April 29, 2000, p. 4.

Jiang Zemin has the greatest scope for such influence. He is not yet formally an elder and has a legitimate voice in some policy decisions as chair of the Central Military Commission. In addition, five members of the PBSC and four regular members of the Politburo are more or less closely allied to him. He also has the greatest support within the wider Central Committee, where 13 of the 198 members are considered his associates, compared to 9 for Li Peng and 7 for Li Ruihuan. (Only about 60 of the 198 members have strong affiliations to any leader, according to Zong Hairen, a sign of how merit has influenced the promotion process.) On economic affairs, two of his allies—Huang Ju and Zeng Peiyan—serve as vice-premiers.

Jiang's major concern will be that his name and reputation be treated with respect. A reversal of the verdict on the suppression of protest at Tiananmen would not please him, since the Tiananmen events brought him to power. He is not likely to favor bold experiments with political reform, but he would view ongoing experimentation with the economic system as normal. Jiang's notion of a broadly more representative Party, the Three Represents, was written into the Party constitution at the 16th congress. But at Li Peng's suggestion, Jiang's name was not mentioned in the revision, a sign that his authority over broad Party affairs will be limited. The theory will be treated as the crystallization of the Party's wisdom. Jiang will not be asked to step forward and interpret its application to future events. That will be left to his successors, who will have a free hand to apply it as they please.

Despite Jiang's impressive factional showing in the top ranks of the new leadership, others in his group—like former education minister Chen Zhili and former foreign minister Tang Jiaxuan—failed to gain Politburo status. A more pointed snub was the inability of Jiang's eldest son, Jiang Mianheng, a vice-president of the Chinese Academy of Sciences, to gain even an alternate seat on the Central

Committee.[16] Jiang thus has been given several signs from fellow Party elites that the use of his power should be limited.

The elder with the most reason to worry is Li Peng. Some analysts have speculated that the Fourth Generation leadership might be tempted to denounce him for the bloodshed in Beijing in 1989, or even put him on trial. Some interpret Luo Gan's appointment to the PBSC as a guarantee to Li Peng that he will be safe in retirement. Li Peng also sought, without success, to install a former PLA general closely involved in the Tiananmen repression, Zhang Gong, as a vice-chairman of the CPPCC, against the opposition of outgoing PLA senior generals. Zhang was instead placed on the body's standing committee.

But post-succession retribution remains a remote possibility because, for now at least, there is little disposition on the part of the new leaders to prosecute any retired leaders. Security in retirement has emerged as another new and valued norm of the Communist elite. During the Cultural Revolution, thousands, perhaps millions of cadres were hounded from office, then exiled or imprisoned and sometimes denied medical treatment. Even the head of state, Liu Shaoqi, was seized and thrown into jail, and died from mistreatment and illness. In the period following the Cultural Revolution, the leaders decided never to repeat that experience. After Deng Xiaoping engineered the retirement of Mao's chosen successor, Hua Guofeng, from all his offices, Hua retained his position as a Central Committee member with the standard privileges of other members and only retired at the 16th congress. When Zhao Ziyang was purged after Tiananmen, he was

---

16. Reports in the Hong Kong media said that Jiang Mianheng even failed in initial voting to win a place as a delegate to the 16th congress from CAS party members, a result quickly reversed by orders from above. See Luo Bing, "Jiang gongzi luoxuan 'shiliuda' daibiao" (Jiang's Son Fails to Be Elected as a Delegate to the 16th Congress), *Qianshao* (Frontline Magazine), October 2002, pp. 6–7; and Chang Yuan, "Jiang Mianheng 'dangxuan' shiliu da daibiao zhenxiang" (The Truth about Jiang Mianheng's "Election" as a Delegate to the 16th Congress), *Qianshao* (Frontline Magazine, Hong Kong), December 2002, p. 9.

placed under house arrest and allowed a life of comfort, although he was politically isolated. Yao Wenyuan, one of the hated Gang of Four, was quietly released to serve out his sentence under comfortable house arrest. (Two of the others died and one is still in jail.) Former Beijing Party Secretary Chen Xitong was sent home on medical parole after he served a few years of his sentence on corruption charges.

Thus, even if the new leaders were eventually to reverse the verdict on June Fourth, it is unlikely that they would openly attack Li Peng, Jiang Zemin, or the memory of Deng Xiaoping, who made the ultimate decisions that led to the bloodshed. A safe, honorable retirement from high office has become too treasured a perquisite among the Chinese Communist elite.

But Li Peng will have other things to worry about. He is vulnerable to investigations of his children's involvement in corrupt state business deals and financial scandals and of his wife's profitable links with business. Li himself has never been accused of corruption, but his wife, Zhu Lin, has helped to protect the activities of his eldest son, Li Xiaopeng, his daughter, Li Xiaolin, and his second son, Li Xiaoyong, all of whom have acquired reputations for making improper use of the family name. Li Xiaopeng and Li Xiaolin have taken charge of two of the biggest power companies in China, Huaneng Power International and China Power Investment, and have used their connections to help the companies gain lucrative contracts, including contracts to help build their father's pet project, the Three Gorges Dam. The involvement of Li Xiaoyong in a futures brokerage house named Xinguoda that collapsed in 1998 has been the subject of periodic protests by investors in the company, who claim that his responsibility has been covered up by authorities and that the Li family should compensate them for their losses. All this could be used by Li Peng's enemies. It would be hard for his followers to protect him from a well-aimed anti-corruption campaign.

Indeed, signs of Li Peng's vulnerability to corruption charges in retirement emerged shortly before the 16th congress when one of the senior officials accused of graft as part of the normal crackdown that precedes major political events was one of his power sector cronies, Gao Yan. Gao was a cadre in Jilin province from 1975 to 1985, where he won Li Peng's favor. Li Peng appointed him president of the State Power Corporation as one of his last acts as premier in 1997. In August 2002, Gao fled abroad after a warrant was issued for his arrest on corruption charges (his location remains unknown). According to Zong Hairen, the warrant was authorized by Jiang Zemin, something that weakened Li Peng's hand in making personnel arrangements for the 16th congress.

Perhaps the most disgruntled retiree will be Zhu Rongji. Zhu has indicated that he is tired of the thankless task of economic reform and wants to have nothing more to do with politics. His silence during the dramatic PBSC meeting where Li Ruihuan was denied reelection reflected his alienation from politics after a decade in the central government. In 2001, he relinquished his honorary position as dean of Qinghua University's school of economics and management to emphasize that he intended to disappear from the public eye completely after leaving office. Whether Zhu succeeded or failed as an economic reformer is much debated in China and outside, but he appears to have no intention of resisting reevaluation of his legacy and, in any case, he will have no power to do so.

Zhu's factional support was reduced virtually to nil in the new leadership. Wen Jiabao, his one undisputed ally, is hemmed in with two vice-premiers loyal to Jiang Zemin, Huang Ju and Zeng Peiyan. The man whom Zhu trusted to run the central bank through a period of complex financial reforms, Dai Xianglong, was kept off the Politburo and sent to Tianjin (the political base of the fallen Li Ruihuan) to serve in the lowly position of mayor. Jiang used the excuse that Dai was in poor health and that the CDIC held a report that he was corrupt (which Jiang made sure was forwarded to Hu Jintao) to exclude him from the new leadership.

Zhu also suffered from attacks on his legacy in the lead-up to the congress. Critics pointed to the growth of the central government budget deficit, the increase in bad loans in the banking sector, a loss of state assets, rising unemployment, and growing income inequality as his main legacies as premier. Fair or not, such criticisms deflated Zhu's reputation at home if not abroad, meaning that his influence as an elder, even on economic issues, will be limited.

Li Ruihuan. The most settled retirement may be enjoyed by Li Ruihuan. He remains the leading standard-bearer of the liberal faction in elite politics. As such, his views might be sought out by any liberalizing leader. Since he was up for consideration as a PBSC member, Li Ruihuan is given a full chapter in *Disidai*. The interest of his life story and the potential importance of his ideas in any political liberalization drive make this treatment worth recounting in detail.

Li Ruihuan is a rough-featured, gravel-voiced former carpenter with a ready smile and a quick tongue. He loves Beijing opera, plays ping-pong and tennis, and likes to watch soccer matches. As a PBSC member, he was a sophisticated political infighter who could manipulate ideological jargon while mixing in bright metaphors, wordplay, and humor. He believes in a minimum of censorship, a position that made him popular with Chinese journalists and writers. He also has strong views about the need to open the Party to greater scrutiny and criticism by the media and the people. Li would support moves to loosen the ban on the formation of non-Communist parties and institute multi-party competitive elections, eventually up to the provincial level. He would also support policies to allow privately owned newspapers, and force the Chinese Communist Party to cease taking financial support from the government budget.

A native of Baodi county on the outskirts of the northern port city of Tianjin, Li left his peasant family in 1951 at age sixteen and found work as a carpenter in Beijing. Accolades for being a model worker allowed him to attend a construction trades college in Beijing, where he caught the eye of then Beijing Vice Mayor Wan Li, who would later rise to Politburo status and become Li's most important mentor. After being chosen for the position of Party secretary at a Beijing building materials factory, Li was sidelined by the Cultural Revolution, along with Wan Li, remaining "under investigation" until 1971. The following year he made the leap to an official position under Wan's patronage, joining the Beijing municipal government's building materials bureau and then its construction commission in Party positions. Later he served brief stints in the union and youth wings of the Party.

In 1981, Li Ruihuan became one of the older cadres to benefit from Deng Xiaoping's Four Transformations policy of promoting younger, more educated officials. At the age of forty-seven, on the recommendation of Wan Li and General Secretary Hu Yaobang, Li was transferred back to his home city of Tianjin to serve as a vice-mayor in charge of construction. Before long he was serving as Party secretary and mayor.

Li won praise for his performance in Tianjin, a city of over nine million people, eighty-five miles southeast of Beijing on the Bohai Sea. After visiting Tianjin in 1987, Deng Xiaoping observed to a colleague, "We should forget the fact that he used to be a carpenter. He's done great things in building that city. He has a good head on his shoulders."[17] Deng was impressed again in 1988 when he read the transcript of a speech Li had just given to a group of conservative teachers of Marxism. In the context of the time, Li's remarks were bold, and they appealed to the arch-pragmatist Deng. Li said that Marxists should be willing to revise theory based on experience, even if doing so contradicts what is written in books, stated by leaders, or believed by most people. The main obstacle to reform, he added, was

---

17. Deng said something similar but in different words at the May 21, 1989, meeting of the Elders; see *The Tiananmen Papers*, p. 262.

ideological thinking that failed to change with the times. Referring to student protests that had taken place in late 1986, Li said:

> The year before last the college students created a disturbance. Was that a big deal? I think not. It was nothing but a few college students. The soldiers, the workers, and especially the eight hundred million peasants did not join in. So what's the fuss? Some of our people [in the Party] were in a panic as if meeting a huge enemy, as if we had been thrown into a rout, but it seems to me that those people did not really understand Marxism.

Talking about the standard of correctness for the Party's work, Li said:

> We often talk about the need to obey the laws of economic relationships. I think we first of all have to obey the laws of the feelings of the masses.... When they've had a child, they want to put it in nursery school; when the kid gets older, they want to give it a desk at school; when he or she graduates, they want to see that there's a job; when he or she gets married, they want to be sure there's housing—these kinds of basic things are all the people want.... But if you get on their wrong side, it doesn't matter who you are, you are done for. As the saying goes, "The water can carry the boat, but it can also sink it."

In 1987, Li was promoted to membership in the Politburo, along with his fellow provincial-level Party secretary Jiang Zemin. Although Jiang was eight years Li's senior, Li's career had moved faster than Jiang's. Li became mayor of a major city three years earlier (1982 versus 1985) and a first Party secretary a year earlier (1987 versus 1988).

In 1989, when Deng Xiaoping and seven other Elders stepped in to deal with the crisis created by the student pro-democracy movement, and were considering how to revamp the Party leadership, Deng praised Li as a "doer" with strong popular support.[18] It was Jiang Zemin, however, who won the top job as general secretary. What seemed to favor Jiang was the time he had invested in currying the favor of the retired leaders, especially Chen Yun and Li Xiannian, the two most influential of the Elders—not least by entertaining their wives every time the couples came to Shanghai (see Chapter 6).

Still, Li was promoted to the PBSC and put in charge of the Party's propaganda and ideology. In the conservative post-Tiananmen atmosphere, he resisted attempts to tighten control both of the state-run media and of creative writing. He said:

> There has never been a novel, a play, or a song that overthrew a government or ruined a country. We have some comrades who overestimate the social capacity of literature and art. They make a major issue out of a small [ideological] error, as if it would create massive disruption, and they even mobilize the troops for a great expedition [a big ideological campaign].

He also said:

> Literary and artistic creation is a highly democratic, highly free, spiritual activity which cannot coexist with excessive interference or mechanical coercion. Works of the spirit have to be rich, multihued, diverse, and dynamic. They cannot be subjected to simplistic unitary standards or demands for uniformity, and they can't tolerate formulaic or mandated styles. There will always be limitations in the knowledge and experience of artists. Their works cannot be flawless [ideologically], nor can artists avoid all [ideological] error. This requires that the

---

18. May 21, 1989, meeting of the Elders; see *The Tiananmen Papers*, p. 262.

practice of literature and art take place in a tolerant and harmonious atmosphere.

In the years after Tiananmen, Li used humorous yet strong words implicitly to criticize Jiang Zemin's and Li Peng's reluctance to promote economic and political reform, and their tendency to defend such conservatism by citing the opinions of the Party Elders. Li said:

> We Chinese people have an old weakness: we cling to some things so hard that we can't let go. We say that heaven doesn't change and the Way doesn't change; that whatever the ancestors said, cannot be done any other way, and whatever they didn't say, cannot be done at all. In everything we take the ancestors' right-and-wrong as our right-and-wrong. This weakness has blocked people's thinking, has stifled democracy and science, has aided ignorance and backwardness, and is a major obstacle to the advance of Chinese society. What is disturbing is that we have some comrades who have not really awakened to this problem. They love to cite the [Marxist and Chinese Communist] classics, as if they are deeply educated in political theory and have strong revolutionary principles. Yet in reality, these comrades are violating the principles of Marxism on precisely the most basic issue of principle [i.e., the principle that practice is the sole criterion of truth].

In 1993, the Party assigned Li Ruihuan to head the Chinese People's Political Consultative Conference. (He also continued to hold his seat on the Politburo Standing Committee.) The CPPCC consists mostly of non-Communist dignitaries and meets annually just before the National People's Congress. Its Standing Committee meets six times a year. Under Li this traditionally quiescent body began to raise questions and voice criticisms about issues such as corruption and the haughty work styles of officials estranged from the public. In internal speeches, Li as CPPCC chair criticized the work of the Party and the State Council, despite protests from his targets that such criticism constituted undue interference. "It's normal to have different views in the course of our work," he argued. "If everyone's view on an issue were the same and there was no criticism or counter-criticism, how could we call this decision-making? We need to protect the freedom to criticize."

In vivid language, Li attacked the vacuous, conformist political style fostered by Jiang Zemin:

> During the last few years, the wind of exaggeration has been rampant in some of our Party and government organs. People talk nonsense, and cadres like to put themselves on display like flowerpots on a stand. Flattery and overstatement get more serious daily. Such incorrect social and political work styles have led to an increasing prevalence of cadres who steer with the wind, so that there's no longer anybody among Party or government officials with any edges or corners [i.e., straight talk]. There are more and more of the "you're okay I'm okay," oily-head-slippery-chest, exquisitely-nimble-in-eight-directions kind of people.

It seemed to irritate Jiang that Li never dropped the habit carried over from the days when they were both provincial Party secretaries of calling him "old Jiang"—something no one else presumed to do once Jiang became general secretary.

There was a frostiness when Jiang Zemin attended CPPCC meetings. Li would speak about the need for the consultative group to supervise the Party and Jiang would not applaud. Li was the least enthusiastic of the PBSC members about publicizing Jiang's theories of the Three Stresses and the Three Represents. His criticisms of Jiang's style of rule were shared by Qiao Shi, another PBSC member and, from 1993 to 1998, head of the National People's Congress. After Jiang arranged Qiao's ouster from the Party leadership in 1997, Li was the only strong liberal left in the top leadership. His relations with Jiang and Jiang's associate Zeng Qinghong grew colder in the period leading up to the 16th Party Congress, as Li lobbied for Jiang's retirement from all posts, and Jiang sought to prevent Li from gaining another term in the PBSC.

In private conversations in the years leading up to his retirement, Li talked more about political reform than any other leader. He placed his hopes in the effectiveness of external constraints on Party power rather than internal codes of conduct. He wanted gradually to expand direct elections of government leaders (now limited to the village level[19]) by stages all the way up to the provincial level, calling elections "the trend of the times and of history." He said that the media should be less constrained by Party censorship and that private ownership of some media should be put on the agenda for future consideration.

Li also spoke frequently about the Party's past, asserting that the Party has yet fully to recognize and apologize for its past errors, including the failure to end illiteracy and poverty and tragedies like the famine of 1959–1961 that was caused by the abortive Great Leap Forward campaign. "We had the courage to conclude that the Cultural Revolution was a disaster, so we should have the same courage to face and learn from other mistakes and harm we have brought to the people in fifty years of rule," he said in 1999. "We should admit our mistakes to the people and to history." He did not say, however, whether that should include the Tiananmen tragedy.

Li enjoyed deep support among cadres in all the hierarchies within

---

19. Strictly speaking, the village level in China is not considered a level of government. The village is said to be a "grass-roots" organization.

which he worked—the Communist Youth League, the labor union federation, the political consultative conference system that goes down to the township level nationwide, and the bureaucracies of Tianjin and Beijing. He was also popular in Hong Kong, including among its property barons and government leaders, because he advocated a hands-off approach to the former colony in the period leading up to its return to Chinese sovereignty in 1997.

Hu Jintao once idolized Li Ruihuan for his good work as Tianjin mayor in the 1980s. Both spent time in the Communist Youth League, although they did not overlap there. The two became closer because of Li's excellent personal relations with Hu Jintao's mentor, Song Ping. Although their political ideas were different—Song is an old-line Communist conservative—Li Ruihuan found an affinity with Song because of both men's down-to-earth, hard-working style and dislike of pretense and exaggeration. After joining the PBSC in 1992, Hu consistently showed respect for Li. Li in turn was a major proponent of Hu's full succession to all three offices held by Jiang Zemin. That closeness helps assure that Li Ruihuan's views will be heard as China's new leaders grapple with the difficult issue of political reform.

6

NEW LIGHT ON THE JIANG YEARS

ALTHOUGH THE INFORMATION contained in *Disidai* relates mainly to the rise of the Fourth Generation, the book also sheds new light on the thirteen-year reign of Jiang Zemin from 1989 to 2002. It probes Jiang's personality, his rise to power, and his style of politics. It reveals the intensity of the political infighting that took place as he consolidated power; it also evaluates his successes and failures as a leader, and illuminates the legacies he leaves to his successors. *Disidai* confirms some information that was previously available from less reliable sources, adds many new facts, and provides fuller explanations for Jiang's actions than we have had before.

Jiang's rise. In contrast to the Fourth Generation leaders described in *Disidai*, Jiang, born in 1926, belongs to a cohort of Chinese who have clear memories of pre-Communist China—including the Japanese invasion and corrupt Kuomintang rule—and thus a stronger visceral allegiance to the ideals of the CCP. The adopted son of a Communist sympathizer who was killed by bandits, Jiang was trained in automobile manufacturing in Moscow in the mid-1950s before returning to a career as a machinery engineer in China. Like the Fourth Generation leaders, his ascent was assisted by a combination of merit and patronage. He proved his ability first in the world of industry and later in

Communist organization. He benefited from Deng Xiaoping's campaign of the 1980s to promote younger leaders: Jiang became a vice-minister of newly created state commissions handling foreign investment and trade in 1980 at fifty-four and then minister of electronics industry three years later.

Jiang also relied on the personal backing of Party elders. For instance, as minister of electronics, he paid a highly publicized visit to the home of Party elder Chen Yun in 1984 to show him some of the latest microcircuitry devices, an event which suggested Jiang was in Chen's favor.[1] Official reports spoke of Chen requesting the visit. But *Disidai* says it was Jiang who took the initiative after hearing that Chen was interested in recent advances in electronics. It was also Jiang who arranged for the CCP's official newspaper, *People's Daily*, to cover the visit, and he had a hand in writing the resulting article, entitled "The Proletarian Revolutionary of the Old Generation, Chen Yun, Is Very Concerned about the Development of China's Modern Industry."

Disidai also confirms the role of Wang Daohan, another elder, in Jiang's rise. Wang, who had fought alongside Jiang's uncle in the civil war and marked Jiang for promotion in the early 1950s, recommended him for his 1980 appointment to the foreign investment and trade commissions and also recommended Jiang to replace him as mayor of Shanghai in 1985. Thus Jiang at an early stage was known to "follow the line of upper-level officials" (*zou shangceng luxian*), a play on the Leninist exhortation for Party members to "follow the mass line" (*zou qunzhong luxian*).

Jiang's four years in Shanghai from 1985 to 1989 are remembered in annual Party Organization Department reports on the leadership group (*lingdao banzi*) of the municipality as a period of uninspired leadership and few results, according to *Disidai*. In comparison to the

---

1. See Gilley, *Tiger on the Brink*, p. 72.

performance of Li Ruihuan in Tianjin over the same period, Jiang accomplished little. The city's finances, state industries, and infrastructure deteriorated during his two years as mayor, but began to improve under Zhu Rongji, who succeeded him in 1987.

Despite this, Jiang was promoted to Shanghai Party secretary in 1987 (and made a Politburo member) when the incumbent, Rui Xingwen, was sent to the Secretariat in Beijing. Rui's transfer was owing partly to his shake-up of the Shanghai Party system, which had angered Chen Guodong, the city's former Party secretary and political patriarch. Ironically, the reforms sponsored by Rui were designed by Jiang's future close ally, Zeng Qinghong.

Jiang was promoted to replace Rui because of his ties to Wang Daohan and Chen Guodong, the city's two kingmakers. Jiang frequently called on these two elders during his tenure as mayor, asking their advice on official matters and talking warmly in the local patois to emphasize his affinities with the Shanghai natives.

In the weeks preceding the killings of pro-democracy demonstrators in Beijing on June 4, 1989, the eight Elders met twice to choose a successor to the purged Party General Secretary Zhao Ziyang. The reasons why they settled on Jiang have never been clear. A number of officials in Beijing who might have been named to replace Zhao outranked Jiang, and other provincial officials drew strong praise from the Elders. But Jiang came up the winner.

The Tiananmen Papers confirmed that two Elders, Chen Yun and former state President Li Xiannian, spoke most strongly on behalf of elevating Jiang. They felt that he was steadfast on political principles because he had padlocked the liberal *World Economic Herald* at the height of the demonstrations in Shanghai. *Disidai* confirms that Jiang's close aide Zeng Qinghong had a crucial part in the decision to close the newspaper. Zeng may have been more attuned to the hardline shift in Beijing than Jiang himself. It was just the first of many instances when Zeng would prove instrumental in Jiang's advance.

Disidai adds another dimension to the choice of Jiang by the Elders: pillow talk. The book reveals how Jiang's assiduous cultivation of the wives of Chen Yun and Li Xiannian helped win them to his cause. Both couples were in the habit of wintering in Shanghai. In the years between 1985 and 1989, Jiang went to inordinate lengths to entertain Chen's wife, Yu Ruomu, and Li's wife, Lin Jiamei. He would visit them at least once a week during their months in the city and make sure their lodgings were satisfactory. Thus, in addition to his ability to "follow the line of upper-level officials," Jiang is credited with the ability to "follow the line of [their] wives" (*zou furen luxian*).

Jiang's emergence as China's top leader thus reflected the largely uninstitutionalized nature of cadre promotions in pre-1989 China, in which personal connections were crucial. Jiang in turn never abandoned his belief in promoting those who cultivated his good graces. Things were different for the Fourth Generation, who advanced at a time when merit was beginning to outweigh patronage. Members of the Fourth Generation want to go further and to break with the legacy of personal patronage in the CCP. Yet it is a legacy with deep roots. Many of the Fourth Generation, as we have seen, got crucial boosts from patrons in moving ahead in their own careers.

Jiang's post-1989 weakness. Despite his assumption of the Party's top job, Jiang remained weak in the years after Tiananmen. The Elders who had chosen him were his only power base. As the first person selected from a regional post to head the CCP, Jiang was not even familiar with the physical layout of Zhongnanhai when he arrived in Beijing in late May. Aware of his vulnerability, Jiang asked to bring with him one aide, Zeng Qinghong, his chief of organization and propaganda in Shanghai. Jiang had closer relations with another deputy Party secretary of Shanghai, Huang Ju. But Jiang made the shrewd choice, knowing that Zeng's personal connections and political skills would be more useful in the snake pit of Beijing politics.

Li Peng was dismissive of Jiang in the early years. He not only controlled the State Council but also exerted the greatest influence on Party matters. Li had to approve any meetings between Jiang and foreign visitors. When Jiang finally broke through the post-Tiananmen US freeze on high-level meetings with China by holding talks with President Clinton in late 1993 in Seattle, the script prepared for his conversation was entirely written by Deng Xiaoping, Li Peng, and others. That explains why, for that first meeting, Jiang stuck so closely to the remarks he was given, to the consternation of the US side.

According to *Disidai*, Yao Yilin and Song Ping, the hard-liners of the post-Tiananmen PBSC, never sought Jiang's advice on any issue. Nor could Jiang exert any influence over Qiao Shi, the third-ranking Party leader, who maintained a tight grip on internal security, Party discipline, and organizational affairs. Even Li Ruihuan, the lowest-ranking PBSC member, who had been put in charge of propaganda, did not obey Jiang and maintained a more open and tolerant atmosphere in the country's media and arts than Jiang wanted.

Jiang relied on Deng Xiaoping and Elders Chen Yun and Li Xiannian for his legitimacy and survival in these years. When Wu Bangguo took over as Party secretary of Shanghai in 1991, Jiang's first instructions to him were to look after these three Elders when they visited the city and to report in detail their remarks and instructions. Li Peng also maintained close ties to Deng and Chen, but more to assert his high rank than to defend his position. So often were Jiang and Li seen going to the Elders to seek advice (*qingshi*) that Li Ruihuan publicly criticized them, calling their behavior ancestor worship.[2]

Jiang's experiences could provide lessons for the Fourth Generation. The presence of elders, the dispersed nature of power in the new PBSC, and Hu Jintao's weak personal power base suggest he may face the same challenges in the early years of his rule that Jiang did. For

---

2. See Li's remark quoted on page 165.

Jiang, a critical part of overcoming that weakness was the purge of rivals at the top.

Purge of the Yang brothers.[3] Despite their cultivation of Deng's good graces, and despite the fact that Deng had warned both of them during and after the Tiananmen crisis never to falter in promoting his program of "reform and opening," Jiang and Li Peng steered a cautious course on economic reforms between 1989 and 1992. Moreover, as Communist regimes collapsed in Eastern Europe and the USSR, they maintained hard-line policies on political and ideological orthodoxy.

To show his dissatisfaction, Deng launched an extraordinary piece of political theater. He made a highly publicized trip to southern China in January 1992, during which he gave several long, pointed talks on promoting reform. Among other statements, he said, "Whoever does not support reforms should step down." Deng's remarks, however, were at first not reported in the Party press.

This only confirmed his disillusionment with his successor. Deng decided to dismiss both Jiang and Li at the 14th Party Congress in October 1992. Under his plan, Qiao Shi, the third-ranking PBSC member, would take over as the core leader, holding the positions of Party general secretary, state president, and chairman of the Central Military Commission. The premiership would go either to Li Ruihuan or to then Vice Premier Zhu Rongji, two liberals who had been steadfast in their support for reforms. Wan Li, another liberal, would remain in charge of the National People's Congress. Meanwhile—and this would have been seen as an extraordinary development—the

---

3. For earlier analyses of the cases of Yang Baibing, Chen Xitong, and Qiao Shi, see Gilley, *Tiger on the Brink*, pp. 195–196, 241–247, and 305–307. On the Chen and Qiao cases, see Joseph Fewsmith, *China Since Tiananmen: The Politics of Transition* (Cambridge University Press, 2001), pp. 165–167 and 193–194.

deposed Party General Secretary Zhao Ziyang would be rehabilitated as CPPCC chairman in exchange for admitting that he made mistakes during the Tiananmen crisis.

Preparations for the Party congress were to be handled by Wan Li, Qiao Shi, state President Yang Shangkun, and Elder Bo Yibo. Yang would make overtures to Zhao about admitting his errors in return for being rehabilitated. Deng began to praise Qiao's speeches and attitudes in internal meetings. The signs were inauspicious for Jiang. For the first time, his decision to bring Zeng Qinghong to Beijing paid off. Zeng, whose own career would also be ruined if Deng's plans succeeded, started by arranging several meetings between Jiang and Li Peng at the latter's home. The two men, hitherto rivals, agreed to cooperate in the interests of their respective positions. In the months after the Southern Tour, they belatedly issued more than twenty documents in the name of Party Central and the State Council promoting Deng's speeches.

Deng appeared to be mollified by the stream of propaganda. But Zeng knew that he needed to give the patriarch a more convincing reason to keep Jiang in office. He undertook the most audacious step of his political career, an attempt to drive a wedge between Deng and President Yang Shangkun.

Doing so was not easy. Yang was one of Deng's closest friends, going back to the time when they fought together in the fledgling Communist armies of the 1930s. Deng had personally brought Yang back to political life after the Cultural Revolution and arranged his appointment as president in 1988. Yang was a frequent guest at the Deng family home north of the Forbidden City, served as an intermediary between the Politburo and the patriarch,[4] and had headed Deng's personal entourage during the Southern Tour.

---

4. For more on Yang's unique role as Deng's confidant and spokesman, see *The Tiananmen Papers*.

Yet on one point, Yang was vulnerable: the growing influence in the military of his cousin, Yang Baibing, a veteran of the civil war who had returned after the Cultural Revolution to take up a series of senior military positions. He was head of the PLA's Political Work Department during the 1989 crisis and afterward was appointed to the added position of secretary-general of the Central Military Commission, whose new chairman was Jiang.

Deng had appointed Jiang to head the military commission in order to ensure the army's fealty to the Party. Yet that fealty was being undermined by the Yang cousins. Yang Baibing had recently recommended 100 officers, many his friends, for promotion to the rank of general. He had also pledged to provide a "protective escort" for Deng's reforms after the Southern Tour, which, although pro-Deng, could be read as a sign of the military's intrusion into politics. Zeng hoped to portray Yang Baibing's behavior as a threat to Party supremacy over the military and use it as an excuse to oust both the Yangs.

In order to get the ear of Deng Xiaopeng, Zeng contacted two close friends—the mayor of Kunming, Liu Jing, and the mayor of Qingdao, Yu Zhengsheng—fellow princelings who had previously served as assistants to Deng Pufang, the patriarch's crippled eldest son.[5] The two approached their former boss and conveyed Zeng's concerns about the Yangs.

Shortly afterward, Zeng met directly with Deng Pufang. Zeng was at pains to explain that Jiang Zemin deeply respected the patriarch's reforms but that his ability to promote them was being curtailed by what he called the "Yang family army." He warned that Yang Shangkun would take advantage of Deng's plan to rehabilitate Zhao Ziyang

---

5. According to a report on August 19, 2001, in the Hong Kong–based *Sing Tao Daily News*, Liu Jing, who later became a vice-minister of public security, was a middle school colleague of Zeng's in Beijing. The *South China Morning Post* reported on October 12, 1992, that Yu Zhengsheng, who has since served as minister of construction and Party secretary of central Hubei province, was a "crony" of Deng Pufang and a fellow princeling of Zeng.

and would seek to reverse the official verdict on the Tiananmen protests and pin the blame on the patriarch himself. He alleged that there was even a danger of a coup by the Yang cousins.

Deng Pufang was sufficiently alarmed by the report to speak with his father about the problem. With the way thus prepared, Jiang Zemin went to see Deng Xiaoping. Jiang brought to the meeting Yu Yongbo, a former high-ranking political officer in the Nanjing Military Region, which includes Shanghai, whom Jiang had installed in the PLA's Political Work Department under Yang Baibing. Deng invited his own closest military adviser, General Liu Huaqing. At the meeting, Jiang raised the issue of the list of 100 officers recommended for promotion. He said that he had delayed approving the list in order to seek the patriarch's views. Yu Yongbo said that there had been little consultation within the PLA on the list and that he believed it was an attempt to weaken Jiang's influence in the military. Liu Huaqing expressed agreement with Yu's analysis. Deng listened in silence.

In subsequent weeks, rumors of the growing Yang family army swirled around Zhongnanhai. Several Elders, including Chen Yun, one of the key figures who had argued in favor of Jiang taking over the top Party position after Tiananmen, expressed displeasure at the growing influence of the Yangs. The other key figure who had chosen Jiang, Li Xiannian, had died in June, but his dislike of Yang Shangkun, who had replaced him as state president, was well known. A veteran general who had fought alongside Jiang's martyred father, Zhang Aiping, also complained to Deng, and recommended that a semiretired general, Zhang Zhen, be reinstalled in the military commission as Jiang's protector.

A few months earlier, Deng had been seething about the failure of the Party leaders to give priority to economic growth. Jiang and Li Peng had already shown their support for faster reforms by encouraging a stream of documents arguing in their favor. Now Deng felt threatened by a nascent military faction, and the threat from the

Yangs seemed the more serious. At the 14th Party Congress in October 1992, Yang Baibing lost all his positions in the military. Meanwhile, Yang Shangkun had been stripped of his responsibilities for making arrangements for the congress, and in March 1993 he was removed from the state presidency. Jiang was reelected as Party general secretary and a few months later succeeded Yang as president. Li Peng kept his post as premier.

Deng's new tack had other repercussions. Zhao Ziyang's one chance to return to politics was lost in the shuffle, making it more likely that he would live out his remaining days in the obscurity of house arrest in Beijing. In addition, Deng had turned to a fading party elder, Song Ping, to help make the revised arrangements for the 14th Party Congress. When consideration was given to elevating a young cadre to the PBSC, Song took the opportunity to recommend his protégé, Hu Jintao.

The purge of Chen Xitong. It was only a matter of months before Zeng Qinghong detected another threat to Jiang's power. This time it came from Chen Xitong, a newly appointed Politburo member, Party secretary of Beijing, and a close ally of Deng Xiaoping and Li Peng.

Following the Southern Tour, Chen had been quick to publicize Deng's speeches, outpacing Jiang by issuing reports on the speeches earlier than the Party Center. In May 1992, Chen was at it again, personally arranging for Deng to visit the Capital Iron and Steel works in western Beijing, a model state enterprise belonging to the municipal government. Afterward, Chen took personal charge of issuing a report on the eighty-seven-year-old patriarch's statements there, sending them to the Central Committee in the name of the Beijing Party Committee and personally conveying them in meetings to senior municipal cadres.

Zeng, who was due to take over as head of the Central Office in March 1993, was angered by the visit. Chen had bypassed the Central Office in arranging it and had not invited a single PBSC member to participate. Zeng believed that Chen, by flaunting his disdain for Jiang's leadership, would weaken Jiang's authority over other local governments and central ministries, who would take it as a cue to go their own ways.

For more than two years, Zeng sought to uncover evidence of corruption that could be used to dismiss Chen. The task was not easy, and Zeng had to be discreet. The Beijing leadership was a watertight kingdom, and Chen's connections to Li Peng were strong. Finally Zeng found an opening. In mid-1994, Party investigators found that officials of the Beijing State Security Bureau had been running an illegal scheme in the Yangtze River city of Wuxi to raise capital for investment. Through a complex path the scheme was linked to Capital Iron and Steel and thence to Chen Xitong. Once that connection was established by investigators, Zeng Qinghong took personal charge of the case.

The question, as with the Yang family incident, was how to convince Deng to go along with the purge. Not only were Chen and Capital Iron and Steel leading supporters of Deng's reform drive, but another one of his sons, Deng Zhifang, controlled one of Capital Iron and Steel's Hong Kong–listed affiliates, a property development company called Shougang Concord Grand Group. Again, Zeng approached Deng's son, Deng Pufang, and convinced him that Chen and his cronies were a threat to the reform drive and to Jiang's authority.[6] After several meetings, they worked out a plan under which Deng Zhifang would give up his stake in the Hong Kong company so as to distance the family from the coming purge.[7] In subse-

---

6. Zeng would in 2003 seek to reward Deng Pufang for his efforts with an appointment as a vice-chairman of the CPPCC. The bid failed, however, due to strong competition for the plum posts.

7. Deng Zhifang resigned as chief executive officer and vice-chairman of Shougang Concord Grand Group and sold his 20 percent stake in the company to another Capital Iron and Steel unit for a nominal $1 consideration in May 1996.

quent months, Zeng and Jiang repeatedly gave their personal assurances to the Deng family that their names would not be drawn into the scandal.

In February 1995, investigators arrested several Capital Iron and Steel executives. Chen was detained on April 26, two weeks after one of his associates, a vice-mayor of the city, shot himself in the head to avoid arrest. Zeng sat in a prominent place on the podium at a meeting of senior Beijing cadres held the next day to explain the purge of Chen and dozens of his cronies. At a Central Committee plenum in September, Chen was expelled from the Politburo, and three years later he was given a sixteen-year jail term on corruption charges. (After serving several years he was quietly sent home on medical parole.) At the same plenum, Deng Xiaoping's former private secretary, Wang Ruilin, was installed on the Central Military Commission, a symbolic act intended to demonstrate Jiang's and Zeng's intention to protect the good name of the Deng family. Just after this purge, Zeng dispatched ministry-level work teams from the Central Committee to every province and major city in the country to inspect their anti-corruption efforts. The message they carried was clear: any local government that did not show its allegiance to Jiang would risk similar sanctions. As a result, reports from local governments to Zeng's office on every aspect of their work rose by 25 percent.

Chen's fall reduced the power of Li Peng. Li had a long association with the city of Beijing. He had served as head of its electricity bureau early in his career and remained an NPC delegate representing Beijing. As a city with the status of a province, Beijing answered directly to the State Council, which in effect meant that Li Peng had controlled the city through Chen Xitong since 1989. Following the purge, Beijing's large Party and government bureaucracies were put under the authority of Politburo member Wei Jianxing for a transitional year. In that period, Li sought to find his own ally to take over the city. But the only candidate of sufficiently senior rank he had available was Luo

Gan, and Li did not want to lose Luo to the comparatively minor post of Beijing Party secretary. Li finally surrendered the city to Jiang's follower Jia Qinglin, who was transferred from Fujian.

The Wuxi fund-raising scheme that led investigators to Chen Xitong also brought about the downfall of a lesser protégé of Li Peng's, a former Wuxi Party secretary whom Li had brought to Beijing in 1993 as a vice-secretary-general of the State Council. This man, Liu Jimin, was linked to the scandal, although he was not accused of any crime. Li Peng had to send Liu Jimin into semiretirement as a CPPCC vice-chairman, thus losing a subordinate in whom he had placed some hope.

Another blow to Li Peng was his loss of control over the foreign ministry. In 1995, Jiang and then Foreign Minister Qian Qichen conspired to get rid of Li Peng's protégé and putative next foreign minister, the senior vice-minister of foreign affairs, Liu Huaqiu, by making him head of the State Council's Foreign Affairs Office. Foreign observers believed that the new title for Liu confirmed that he would be the next foreign minister. In fact, the additional title was a prelude to his being removed from the foreign ministry altogether. That plan came to fruition in 1998, when another vice-minister, Tang Jiaxuan, became foreign minister. Tang, a Japan specialist, was considered by people in the foreign ministry to be less qualified than Liu Huaqiu, who, having served as director of the American and Oceanic Affairs Department, had more experience in relations with the United States, which were considered more strategically and economically important. But Jiang and Qian opposed Liu, who had often reported directly to Li Peng over the head of Qian. Before the purge of his ally Chen Xitong, Li Peng would probably have been able to have his way, since the foreign ministry comes under the supervision of the premier. Now he could not. Six years after Tiananmen, Jiang had begun to emerge from the shadows of others as an independent center of power.

The purge of Qiao Shi. The consummation of Jiang's consolidation of power came at the 15th Party Congress of 1997. By this time, with the death of Deng Xiaoping in February, Jiang's position as dominant leader was no longer in doubt.[8] But his ability to use that position to

---

8. By the time of Deng's death, the two Elders who had had the most say in choosing Jiang to rule in 1989, Li Xiannian and Chen Yun, had already died. Only three of the eight Tiananmen-era Elders were still living, and two of them, Peng Zhen and Yang Shangkun, would die before the end of 1998. (The last of the eight Elders was Bo Yibo, who is still alive.) As long as Deng lived, Jiang had had to pay heed to the patriarch's views on policy and personnel issues, views that were conveyed to him mainly by Deng's daughter, Deng Rong. With Deng's death, Jiang could move in new directions with greater assurance.

This change in the structure of power was shown by the sidelining of one of Deng's favorites, Li Tieying, a story which is told in passing in *Disidai*. Li's mother was Deng's second wife, who had left him for another man. Far from harboring resentment, Deng cherished Li as a reminder of his lost love. Since his own two sons had little interest in politics, Deng considered Li his political heir.

Jiang Zemin's sentiments toward Li Tieying were different. Li had succeeded Jiang as minister of electronics industry in 1985, and had reversed many of Jiang's policies and deprived many of his associates of their power. Among those pushed aside was Zeng Peiyan, whom Jiang had made director of the ministry's General Office. Moreover, Li Tieying was loyal to Li Peng. Both spoke Russian, Li Peng having studied in the Soviet Union and Li Tieying in Czechoslovakia in the 1950s.

Li Tieying had joined the Politburo in 1987, and was given responsibility both for the education and then the economic reform portfolio in the cabinet between 1988 and 1997. At the Party congress after Deng's death in 1997, Li retained his Politburo seat but was left without any major job when Zhu Rongji refused Li Peng's suggestion that he retain a seat in the State Council as a vice-premier. After intense talks among Zhu, Li Peng, and Jiang Zemin, Jiang suggested that Li be given the empty position of head of the Chinese Academy of Social Sciences. Jiang called Li Tieying into his office and told him not to fret about the demotion.

Like former Party General Secretary Hu Yaobang after 1987 and former military strongman Yang Baibing after 1992, Li Tieying became a powerless Politburo member. At the 16th Party Congress of 2002, he lost his Politburo seat even though he was four years below the informal retirement age of seventy, taking up a position as an NPC vice-chairman. Jiang's friend Zeng Peiyan was promoted to the Politburo and made a vice-premier, enjoying more authority than the man who removed him from office many years ago.

realize his vision of China's future remained constrained. The biggest obstacle was Qiao Shi, chairman of the National People's Congress. Two years older than Jiang, Qiao was the ranking liberal in the Party, having served on the PBSC since 1987. Since taking over the NPC in 1993, Qiao had put emphasis on building the legal system, on the supervision of government by the national and local parliaments, and on constitutional norms. Within Zhongnanhai, it was said that Qiao and Li Ruihuan (then in charge of the CPPCC) were attempting to create a "balance of powers" between, on the one hand, their two assemblies and, on the other, the executive authority of Jiang's Party Center and Li Peng's State Council. Qiao's speeches rarely mentioned the need to support Jiang, whose own vision of the Party's role was quite different. There was clear tension between the two men.

Whenever Qiao attended meetings of the full Politburo, Jiang was nervous and uncharacteristically subdued. If Qiao remained in office, he would likely undermine Jiang's efforts to have his theories accepted as Party doctrine with the same status as those of Mao and Deng. In addition, if Qiao continued as chairman of the National People's Congress, Jiang would have to allow Li Peng to become president of the People's Republic of China. Li was limited to two terms as premier, which were coming to an end; he was too young to be forced to retire; and the NPC chairmanship and state presidency were the only jobs that were, according to protocol, appropriate for his next posting.

From late July to mid-August 1997, senior Party leaders met in the seaside resort of Beidaihe to draw up the final list of top appointments to be announced at the 15th Party Congress. Jiang and Zeng Qinghong shuttled back and forth between Beijing and Beidaihe seeking the support of elders to persuade Qiao to retire. There was at that time no fixed retirement age for central leaders, even though the PRC had developed a series of rigidly enforced retirement ages for workers, professionals, and officials up to the rank of minister. Since Qiao

Shi was in good health; there was no reason to expect him to retire voluntarily even at the age of seventy-three, and no strong reason to ask him to retire. The only hope was to find one of the elders to intercede.

The top five elders at this time were Yang Shangkun, Wan Li, Song Ping, Bo Yibo, and Song Renqiong. Jiang had poor relations with Yang after engineering his fall from power in 1992. Wan Li was an ally of Qiao's, with little respect for Jiang. Song Ping was considered a conservative in the Party ranks and in the atmosphere of the time commanded relatively little prestige, and in any case he was less senior than Qiao. Song Renqiong was in poor health and little involved in politics. Bo Yibo was the only one who could be of assistance.

Bo had supported Jiang's accession in 1989 and the two had remained on friendly terms. Bo had upheld Jiang as "the only core" in a 1994 *People's Daily* editorial which supported the idea of passing the torch to younger leaders. Jiang frequently sought advice from "elder Bo," as he called him. However, it was Zeng Qinghong's good relations with three of Bo's sons—Bo Xiyong, Bo Xilai, and Bo Xicheng—that provided the critical help in persuading their father to take Jiang's side. Zeng held several meetings with the sons during the summer months and on one occasion flew Bo Xilai, then mayor of Dalian, to Beijing for consultations. Making arguments about Qiao's age and long tenure on the PBSC, Zeng was able to convince them to persuade their father to try to bring about Qiao's retirement.[9]

At the end of August 1997, the full Politburo met in Beijing. The only issue for the upcoming congress that was not resolved was the lineup of members of the PBSC. Jiang and Zeng invited Bo Yibo to attend the meeting as a special guest. Arriving to gasps of surprise, Bo spoke about Party history and how a balance of youth and experience had helped preserve its rule. "In order to ensure the continuation of

---

9. Bo Yibo's role in Qiao Shi's retirement was reported in Willy Wo-Lap Lam, *The Era of Jiang Zemin* (Singapore: Prentice Hall, 1999), pp. 335–336.

the leadership as well as its youthful invigoration, I suggest that we set the age of seventy as the cutoff age and that everyone who is above this age should retire, excepting of course Comrade Jiang Zemin. Even though this is a collective leadership, we still need a leader, a core. Jiang Zemin is that core," he said.

Jiang, who had turned seventy-one just days earlier, spoke next. "I previously considered stepping down at the 15th congress but I felt that this would not be good for the Party's smooth succession and the continuation of our work. Instead, I'll step down at the 16th congress [in 2002]."

The surprise attack on Qiao Shi caught everyone off guard. Qiao had never expressed any desire to step down, and many members of the NPC Standing Committee wanted him to remain in office. But he had little choice in the face of the sudden suggestion by the much-respected Bo. He accepted his fate with little protest. At the 15th Party Congress, Qiao lost all his positions in the Party hierarchy. He was still NPC chairman until the following March, after which he went into retirement. At the close of the congress, the official news agency Xinhua issued a special interview with Bo Yibo in which he urged delegates to "unswervingly rally around the Central Committee with Jiang Zemin at the core."[10] In 2000, Bo's son Bo Xilai became the governor of Liaoning province.

The years of preeminence. The 1997 purge initiated the years of Jiang's preeminence. Until 1992, Jiang was subordinate to others and from then until 1997 he was constrained by several equal power centers. From 1997 onward, a new Jiang emerged. His personality came more into the open and his personal views on policy issues gained more prominence.

Jiang had the denigrating nickname "show-off expert" (*fengtou*

10. Xinhua, September 18, 1997.

zhuanjia) inside Zhongnanhai, a tribute to his love of attention. He peppered his Mandarin with words from other languages and dialects —Russian, English, Cantonese, Shanghainese, even a little Spanish and Romanian. When he traveled to the regions, including Hong Kong, he did so with a phalanx of security men and hangers-on. When he stopped to engage with commoners, it was to lecture rather than to listen. Many in the Chinese leadership had been schooled in a more sober and restrained sort of social behavior, and they found Jiang's style contrived and wasteful. Li Ruihuan criticized Jiang for engaging in "empty talk" rather than "real work" and called his travel style "bothering the people." That personality came naturally to him. But after 1997, its frequent expression also reflected Jiang's having attained a secure hold over the leadership.

Jiang promoted many of his allies during the 1997–1998 leadership reshuffle. One prominent appointment was his friend Chen Zhili to minister of education after five years of having his plans to bring her to Beijing frustrated by other PBSC members (see below). People inside Zhongnanhai now talked about the Shanghai "Gang of Four": Jiang, Zeng Qinghong, Shanghai Party Secretary Huang Ju, and Chen Zhili. Jiang made his new protégé Li Changchun the Party secretary of Guangdong province. His ally Jia Qinglin, recently appointed Beijing Party chief, joined the Politburo, while Zeng Peiyan was put in charge of the State Development and Planning Commission. Jiang's eldest son, Jiang Mianheng, was made a vice-president of the Chinese Academy of Sciences.

In the past, Jiang had been sensitive to charges that he was promoting his cronies to higher office. Qiao Shi was one person who had criticized his failure to promote cadres from diverse backgrounds and regions, from the "five lakes and four seas," as a Chinese idiom put it. After 1997, Jiang acted with less concern for those criticisms.

Still, it would be wrong to say that he was free of constraints. While he no longer had any serious rivals, Jiang's word was not law.

Most importantly, the National People's Congress under Li Peng and the CPPCC under Li Ruihuan remained outside his control. Even though their weak institutional power made them of limited importance, these were at least platforms for criticism of Jiang's rule. Li Ruihuan in particular made frequent remarks that did not name Jiang but were obviously critical of his style of governing.

The limits on Jiang's power could be seen in some proposed appointments that never got approved. Chief among these were his attempts to bring Shanghai Party Secretary Huang Ju to Beijing. Huang was twice denied a position in Beijing despite being a Politburo member since 1994 and being reappointed in 1997. Since he was one of Jiang's closest allies, this failure stood as a mark of the limits on Jiang's power.

In light of the Jiang experience, one should not expect Hu Jintao to put a clear mark on policy until his second term, starting in 2007. By then, Luo Gan will have retired and Hu will have had time to formulate his own vision for China's future.

Jiang's women. Jiang's relations with women became more active as his power grew. *Disidai* identifies four women as his favorite female friends, although it leaves ambiguous whether the relationships were sexual. Two are politicians and two are artists. All four were beholden to Jiang for advancing their careers.

The best-known was Chen Zhili, a former minister of education. Chen, a Fujianese, spent two years studying materials science at Pennsylvania State University in the early 1980s. In 1984, she joined the Shanghai science and technology commission as deputy Party secretary. The following year Jiang Zemin was appointed mayor of the city, and the two quickly became friends. In 1988, Jiang made Chen a member of the city's Party standing committee and head of propaganda. Chen frequently visited Jiang at his home in Shanghai in those days. Jiang is married to his high school sweetheart, Wang Yeping, who has long suffered from ill health. On one occasion in 1988, Jiang was seen standing outside his residential building waiting for Chen to visit after she had returned from a business trip. At the sight of her, he snapped his fingers gaily and accompanied her inside.

Chen was at Jiang's side throughout the 1989 pro-democracy demonstrations in Shanghai, providing important assistance in her capacity as propaganda chief when Jiang closed down the liberal *World Economic Herald* newspaper. From 1993 onward, Jiang tried to arrange a high post for her in Beijing but met resistance from other Politburo members. Finally, in 1997 he found her a job as vice-minister and Party secretary of the State Education Commission and a spot on the Central Committee at that year's 15th Party Congress. When she was nominated for minister of education at Jiang's behest the following year, 10 percent of the delegates to the national parliament either voted no or abstained on the vote to confirm the post, the worst showing of any new minister.

Chen won praise for shaking up higher education in China. She merged 450 undistinguished universities into 188 larger ones, expanded college enrollments by one million students a year, and stressed the importance of the Internet in higher education. But her attempts to implant Jiang's ideological theories in the schools met with resistance. She was the only cabinet minister able to drop in on Jiang's office at any time, a privilege denied even to full Politburo members. Resentment of her close association with Jiang foiled her hope of joining the Politburo in 2002. She was made a state councilor with the lowest NPC support—87 percent—of any member of Wen Jiabao's new cabinet.

The other politician was Huang Liman, who was the secretary of the General Office of the Ministry of Electronics Industry when Jiang became minister in 1983. She was later sent to the open city of Shenzhen, near Hong Kong, as a junior administrator for the city's Party committee. She languished there until Jiang became the Party's top leader in 1989. From then on she was promoted quickly, reaching the position of Party secretary of Shenzhen in 1998. Jiang was said to adore the company of Huang, who made a point of visiting him during each of her approximately monthly trips to Beijing. She was known as an ardent disciple of Jiang's leadership and theories, speaking of him at meetings in terms that embarrassed those present.

In Guangdong province and Shenzhen, Huang's reputation among colleagues was that of a weak leader. She was considered uncreative and bureaucratic, traits that are especially unsuited to the supposedly path-breaking city of Shenzhen. Her husband and two sisters were alleged to have traded on her name in Shenzhen, a city of cowboy capitalism. The criticisms of Huang hurt the reputations of Li Changchun, who promoted her at Jiang's request, and of Zeng Qinghong, who as head of the Organization Department helped arrange the promotion. Like Chen Zhili, her close association with Jiang eventually proved her undoing. At the 16th congress, Huang barely made it onto the list of alternate members of the Central Committee, receiving the third fewest votes, an obvious snub to Jiang from the Party rank-and-file.

Jiang is also close to two other women whose attractions seem more romantic than political. He is said to have admired from afar the actress Wang Xiaotang in the mid-1950s when he helped manage Communist China's first automobile factory in the frigid northern city of Changchun, also the site of the military's August First Film Studio where she worked. Once he became chairman of the Central Military Commission in 1989, he had a perfect excuse to inspect the studio, and get to see Wang. Soon she was promoted to head the studio and was appointed a major general in the PLA.[11]

Finally, Song Zuying is an ivory-skinned, long-haired beauty in her thirties who is the toast of the PLA, where she works in the naval

---

11. Wang has apparently been giving support to Jiang's policies in her work as an actress and director. For example, she directed a movie released in 2001 called *Fragrant Experiment* (*Fengfang shiyan*), which is about the campaign to develop China's poor western hinterland.

cultural troupe as a singer and dancer. Jiang's admiration of Song is often displayed in public when he attends one of her performances and appears on stage to lead a few songs. Jiang often holds her hand as they sing together.[12] Like Wang, Song was always careful to keep her greatest fan at a respectable distance in public. But her career benefited greatly from the friendship. In addition to enjoying the highest level of state support for an artist, she is a delegate to the NPC.

Jiang thought. With Deng Xiaoping deceased and Qiao Shi out of the way, Jiang was in a position to put his stamp on the CCP and its ideology. Before 1997, he had sponsored new approaches or new slogans concerning several issues—among them, reunification with Taiwan, anti-corruption and crime-fighting efforts, regional redistribution of wealth, social morality, and patriotism. In many ways, Jiang was addressing the failures of the reform era led by Deng. Yet Jiang's proposals called for little more than mundane adjustments of policy, short of what would be required for him to be remembered as a visionary. To make such an impression, Jiang had to have an effect on the Chinese Communist Party itself: he had to come forward with a new conception of its mandate and its basis for action.

From 1997 onward, Jiang made several attempts to remold the CCP. The vision he espoused was a neo-authoritarian one, in which the CCP would be a party of modernizing, educated elites who could discern the national interest without recourse to the messy processes of democracy. The Party would also be a more disciplined body with an esprit de corps recalling its origins in the 1930s and 1940s. These two approaches to reform were articulated in separate policies, the Three Stresses and the Three Represents.

---

12. After a performance in July 2000 where Song performed, Jiang mounted the stage and held her hand. Xinhua reported that Jiang's move ensured that the event was "pushed to a climax again and again." Xinhua, July 30, 2000.

The Three Stresses campaign was Jiang's attempt to save the CCP from internal collapse at a time when the Party was threatened by rampant corruption and regional disobedience to central and provincial dictates.[13] If he could reverse the trend, he would not only bolster his own position but would also be remembered as a hero in Party history. The campaign's title referred to the need for Party cadres to lay stress in their daily work on three things: political probity, studying Party documents and ideology, and maintaining an upright lifestyle. Jiang had put forward the idea as early as 1995, comparing it to the Party rectification campaigns launched by Mao in Yan'an in the 1940s. But the campaign was torpedoed by Qiao Shi and Li Ruihuan, who believed it was an attempt at self-aggrandizement.[14]

With Qiao Shi gone, Jiang was in a position to relaunch the campaign. It was fortuitous that Elder Song Ping in mid-1998 made an appointment to see Jiang to express his concern about growing corruption among cadres. Jiang saw the opportunity to use Song's concern for his own ends and dispatched Zeng Qinghong to visit Song on three occasions, accompanied by Song's protégé Hu Jintao. After planning by the three, Zeng, in October 1998, presented the Secretariat's proposal for the Three Stresses campaign to the Politburo, and in December Hu Jintao went on television to launch the campaign. Cadres were expected to put aside their daily work to write self-criticisms, hold meetings to discuss their styles of work, and go to the countryside to pass the gospel to others.

Li Ruihuan remained opposed to this campaign, urging Jiang to "talk less theory and do more real work." Premier Zhu Rongji and

---

13. We borrow here also from Zong, *Zhu Rongji zai 1999*, pp. 138–176.

14. In a rare example of elite political feuds leaking into the mainland press, Li Ruihuan was quoted in a Guangdong newspaper in early 1996 as calling the exhortation to "emphasize politics" a departure from the Party's proper focus on economic development and living standards. See Gilley, *Tiger on the Brink*, p. 267.

NPC Chairman Li Peng were lukewarm to the idea. A liberal Politburo member, Tian Jiyun, called it "a joke," arguing that mere sloganeering would not ensure disciplined cadres. Party elders were even more dismissive, seeing the campaign as a sign that Jiang was trying to build a personality cult. A retired senior general, Zhang Zhen, said that the campaign was an attempt to force fealty to Jiang "but he is not up to scratch as a leader whom cadres want to obey." Qiao Shi, from retirement, expressed dismay that Jiang "dares to do this" and called it "Three Stresses in name but a personality cult in nature." The leftist ideologue Deng Liqun commented, "This is just to establish personal authority. I oppose personal authority most of all.... What right does he have to do this? He's not even as good as [Mao's ill-fated successor] Hua Guofeng." Within Zhongnanhai, staffers circulated jokes about the campaign.

Jiang responded to the criticisms at a Politburo meeting in March 1999:

> Some people say the Three Stresses are designed to build up my personal authority. I, Jiang Zemin, am not covetous, do not grab power, and even less do I have the intention of erecting monuments to myself. I have launched the campaign for no other purpose than to rectify the Party's work style and purify the ranks of the Party's leading cadres, so that our Party will not continue to go down the road of corruption. We must be worthy of our predecessors![15]

Despite the disapproval of older members of the Politburo, younger leaders who wanted to curry favor with Jiang—among them Hu Jintao, Wen Jiabao, Wu Bangguo, Jia Qinglin, Huang Ju, Li Changchun, and Bo Xilai—promoted the campaign. While mainly a means of

---

15. Zong, *Zhu Rongji zai 1999*, p. 153.

asserting Jiang's authority and shoring up the Party from the inside, the Three Stresses campaign also helped Zeng Qinghong to gain a stronger grip on the dossiers of provincial cadres (see Chapter 3).

The Three Represents campaign, by contrast, was more widely endorsed in the Party. The Three Represents called upon the Party no longer to think of itself as representing only the workers and peasants, its traditional Marxist constituencies. It was now to represent "the interests of the vast majority of the population" as well as "advanced productive forces" and "advanced cultural forces." These were code words for making the party more urban and bourgeois.

The Three Represents grew out of policy papers by Jiang's advisers, among them Wang Huning and Teng Wensheng, and conclaves of Party theorists convened by Zeng. Their shared belief was that the CCP could no longer ignore the growing middle class, which identified more with the educated and well-off members of society than with workers and farmers. Bringing middle-class people into the fold of the CCP was critical if the Party was to maintain its influence. Zeng was particularly keen to have leading private businessmen in the Party. The CCP should be composed of "excellent elements" (*youxiu fenzi*) and "advanced elements" (*xianjin fenzi*) no matter what their backgrounds, Zeng argued. "The great door to CCP membership should be opened to all advanced elements of the Chinese people. If we do this we can solidify our Party and we will face no dangers," Zeng said.

Jiang launched the Three Represents at a meeting with cadres in Guangdong in February 2000, and a full transcript of the meeting and commentary on the doctrine was issued by Xinhua the following month. Then, in a speech on the Party's eightieth anniversary on July 1, 2001, Jiang invited leading private entrepreneurs to join the Party's ranks.

As with the Three Stresses, Hu Jintao had primary responsibility for running the campaign, while the Party propaganda chief, Ding Guan'gen, a Jiang loyalist, made arrangements for media coverage.

As before, cadres were expected to put aside their regular work and arrange meetings to study the materials coming off the presses in Beijing. Zeng personally visited several provinces to inspect the progress of the campaign. Southern farmers became angry when the spring planting season in 2001 was disrupted by the campaign, as village cadres remained in Party offices attending Three Represents education sessions. In the end, Jiang's theory was written into the CCP constitution at the 16th congress, but without any reference to Jiang himself. For Hu Jintao, the lessons are two-sided: grand theorizing is a tool of leadership in China and may be necessary to consolidate power. But it can also be seen as self-aggrandizing and may face resistance.

Relations with Zhu Rongji.[16] Although Jiang and Zhu had been friends and allies since their days together in Shanghai, after 1997 their relations deteriorated. Jiang was in the period of his greatest power and was less inclined to make allowances for the views of others. Zhu meanwhile, as vice-premier until 1998 and thereafter premier, was undertaking difficult reforms in several economic fields and was also less inclined to make concessions to middle-of-the-roaders like Jiang. In two instances in 1999, Jiang responded to political crises by pinning the blame on others and disregarding the views of some fellow PBSC members. In both cases, Zhu found himself dissenting from Jiang.

When 20,000 adherents of the Falungong religious sect demonstrated silently in front of Zhongnanhai in April 1999, Jiang immediately blamed Luo Gan for failing to detect the planned protest ahead of time even though the police had been monitoring the group since 1997. In fact, Jiang had been given reports on Falungong's activities and had not given them sufficient attention. He labeled the gathering a "serious political incident" and ordered a harsh crackdown. Zhu

---

16. This is based on Zong, *Zhu Rongji zai 1999.*

Rongji and some others advocated a more tolerant line. Zhu said that the sect's popularity was a reflection of the difficulties of economic transition and should be treated with more understanding. The second incident came on May 8, 1999, when US warplanes that were bombing targets in Belgrade hit the Chinese embassy in the city, killing three PRC nationals and setting off anti-US demonstrations across China. The US claimed the bombing was a mistake, but the Chinese judged it to be intentional, a signal to China not to challenge American policies. Jiang had invested heavily in the improvement of China's relations with the US under President Clinton and did not want to denounce Washington publicly. He maintained his silence despite reports of popular anger over his cautious attitude. One of the many protest posters whose contents were reported to the Politburo by security agencies read, "Jiang Zemin—the turtle that pulls in its head."

At a Politburo meeting following the Belgrade bombing, Jiang proposed that Hu Jintao appear on television to address the nation in his capacity as vice-president. Hu did so two days after the event, when he read a conciliatory speech that only inflamed public anger. Many hard-liners in the Politburo blamed Zhu Rongji for making the US believe that China's embassy could be bombed with impunity. Zhu had just returned from a visit to the United States, and was seen as the most pro-American member of the top leadership, even though he had done nothing in his US dealings without Jiang's authorization. But Jiang allowed the private criticisms to rain down on Zhu, never speaking out in his defense.

Meanwhile, Jiang's growing sense of his own power could be seen in his interference in Zhu's economic work from late 1998 onward. In fields as diverse as finance, agriculture, poverty relief, and finally entry into the World Trade Organization, Jiang began to assert his views. The two men seldom saw eye to eye on these issues. On state enterprise reform, Jiang had more faith in the potential for state firms to survive, and a deeper appreciation of their political role in a

Communist state. In 1999, Jiang simply took the issue away from Zhu by convening a conference of officials on state enterprise reform. He encouraged state enterprise managers to think less about the bottom line and more about the political role of state firms in maintaining CCP rule. In Zong Hairen's words, "[Jiang] talked about the economy from the angle of politics, he talked about development from the angle of social stability, and he talked about management from the angle of Party leadership."

On the issue of the WTO, Jiang shared Zhu's opinion that China should join it but wanted to take the credit for reaching the deal with the US that would clear the way for China's entry. Although he had authorized Zhu to make concessions to reach a deal during a trip to Washington in April 1999, Jiang balked when Zhu later concluded an agreement. Jiang delayed giving his approval until he could rap the gavel himself and appear before the TV cameras to toast the moment during a visit to Beijing by US negotiators in October. Although Zhu was criticized in Beijing for offering too much in his April visit, the deal that Jiang eventually approved contained even more concessions.

When it came to plans for the fiftieth anniversary celebrations of the PRC on October 1, 1999, Zhu argued for modest celebrations to save money. The Politburo resolved that the scale and cost of the celebrations should not exceed those of the thirty-fifth anniversary in 1984. But Jiang laid on an additional $22 billion to increase the wages of state workers and pay for other new expenditures that would stimulate the economy before the anniversary. Jiang also endorsed the start of sixty-seven new major infrastructure projects in Beijing, among them roads, subway stations, and theaters. Clearly he wanted the anniversary to serve as a celebration not only of the national founding but also of the Jiang era. As the person in charge of monetary policy, Zhu was the main critic of the splurge, arguing that it was unfair to other regions and would cause inflation. But he was overruled by Jiang, who evidently felt that it was his time to shine. Jiang scheduled himself to read a grand speech on the achievements of the PRC from the Tiananmen rostrum on the day of the anniversary (just as Mao had done a week before the PRC's founding); he then rode around the square in an open sedan inspecting the military (just as Deng had done in 1984).

Jiang defended the costs and pomp at a Politburo meeting in which he turned the anniversary into an issue of confidence and pride in the country. "In celebrating the fiftieth anniversary," he said, "we should mainly calculate political accounts and not let ourselves be tied down to calculating economic accounts." Zhu frowned when standing alongside other PBSC members on the Tiananmen rostrum and appeared too preoccupied to sing the national anthem.

Jiang's legacy. By consolidating his power and staying in office until the end of his term, Jiang contributed to the institutionalization of Party politics. No political disaster occurred on the scale of Tiananmen during his tenure. The Party's grip on power seems more secure when he leaves office than when he took it. His reluctance to retire as scheduled from the military commission in 2003 clouds his legacy. It suggests that the retirement of Hu Jintao, whose successor remains undetermined, may prove just as difficult to manage.

According to *Disidai*, Jiang's one undisputed gift to his successors is to have improved China's relations with the West in general and the United States in particular. In doing so, he not only raised his own stature but also undermined that of Li Peng, whose anti-US sentiments were well known. Jiang's gregarious personal style and middle-of-the-road attitudes on most policy issues enabled him to work with both conservatives and liberals in the Chinese leadership. With their help, he kept economic growth steady and expanded the CCP's constituency in a rapidly changing society.

On the other hand, Jiang did little to address rural economic stagnation or the emergence of a national AIDS crisis. He slowed state enterprise reform, and was unwilling to modify the Party's authoritarian style of governing. These are some of the prominent issues that China's new rulers will have to address during their five to ten years in office.

7

DOMESTIC REFORM AND DEMOCRACY

THE ULTIMATE IMPORTANCE of the political maneuvers we have traced lies in the effects they have on policies. The Fourth Generation comes to power with the fundamentals of Deng Xiaoping's "reform and opening" program beyond debate. But significant problems remain in the economy, in social life, in relations between the state and society, and within the Party itself. The statements of the new leaders excerpted in the investigation reports give hints about how they intend to handle these problems. Although the views of the nine who made it into the PBSC will count most, elite opinion is also reflected in statements by the fallen liberal leader Li Ruihuan, by candidates for Fifth Generation leadership status, and by members of the wider Politburo. We cannot read their remarks as campaign manifestos, intended to criticize existing policies; they are explanations and defenses of those policies, often stated in general terms, by officials already serving in high positions. Nonetheless, because they are expressed in each person's own words (sometimes, to be sure, drafted by secretaries) and delivered mostly before inner-Party audiences, they help us discern the new leaders' particular concerns and ways of thinking about the issues facing them. Read in context, they offer clues to the possible course of reform in the coming decade.

Economic growth and unequal incomes. The Fourth Generation leaders all believe that the first requirement for China's continued development and stability is fast, indeed breakneck, economic growth. The consensus of the leadership under both Deng and Jiang was that an average annual 8 percent growth rate, mostly export-led and fueled by foreign investment, was the key to political stability because it provided jobs and a rising standard of living for enough people to give the regime a base of support. For three of the top Fourth Generation leaders—Hu Jintao, Zeng Qinghong, and Luo Gan, none of whom has any experience in economic administration—Deng's slogans calling for "reform and opening" and a "socialist market economy" are uncontroversial. But they must leave implementation to the technocrats who serve with them—especially Premier Wen Jiabao and Executive Vice Premier Huang Ju.

Wen Jiabao will be the leading official in charge of the economy. He and others have articulated a vision of growth based on domestic consumer demand which is different from the two macro-visions that have guided China's growth strategy in the past: the vision of growth based on large state-owned conglomerates, which was promoted in different versions by the conservatives and by Zhu Rongji, and the reformist vision of export-led growth that was articulated by Zhao Ziyang in the late 1980s. Wen differs from the latter vision in wanting economic growth to be stimulated largely by domestic rather than by foreign demand. He differs from the former vision in wanting domestic demand to come more from consumers than the state. According to Wen:

> The long-term strategic direction for China's economic growth has to be rooted in the expansion of domestic demand. Pushing economic development based chiefly on domestic demand requires good handling of "five combines"—we have to combine the expansion of domestic demand with strategic readjustment of the economic structure, deepening of economic system

reform, increasing employment, improvement of the people's standard of living, and sustainable development.

Another high official who has spoken about expanding domestic demand is the Fifth Generation's Li Keqiang, who is now first Party secretary in Henan. His words have added weight because between 1988 and 1995 he took a doctorate in economics at Peking University. Li asserts that economic growth should result in increases in disposable real incomes, and rejects the excessive attention to GDP figures. "The basic measure of whether a locality's economy has grown is whether people's living standards have improved," he said. He has called stimulating domestic demand "a critical ingredient" in maintaining economic growth, and would encourage it through measures such as selling off state housing to create a bigger residential real estate market, and loosening migration controls on peasants so as to encourage urban development.

In another shift from policies of the past, the new leaders think that domestic demand should be increased by reducing income inequality rather than by allowing it to increase. The initial stages of economic reform saw rapid growth in coastal regions, urban areas, and favored industries like automobiles and telecommunications equipment. Privatization policies allowed entrepreneurs, many of them ex-officials, to get rich. China's Gini coefficient—the measure of overall income inequality in which a figure of 0 represents perfect equality and 1 represents perfect inequality—rose from 0.15 in 1978 to about 0.43 by the turn of the century, according to both official Chinese and World Bank figures.[1] Some economists in China say it is higher. This has led to a growing sense of injustice—not only among citizens generally but, the documents show, among the leaders.

---

1. Chen Shaohua and Wang Yan, "China's Growth and Poverty Reduction: Recent Trends between 1990 and 1999," IBRD Working Paper, July 2001.

While he was still in office, Li Ruihuan was outspoken on this issue. While visiting the poor in the northwestern province of Shaanxi in 1999 he said: "The CCP has been in power for fifty years but there are still thirty million people in poverty and fifty million people without primary education. This is our failure [*guoshi*], our sin [*zuiguo*]." In Shandong in 2001 he commented:

At this point, we should give more attention to especially disadvantaged people, such as the furloughed[2] and unemployed, retired staff and workers, and people in the villages who still don't have enough to wear and eat. We need to create a series of channels to give them enough food to eat, clothing to wear, and guarantees for basic livelihood that are laid down in policy, paid for by [their original] work units,[3] and have guaranteed [backup government] financing.

Wen Jiabao has urged city governments to allocate funds and set up programs to guarantee a minimum livelihood for all urban residents. He has described this as "a companion project to state enterprise reform and an important measure for social stabilization." He adds:

Raising the people's standard of living is the basic starting point for various projects. Clearly we need to undertake effective measures to raise the incomes of residents, and especially the family incomes of farmers and lower- and middle-income residents of small towns, and work to raise the purchasing power of these residents.

---

2. Many state enterprise workers in China are laid off by being "furloughed" (*xiagang*), which means they continue to draw a minimal stipend from their enterprise, but not enough to live on.

3. Traditionally social welfare in China was handled by work units, not by government agencies. The system is moving toward government financing. Li here seems to be saying that work units should be required to contribute money to government social welfare funds.

Li Keqiang agrees, stating, "In our province [then Henan], guaranteeing and even raising the incomes of the low-income groups is extremely important."

Reducing inequality and increasing domestic demand require that farmers have higher incomes. Incomes in the countryside rose rapidly in the first years of the Deng Xiaoping reforms after the rural communes were dissolved and agriculture was effectively privatized; but since the mid-1980s the government has held down the rate of increase in prices of agricultural products and instead allowed peasants to solve problems of making a living by leaving the land for low-paid urban manufacturing and construction jobs.

The farmers have a powerful ally in the new premier. Wen has pressed rural governments to provide basic health care and retirement benefits for peasants while encouraging the peasants to supplement public health care by participating in voluntary commercial insurance plans. He also believes that the government must invest greater resources in rural infrastructure, such as electricity, transport systems, and water supplies. He has emphasized that supporting agriculture and the broader rural economy is the "key support" (*zhongdian zhichi*) of the central government in macroeconomic strategy, suggesting that the industrial and high-tech investments usually favored by officials should come second.

However, as is often the case in China, local bureaucratic resistance can prevent the goals of the central rulers from being realized. The troubled attempts at rural reforms in Henan province by Li Keqiang demonstrated the problems. The investigation report on Li shows how local cadres foiled his three efforts to make major progress on rural issues. The first involved his program to equalize electricity rates between urban and rural areas. Li found rural electricity companies refusing to make the required decreases since they needed to charge high fees to cover salaries for their many employees. A year into the reforms in 1999, rural rates remained roughly twice as high as those in urban areas. Second, Li tried to solve chronic water short-ages faced by 2.2 million people in Henan by imposing rationing on urban factories and residential areas. But urban units that exceeded their quotas were never fined, or they bribed their way out of fines. Third, Li wanted to replace a plethora of fees imposed on peasants with a single tax, a reform that would have cut 2.3 billion yuan from the rural tax burden. But while the new single taxes were imposed, many fees remained or were revived, mainly owing to bloated payrolls in the province's 2,145 township governments.

Wen Jiabao has attacked this type of obstructionist bureaucracy in rural areas. He said:

> The work style of rural cadres can be changed only by focusing on implementing rural tasks and resolving pressing rural prob-lems. When doing anything in the countryside, we must respect the wishes of the peasants, respect their autonomy in production, and absolutely not use force and orders against them. Rural cadres should spend more time in the countryside talking things over with peasants, understanding their desires and hopes.... Rural cadres must pay attention to the situation in rural areas. They should especially pay attention to those struck by poverty or natural disaster. Rural cadres must implement every policy and regulation of the central government with no variations.

By raising incomes and living standards, the new leadership's redis-tributive policies could help consolidate the regime's popularity. Although not made explicit and perhaps not even intended, the policy of encouraging growth based on domestic demand could have two other important consequences. It could make the China market a reality for both Chinese and foreign firms. And it could increase China's freedom of action in foreign policy by diminishing its depen-dence on the American market.

State enterprise reform. A second economic issue has been increasingly important since urban reforms began in the mid-1980s: what to do about unprofitable state-owned enterprises (SOEs). Under Mao Zedong, the state's large and medium-sized enterprises dominated mining, heavy industry, transport, commerce, and most manufacturing. Because of inefficient management and outdated equipment most of them have proven unprofitable under the market discipline of Deng's reform era. For nearly two decades Chinese officials encouraged the growth of various kinds of non-state-owned companies and sold off the assets of loss-making state corporations to domestic and foreign entrepreneurs. SOEs now account for only about a quarter of China's GDP, according to the World Bank.[4] What remains in the government's hands are the most inefficient and bloated companies, which is why more than half of the loans made by state banks are not repaid and why workers and retirees frequently demonstrate over unpaid wages and pensions.

During his term as premier, which started in 1998, Zhu Rongji promised to resolve these problems. His plan was to create a trimmed-down state sector of efficient, profitable, high-tech enterprises, along the lines of the state sector in contemporary Germany or France. He wanted to sell off to private investors (foreign or Chinese, in some cases including the enterprise's own workers) SOEs that did not occupy leading positions in their sectors. He also wanted to invigorate key state enterprises in sectors considered to have important national security implications, like armaments, telecommunications, banking, energy, and airlines, by subjecting them to greater market discipline. Zhu's efforts were undercut by Jiang Zemin, who insisted that public ownership must remain dominant in the economy. This view ruled out faster privatization or rapid cuts in state subventions

---

4. Neil Gregory, Stoyan Tenev, and Dileep Wagle, *China's Emerging Private Enterprises: Prospects for the New Century* (International Finance Corporation, 2000).

to important enterprises.[5] The new generation thus inherits a cautious, ambivalent SOE policy that has had only modest success. To judge by their statements, however, the Fourth Generation leaders intend to continue it, and the differences among them are matters more of nuance than of principle.

Wen Jiabao is on the reformist end of the policy spectrum in favoring faster privatization for recalcitrantly inefficient SOEs. The Party Center's policy has been to "grasp the large and let go of the small" (*zhuada fangxiao*)—i.e., to sell off small SOEs while pouring new money into big ones. Wen has argued for a modified understanding of this slogan, saying that it should not be treated as "an absolute standard." He implies that some large enterprises that are losing money can also be sold off, so long as they do not occupy sectors that are important for the state to control. He said:

> Is "large" really the best thing? We've had a lot of lessons on this. [The bankruptcies in the late 1990s of] Guangdong International Trust and Investment Corporation and Hainan Development Bank showed us that having huge assets was often just a show. Many other large SOEs also look great just because they are big. By contrast many high-tech enterprises are small in scale but they are very vibrant. We should correctly understand the meaning of "grasp the large and let go of the small." We should not take it as an absolute standard if it is taken to mean just paying attention to the scale and not to the strength or competitive capacity of an enterprise.

Wen is thus ready to continue Zhu Rongji's policy of trying to privatize many state-owned enterprises by ordering them to issue

---

5. This contretemps between the two is mentioned in *Disidai* but given a fuller airing in Zong Hairen's *Zhu Rongji zai 1999*.

stocks. This policy has resulted in stock market listings, or planned listings, of major state companies in sectors previously considered strategic, like banking (Bank of China), air transport (China Eastern, Air China), resources (PetroChina) and telecommunications (China Mobile). Moreover, Wen says, even those state enterprises that cannot be sold outright can be partially "transferred" (*chanquan zhuanrang*), which means giving or selling stocks in the company to the workers and staff while retaining partial ownership in the hands of the state.

On the more cautious side of the policy spectrum are Executive Vice Premier Huang Ju as well as NPC chairman Wu Bangguo and CPPCC chairman Jia Qinglin. Huang's and Wu's Shanghai-based careers left them more familiar with the state-owned sector, believing that many SOEs must and can be saved. Wu has said:

> The goal of carrying out reforms to bring [the SOEs] out of difficulties in three years has been achieved, their economic efficiency has been greatly improved, the realized profit of state-owned and state-majority-owned industrial enterprises[6] was four times as high in 2000 as in 1998, and in the first seven months of this year [2001] profits again increased 20.4 percent over the same period last year. We have explored a road of development for state-owned enterprises which suits the national conditions of China.

On this basis Wu calls for further state investment in SOEs to upgrade their technology as well as to improve their management.

Wu has also advocated what market advocates denigratingly call picking winners—that is, the government investing money in places

---

6. *Guoyou konggu gongye qiye*, industrial enterprises in which shares have been issued and the majority of shares are held by the state; considered a subcategory of state-owned enterprises.

and sectors that it believes will be profitable. For example, the investigation report on Wu quotes him as announcing in his capacity as deputy premier that the government will financially support the development of "software production bases" in ten cities around the country; on another occasion he said that the government would close down small coal mines in order to consolidate the industry around large mining enterprises that extend across regions and have ample capital.

The wider leadership sides mostly with the reformers on the question of SOEs. Zeng Peiyan, a Politburo member and chairman of the State Development Planning Commission, has been loyal to Jiang, but he is less concerned than Jiang with the political role of the state sector and more with its efficiency. Wu Yi, a Politburo member and vice-premier in charge of foreign affairs, is an advocate of opening the Chinese economy to global competition. The Fifth Generation leader Xi Jinping worked chiefly with private investors from Taiwan during his years in Fujian; he said then that he believed in "opening up a green lane" for private enterprise. He issued a directive that

> whatever fields of economic activity are not expressly forbidden by state law and regulations, non-state-owned enterprises are permitted to undertake, and whatever foreign-invested enterprises are allowed to do, domestic-invested private enterprises are also allowed to do.

Environmental protection. Wen Jiabao has expressed more forward-looking views than any of his predecessors or colleagues on matters of environmental policy. Commenting on the Great Western Development Plan, which calls for pouring central government money into Xinjiang to exploit the region's resources and tie it more closely to the rest of China, Wen has argued for step-by-step development that pays attention to high environmental standards. If his advice is followed, it would be a dramatic departure from the Communist state's tradition of hastily executed megaprojects. Moreover, he has said:

> We must accelerate the work of returning land to cultivation, restoring forests, and restoring grasslands, and must firmly resist the excessive and recklessly predatory exploitation of various kinds of resources. We must strengthen ecological and environmental construction in the western region.

Similarly, in commenting on the grand plan that has been proposed for a network of canals and aqueducts to carry huge amounts of water from the wet south to the dry north—three separate systems of 1,000 miles each, costing a staggering $58 billion—Wen voices rare words of caution:

> The south–north water transfer project is a complicated, systemic project which affects the entire [national] situation. We have to make scientific comparisons and detailed plans. We must conserve water before moving it, control pollution before turning on the tap, protect the environment before consuming water. We must fully think through the economic, social, and ecological effectiveness of transporting water. We must undertake full-scale planning, scientific confirmation, and careful decision-making with regard to the eastern, central, and western lines. There must be no hasty start to the work before we have undertaken scientific, full-scale confirmation. Water conservation must be tried before undertaking water transfer.

Wen went on to suggest that before moving any water, China should raise water prices and impose fees for pollution. The passion of his arguments suggests the strength of the Party consensus for the opposite view, which favors spectacular engineering projects like the controversial Three Gorges Dam in Hubei province that was begun during Li Peng's premiership and is still under construction. Wen's environmentalism apparently reflects his early experience as a geologist in arid Gansu, as well as his experiences as the vice-premier in charge of environment in Zhu Rongji's cabinet.

In addressing ways to protect the environment, as governor of Henan Li Keqiang emphasized the damage done by unbridled economic development; he advocated making local Party chiefs personally responsible for mitigating environmental damage:

> The main leading comrades at every level and in every department must give sufficient attention to environmental protection work. The "first hand" [Party secretary] must take responsibility for environmental work in his locality. He must earnestly take lessons from the environmental accidents that have occurred in some places, make inferences from all known facts and take warning, resolutely eliminate potential environmental disasters, and thoroughly clean up problems. Environmental officials should be aware of the problems that can arise from economic development, ensure that new projects meet environmental criteria, and make use of the strength of the whole society through guidance and mobilization to take part in environmental protection work.

Health and education. Issues of health and education have grown in prominence as the socialist welfare state has collapsed. In rural areas, free health care is now largely a thing of the past, creating a crisis of medical care for peasants. Schools at all levels are chronically underfunded and impose illegal fees on students, forcing many from poor families into the workforce before they complete the legally mandated nine years of education. Consistent with their own highly educated backgrounds and their concern for creating a political system headed by an educated elite, the Fourth and Fifth Generation leaders intend to continue modernizing and expanding China's educational system.

The investigation report on Li Keqiang praises him for developing a plan to expand basic education in Henan so that all of the province's 27 million school-age students could attend for the compulsory nine years. His boldest stroke was to order that funds earmarked for rural teacher salaries, which had frequently been embezzled or diverted by township governments, should be placed in escrow accounts under the control of county governments starting in 2002. He also allocated new funds to rebuild crumbling rural schoolhouses. Moreover, Li lobbied in Beijing for the right to establish a national-level university[7] in his province, pointing out that Henan has the largest population of any province in China and that only 7.5 percent of its secondary graduates go on to further education.

Health issues appear less frequently in the investigation reports quoted by Zong Hairen. Perhaps this is because they are so intertwined with the issues of SOE reform and rural development, which must be resolved to provide funding for health care. But one issue that gains attention is HIV/AIDS.

The Beijing leadership has recently become aware of this problem, which according to international agencies threatens a potential crisis for the new leadership. The United Nations agency overseeing global efforts, UNAIDS, says that China in the coming decade may have the world's largest number of AIDS victims. It estimates that the total number of infected persons in the country reached 1.25 million at the end of 2001. Without a change of strategy, the agency says, there will be at least 10 million AIDS sufferers in China by 2010.[8]

Li Keqiang is the person who has confronted this problem most

---

7. *Guojia zhongdian daxue*, that is, a university placed administratively directly under the national Ministry of Education and whose budget comes from the central government.

8. See UNAIDS, Beijing, "HIV/AIDS: China's Titanic Peril," June 2002.

directly, again in his role as governor of Henan. Starting in 1992, officially sponsored blood purchasing centers in the province's rural areas extracted plasma from donated blood and then reinjected mixed batches of the remaining blood elements back into donors. This ill-advised practice was thought to promote donors' health and allow them to sell blood more often. Instead, it led to the HIV infection of tens of thousands of peasants. According to the Party's investigation report on Li, the number of infected people in rural Henan in 2001 stood at between 500,000 and 700,000. If accurate, this figure would represent a vast increase over published official estimates of HIV/AIDS sufferers in the province. Provincial officials contended that there were only 1,500 cases in the province in 2001, although unofficial estimates were as high as a million.[9]

The Henan AIDS crisis began to come to light in 1996 when a doctor in the province named Gao Yaojie discovered that one of her patients was infected. Gao traced the source of the infection to the blood collection stations and in 1998 filed a report with the provincial government. That was the year that Li Keqiang took over as governor. It was his first position outside the Communist Youth League system and an opportunity to show his mettle by launching politically successful economic development policies. He was faced with the prospect that his term as governor would be dominated by responding to a health crisis among the rural poor.

The Party investigation report says that Li acted on Dr. Gao's report by banning blood collection stations and launching publicity campaigns against them in rural areas. But, says Zong Hairen, Li's response lacked follow-through. He never personally visited any of the worst-affected areas or talked to any of the infected people. While instructing local governments to set aside funds to deal with those

---

9. See Elisabeth Rosenthal, "Spread of AIDS in Rural China Ignites Protests," *The New York Times*, December 11, 2001, p. 1.

infected, he did not ensure that the order was followed. He required local governments to build HIV treatment and prevention centers but was unaware that the stations closed as soon as visiting inspectors left them. He sought to impose a news blackout on the problem, but the attempt failed. The tragedy was first brought to light by reporters in China, and then covered extensively by the foreign press.[10] The inadequate government response impelled some of the Henan AIDS victims to take their problems to the streets. Mass protests by victims at local government offices are now common, and some victims have begun roaming large cities threatening to jab infected needles into passers-by.

Disidai adds that many senior leaders in Beijing blame this desperate behavior on the ineffectiveness of Li Keqiang. In 2001 the deputy minister of health, Yin Dakui, publicly acknowledged for the first time the woeful inadequacy of the official response. "In some regions, leaders and the general public have not fully realized the hidden dangers of a large-scale epidemic," he told a news conference in Beijing. "They are worried that once the problem is revealed it will harm their social and economic development."[11] At the same time, *Xinwen zhoukan* (Newsweekly), the Chinese magazine that has been at the forefront of covering the crisis, quoted Dr. Gao as saying that Henan leaders were afraid the crisis would "affect their chances of promotion."[12]

In retrospect, the growing disillusionment with government effectiveness in dealing with the AIDS crisis laid the groundwork for the sharp public reaction to the government's mishandling of SARS in the early months of Hu Jintao's rule. Hu Jintao and Wen Jiabao had to

---

10. See Elisabeth Rosenthal, "In Rural China, a Steep Price of Poverty: Dying of AIDS," *The New York Times*, October 28, 2000, p. 1, and "Spread of AIDS in Rural China Ignites Protests," p. 1.

11. Elisabeth Rosenthal, "China Now Facing an AIDS Epidemic, a Top Aide Admits," *The New York Times*, August 24, 2001, p. 1.

12. May 28, 2001, pp. 30–33.

fire the minister of health and the mayor of Beijing to assuage public dissatisfaction, and government media fought a long—some believe losing—battle to regain a measure of public trust in the government's health policies.

Law, order, and human rights. While they will seek to alleviate conditions of hardship that could lead to social unrest, the Fourth Generation leaders also believe in a strict and well-publicized legal system as a way to control social disorder. Although the aim of the system is to uphold Party power, some of the new generation's reforms may help lay the basis for a fairer and more independent legal system, including police, prosecutors, defense lawyers, and judges. Occasionally the leaders even resort to the language of human rights, which the Party until recently rejected as a foreign imposition.

Li Changchun was a strong advocate of legal aid programs during his tenure as Guangdong Party secretary. Citizens have the right to sue government agencies under China's 1993 Administrative Litigation Law, but few poor people do so because of the cost. Li told colleagues:

> Many of us seated here are probably the offspring of peasant families. We know how hard life can be. We must, with deep feeling, do a good job of protecting the disadvantaged. We must do a good job of legal aid; we must protect their legitimate rights and interests.

In 1999, under Li's prodding, Guangdong adopted the first set of legal aid regulations in the country. They allow poor people to apply for grants to sue government agencies (unlike legal aid programs in the US, they do not assist criminal defendants). The province soon led the country in allocating funds to support nearly two hundred government and private legal aid agencies that brought tens of thousands of suits—many of them, remarkably enough, on behalf of migrant workers drawn to Guangdong by the booming export economy. Li used the language of human rights to explain his backing for the program. He said:

> Under market conditions there can be differences in the possession of wealth, but not in access to justice. Society can tolerate a certain degree of difference in wealth, but it cannot tolerate one group of people trampling on and seizing the legitimate rights and interests of another group of people.... For citizens, legal aid is a basic human right. As long as he meets the requirements, every citizen has the right to have it. On the part of the government, legal aid is a duty and a responsibility, not a charitable arrangement that we can either provide or not.

Keeping order through the police and legal systems will be the responsibility primarily of Luo Gan. Judging from his past record and statements, his methods of social control may be boldly reformist in some ways, and may sometimes even improve protection of human rights, although that is not his primary aim.

Luo has worked to reform the old Maoist "household registration system" (*huji zhidu*), which tied peasants to the land, by creating a single national registration status for all citizens. In 1992, Luo convened a drafting group to propose reforms to the antiquated system which, since the 1950s, had assigned every citizen a permanent personal status as a resident of the locality where he or she was born. People were forbidden to move, except in unusual circumstances. The original intent of the system was to prevent a flood of peasants into the cities, and later, to allow the Party to enforce agricultural collectivization. Persons tied to the rural areas were called peasants (*nongmin*). Their living standards and social welfare entitlements were inferior to those of urban residents (*jumin*). If a peasant managed to migrate to a city, he lived there as an outsider, with no right to housing, medical care, or education for his children. Even if he or she married an urban resident, a peasant did not gain the right to urban residency status.

In meetings of the State Council Luo argued that this system had ossified into an unfair, counterproductive status hierarchy of two hereditary social groups. Now that economic reform was causing laborers to move around the country, the registration system was creating an underclass of rural migrants in the cities and generating an illegal market in urban residency permits. He said that the system violated citizens' rights guaranteed in the PRC constitution and subjected China to criticism from international human rights groups.

Luo therefore proposed far-reaching reforms, including a single nationwide registration status for all Chinese citizens. He favored relaxed controls over internal population movements and a single system of entitlements for persons of urban and rural origin alike. The State Council approved Luo's proposals, but so far they have only partly been put into effect. If Luo has his way, peasants will be able to migrate to the cities as long as they have work there, and any Chinese citizen will be able to get a passport for foreign travel with ease. In fact, Luo has gone so far as to say, "We have too many people. We should encourage our people to leave and settle abroad. There are a lot of nice places to live in the world. If every country had some of us Chinese we would feel very proud."

Luo has ordered more funding to improve the administration of police and courts. In the late 1990s, he was impressed with Western criticisms of China's abuse of the death penalty, mistreatment of prisoners, and judicial corruption. He issued orders forbidding the police to use torture to extract confessions, urged the courts to approve death sentences only when the evidence was firm, and forbade the common practice of setting targets for the number of criminal convictions. (Notwithstanding these orders, groups outside China report that torture continues and that over two hundred members of Falungong have allegedly died in detention; it is not clear what view Luo took of abuses in such cases.) Luo also arranged for an annual increase in budget appropriations in order to improve prison conditions, although much of the money was siphoned off by officials before it found its way into the prisons.

Luo's expressed motives for these reforms emphasize administrative efficiency rather than prisoner rights. Luo is not alone in this sense of priorities. For example, alluding to the authoritarian city-state of Singapore, Wen Jiabao has stated, "We should learn from the Singapore experience of ruling the nation through law. Otherwise a country as large as ours lacking a detailed system of management through laws will surely confront chaos."

The importance attached to maintaining social order is underscored by a chilling increase in executions and police killings under Luo Gan. From 1997 onward, Luo intensified a standing campaign instructing the police to "strike hard" (*yanda*). He passed on instructions from Li Peng to the police that political dissidents of all stripes should be "totally eliminated." In March 2001, he told a meeting of security officials in Beijing, "The struggle with our enemies is far from over. On no account can we treat this matter lightly," and called for vigilance against a variety of political enemies, including dissidents at home and abroad, critics of Beijing's bid to host the 2008 Olympics, overseas supporters of Chinese worker demonstrations, officially unauthorized religious groups, and critics of the government's position on the 1989 Tiananmen incident.[13] In a speech on July 8, 2002, Luo ordered police and courts nationwide to "push forward the 'strike hard' campaign...to create a good social environment for triumphantly convening the 16th Party Congress."

The internal investigation report on Luo reveals with apparent satisfaction that more than 60,000 people were put to death in China

---

13. Zong Hairen, "Luo Gan jianghua suowei helai," *Xinbao*, March 6, 2001, p. 9.

during the four-year period between 1998 and 2001, an average of 15,000 a year. The language of the report implies that the figure includes both death sentences and the killing of alleged criminals apprehended in the act or in flight. The report notes that the annual average of 15,000 deaths at the hands of the police is the highest since the start of the reforms. To place the figure in perspective, Amnesty International reported 2,468 executions in China in 2001 based on public records, which it said accounted for 81 percent of the known worldwide total. Its analysts have variously estimated the true figure for China to be two to four times higher. According to the investigation report, however, the true figure was six times higher, although it is not clear how many were judicial executions and how many were police killings.[14] On that basis, China in 2001 accounted for something closer to 97 percent of the world's executions.

Political reform. The prospects for political reform in the next five years were damaged by the exclusion of Li Ruihan from the new leadership. For over a decade under Deng Xiaoping and Jiang Zemin, despite rapid economic and social change, few changes were made in China's political system. The statements of the Fourth Generation leaders excerpted in the investigation reports suggest that several of them take the problems of China's sclerotic political system seriously. But none went so clearly on record as Li Ruihan in proposing

---

14. When China reformed its criminal code in 1979, it put seventy-three capital offenses on the books, including petty theft and fraud. Today, the figure stands at sixty-eight offenses. In 2001, people were executed for bribery, pimping, selling harmful foodstuffs, and stealing gasoline. The law allows the death sentence for theft of as little as $60,000. The state media commend the achievements of police in apprehending thousands of suspects in the course of just a few days and the ability of local courts to complete trials in record time. Successful appeals against death sentences are almost unheard of. None of the new leaders is known to disagree with the view that the execution of thousands of criminals every year is necessary to maintain stability.

to subject the regime to scrutiny by people outside the Party, an idea that was last seriously considered in the late 1980s before the Tiananmen incident.

The Fourth Generation leaders are not significantly concerned about a threat to Party rule from political dissidents. They are confident that the security agencies can harass, threaten, jail, or exile anyone who explicitly aims to overthrow the CCP. But they worry about a weakening of the Party's ethos of public service and a consequent decline of popular support. As Li Ruihan put it,

> To be sure, the CCP ranks have grown quantitatively to over sixty million.... But why is it that our unity, our attractiveness are weaker than they have ever been? Why does no one feel honored or have a sense of historical mission to be a CCP member or cadre? This is the biggest danger today, and the fuse for potential social turmoil.

Li saw cadres serving their own rather than the public interest as the main source of popular dissatisfaction with the regime:

> To be sure, people's living standards today are greatly improved over what they were in the Fifties and Sixties or even the Seventies. In some places they have even reached, or gotten close to, the level of mid-level developing countries in Asia or in the world. But take notice: Which section of the people are those [who are better off]? [They are Party members who have benefited from power to gain wealth.] This is why feelings of anger, cursing, resistance, and oppositional emotions have risen to an all-time high. To be sure, people enjoy freedoms under the constitution that are the broadest freedoms in our history. But take notice: Which group of people enjoy freedoms and rights that go beyond those guaranteed in the constitution? This is why

people's criticism, denunciation, resistance, and cries of opposition to the Party and to leading cadres have come to the boiling point.

On the same theme, Hu Jintao said:

The biggest danger to the Party since taking over has been losing touch with the masses. This is also the error we have been most prone to make. If we want something to happen below, we have to do it first at the top. If we want the people to stop something, the leaders should first stop it themselves.... To improve the Party's work style, we need in the end to focus on the core issue of the inextricable link between the Party and the masses.

Wen Jiabao voiced similar concerns, saying that "problems which involve betraying the interests of the Party and the people are quite widespread and quite serious." From his vantage point in Guangdong, Li Changchun has also noted how the Party's internal inefficiency and declining popularity threaten the larger project of China's emergence as a great power on the world stage: "If we don't refurbish the [political] system, we will find it hard to exploit our advantages in international economic competition and to make a good showing in international political rivalries."

Members of the Fourth Generation are split into two camps about how to address the problems of the Party. One group—which includes Hu Jintao, Wen Jiabao, and Luo Gan—believes in strengthening internal Party mechanisms to rectify the behavior and quality of cadres. Another group—which includes Zeng Qinghong, Wu Guanzheng, and assorted modernizers in the Politburo such as Wang Zhaoguo and Wang Gang—believes in expanding external mechanisms such as competitive elections and a free media. Both sides believe that their preferred methods would improve the quality of governance offered by the CCP and thus its popularity among the people.[15]

The internal solutions have been described by Hu Jintao. He has said that the Party should do a better job of recruiting, evaluating, training, and promoting its cadres; his proposals were partly embodied in new regulations issued in July 2002, which specified a rigorous process of deciding on promotions through investigations, hearings, and examinations. Hu commented:

> At present there are many pressing problems of Party work style. Many of these problems relate to the extremes of the current political system as it is practiced.... This is because our system of selecting, evaluating, and examining cadres is not perfected, while our [inner Party] democratic and competitive mechanisms are not being implemented.... We need to work on three areas: cadre selection, organizational leadership, and the systems for exercising power (*quanli yunzuo zhidu*).

Hu's view is seconded by Wen Jiabao, who says that the Party should tighten its ideological and political training and pay more attention to recruiting and promoting cadres who are as ideologically and ethically committed as they are technically proficient. Wen also favors tougher inner-Party investigations: "We need to use Party discipline and the state's laws[16] to control the problem of corruption by

---

15. The choice between internal and external mechanisms for controlling the Party is an old one, discussed by Harry Harding, *Organizing China: The Problem of Bureaucracy, 1949–1976* (Stanford University Press, 1981).

16. Party discipline refers to internal Party regulations, enforced by the disciplinary inspection commissions at various levels. Normally Party members are investigated and punished by the Party first; then, if the Party authorities deem it appropriate, they are turned over to the government to be tried under the government's legal system.

cadres. We need to strengthen both in order to close the loopholes which allow corruption to take place."

Hu and others argue for an expansion of competitive elections inside the Party. Indeed, this is already happening slowly. For example, provincial Party congresses are increasingly presented with multiple candidates for Party positions (including the position of delegate to the 16th Party Congress). Examples in earlier chapters show that even a modest opening of Party elections leads to some loss of top-down control. At various times in the 1990s, favorites as well-connected as Li Keqiang, Xi Jinping, and Bo Xilai (and also Xiao Yang, the mayor of Chongqing[17]) failed to win election as Central Committee members or alternates despite the top leaders' support. *Disidai* also mentions the case of Wang Gang (now the Politburo's sole alternate member), whom Party colleagues voted onto the delegates' list for the 13th and 14th Party congresses despite his not having been nominated by the Organization Department.

Elite Party opinion sees such unscripted events as reflecting a failure

---

17. The example of Xiao Yang was given by Zong Hairen in an interview. According to Zong, on the eve of the 14th Party Congress of 1992, Jiang Zemin presided over a meeting of congress delegation heads. Jiang had three specific "suggestions" for voting. Two of them were duly accepted and realized. One was to reelect Mao's successor Hua Guofeng to the Central Committee in a show of respect for the late chairman. The second suggestion was that military officers Zhang Zhen and Liu Huaqing should be reelected to the Central Committee so they could "play a bigger role in the CMC." Delegates were not told that Liu was to join the PBSC and Zhang would become a CMC vice-chairman as part of the crackdown on the military following the scandal over the Yang brothers. But they voted for them anyway.

However, the third suggestion was foiled. Jiang suggested that Xiao Yang, then Party secretary and mayor of Chongqing, should join the Central Committee so he could "play a bigger role." Jiang's plan, not revealed to delegates, was for Xiao to become Sichuan Party secretary and a member of the Politburo. Delegates, especially those from Sichuan, voted against Xiao, forcing him to accept alternate status and the lower post of Sichuan governor. In contrast, the more popular Xie Shijie, a deputy Party chief of Sichuan, was elected to the Central Committee, forcing Beijing to switch its previously planned assignments for the pair and make Xie the new Party secretary in the province.

of "ideological and organizational work" to ensure that delegates vote as the top levels want them to. Indeed, this is just the argument for inner-Party competitive elections: they require greater effort by the Party authorities to work with the rank and file. In short, when Hu Jintao says that the Party should employ more "democratic and competitive mechanisms," he means that it should pay more attention to a cadre's popularity with his subordinates before promoting him. In keeping with this vision, Hu's early moves for political reform after taking power were more symbolic than substantive. He and Wen Jiabao spent holidays among peasants and workers, humbly sought lectures on policy issues from experts, and canceled the elitist Beidaihe beachside conclave in the summer of 2003.

The kinds of elections Hu has in mind would influence advancement only within the Party, and would not be extended to government posts for which non-Party candidates might compete and in which ordinary citizens would vote. Li Ruihuan, on the other hand, supported a bolder vision of developing external mechanisms to discipline the Party. Li supported inner-Party elections, but he argued that internal mechanisms alone would not be enough to fix what is wrong with the Party system. Said Li:

> We in the CCP cannot seem to implement successful supervision of ourselves.... Over the course of twelve years we have had eight or nine documents, but still no top leader is willing to reveal his income or property, or that of his spouse or children.[18] Why did an advanced political party, a Party that represents the interests of the broadest number of people [as stated in Jiang Zemin's theory of the Three Represents], come to this pass?

---

18. The documents that Li Ruihuan refers to require Party and government officials above a certain level to fill out forms, but the forms are not made public. Li's point is that the forms have never been taken seriously.

> Where in Marxism or Deng Xiaoping Theory does it say the Party should fear the people, fear supervision by society, fear reforming itself, fear the rule of law, fear telling the people about our own and our families' incomes? Comrade Xiaoping's theory has a clear statement: If we don't reform ourselves we will die. Twenty years' practice shows that this theory is correct.

"If we want to change the situation," Li also said, "and to effectively prevent and check corruption, we must constrain and supervise power." To underscore his point, Li offered generous praise for freedoms in the United States: "There's a lot to study from the US. They can denounce their president but can't libel a commoner. We cannot control corruption, while in the US, even though they have scandals, no one would dare to just demand bribes like they do in China. That's because they have a strict system of restraints and a complete legal system."

Party thinkers who advocate external mechanisms draw on classic instruments of democracy like competitive elections, a free press, and independent courts. However, they conceive of these instruments not as ways to challenge or constrain the regime itself, but as forms of "supervision" (*jiandu*) of cadres that supplement the Party's internal systems of competition, control, and discipline.

In this spirit, Li Ruihuan suggested immediately extending the direct competitive election of government leaders (so far limited to the village level) to the 50,000-odd township (*xiangzhen*) governments. (Such elections have so far been carried out in about a dozen townships as experiments without approval from higher levels.) Three to five years later, Li said, direct elections should be expanded to counties and cities, and later to entire provinces. Direct competitive elections, he said, "are the natural trend of the times, and of history." He did not say so, but the earlier experiences of the villages and of county-level people's congresses suggest that while candidacy in such elections would be open to non-Party members, no organized opposition party would be allowed to compete. Party cadres would have an incentive to please the voters, but the Party as a whole would face no organized challenge.

Interestingly, Li does not seem to have said anything about expanding the power of the people's congresses themselves at the national or local levels. This is consistent with his emphasis on exposing the wrongs of particular cadres rather than on setting up alternatives to Party power.

Li also suggested reducing Party control of the media and allowing private ownership of some newspapers:

> It is crucial to strengthen the supervision [of our work] by news [media] and public opinion. We should allow people to express their true feelings through the news media, and to exercise supervision over Party and government through the news media. We need to give the news media a broader space [in which to express views]—so long as they don't violate the state constitution, we should allow different voices to be expressed through the media. We really don't need all the media to express a single voice the way a Party newspaper does.... Do some local or specialized news media all have to express a single voice the way a Party newspaper does? That question is worth thinking about. We should look into the question of allowing privately owned papers (*minjian banbao*) and analyze the pros and cons, and at the appropriate time put this on the agenda.

Li, again, only hinted at his larger plans, but he seemed to assume that media criticism would be limited and constructive and would not challenge the Party's dominance. Zong Hairen suggests that Li may have envisioned lifting controls on publications and broadcasts having to do with economic, cultural, and environmental matters, and with lifestyle, while keeping control of discussions of politics and religious issues. It was not clear how far Li had thought through the likely consequences of this strategy. Based on the recent history of the Chinese media, the bolder journalists would migrate to the newspapers concerned with lifestyle and economic matters as these gained more freedom, and would use them to probe indirectly into sensitive political issues, for example, by asking who appointed particular stock market regulators or why certain dramas cannot be performed.

With Li in retirement, the forces for political reform in the new leadership are weakened. The seventh-ranking PBSC member, Wu Guanzheng, was Li's choice to join the PBSC and inherits his mantle as its most liberal member. Befitting his relatively modest status as a provincial Party secretary in the Jiang Zemin years, he articulated no broad visions. But his practice of "scientific decision-making" as the head of government in Wuhan city and Jiangxi and Shandong provinces in the 1980s and 1990s (see Chapter 4) suggests his probable sympathy for some of Li Ruihuan's ideas. For example, Wu has stated:

> The development of the Chinese economy must depend on the development of science and technology. In a country like China, a large country with high population and insufficient land, lacking in resources, it is necessary to stress management by targets and scientific decision-making, it is necessary to give attention to order and efficiency [in decision-making]. Lack of order and confused goals will lead not only to great waste of resources but to major policy errors and push China back to a state of stagnation.

Although scientific decision-making sounds technocratic, in the Chinese context it connotes a more democratic style of government because it allows non-Party experts access to information, a right to criticize, and a voice in setting goals. Thus, for example, in the midst of the SARS crisis that erupted after the first edition of *China's New*

Rulers was published, Wen Jiabao made a speech at Beijing's Qinghua University where he said that scientific decision-making requires open information flows and public input into government.[19]

The eighth-ranking PBSC member, Li Changchun, advocated allowing enterprises to go bankrupt as mayor of Shenyang; and he was in favor of providing legal aid to citizens when he was Party secretary in Guangdong. Both reforms again have a technical veneer but larger political implications—bankruptcy reform because the state-owned enterprises are central to the Chinese systems of government finance and Party control, and legal aid because it allows ordinary citizens to challenge decisions by government officials. Both reforms gave added power to the usually obedient Chinese courts.

Other Politburo modernizers who favor greater openness in government include Wu Yi, who at the height of tensions over China's talks with the US over WTO entry suggested that the leadership should establish its bottom line on concessions by conducting a nationwide opinion poll, and Wang Zhaoguo, who advocates that the PRC's lifeless "democratic parties" play "a more independent role."

Wang Gang, head of the Central Office since 1999 and a Politburo alternate member, is a strong advocate of the popular petitioning system called "letters and visits" (*xinfang*) through which the ordinary citizen can bring complaints about anything from bad roads to corrupt cadres directly to the government and Party offices concerned. Wang previously ran the Party and government letters and visits bureaus. In that capacity, he lobbied Hu Jintao, Zeng Qinghong, Jiang Zemin, and Zhu Rongji to raise the bureaucratic rank of the letters and visits bureaucracy nationwide and to increase staff pay. As a result of his efforts, in 2000 the State Bureau of Letters and Visits was established as a subministry-level organ, replacing the letters and visits bureau formerly inside the State Council General Office. Wang then

---

19. Quoted in *Nanfang zhoumou* (Southern Weekend), May 8, 2003.

convinced Zhu to attend a national meeting of letters and visits staff in September 2001, the largest such meeting on record. Just how many complaints are actually received and what is done about them are questions that remain unanswered in the documents quoted in *Disidai*. But the decision to upgrade the offices was remarkable—all the more so because it was the sole exception to the shrinking of the central government carried out as one of his principal reforms by Zhu Rongji.

Whether there will be real movement on political reform may depend on the calculations of Zeng Qinghong. Zeng is not reported as having said much on the subject for the record, either because his work assignments have not given him the opportunity or because the writers of his investigation report purposely left such statements out. His strongest statement is that China should not emulate the American system. "America has many things that we need to study," he has said, "but we Chinese would not like to follow the American model. When we carry out bold political system reform, it has to be on the basis of national unification, ethnic cohesiveness, and social stability." But according to Zong Hairen, Zeng has said privately that he would like to see the ban on the formation of opposition parties lifted. He has told friends he would also favor the expansion of direct elections to the county level or higher, and a more independent press.

There is no indication that Zeng Qinghong or any other member of the new PBSC would allow an opposition party to grow strong enough to threaten the CCP. Nor would they relax the ban on independent worker, peasant, and student organizations of the sort that briefly arose in 1989 and—in the hard-liners' view at the time—threatened Party rule. They have given no indication that they would allow citizens freely to exercise their constitutional rights of association and demonstration. Although all these measures have been advocated by more radical reformers in the Party, the leaders' view is summarized as follows by Zong Hairen:

If they allowed all workers and peasants to set up their own organizations, all intellectuals and students to comment on public affairs at all times, all worker and peasant groups to march on government offices all the time, the government would be engaged in constant talks with these groups. It would seriously impact China's economic development, and foreign investors would lose confidence in China.

Conclusion. The investigation reports do not reveal a Chinese Gorbachev among the new leaders—someone who thinks the Party's problems are so severe that they require changes great enough to risk the Party's existence. Their policy recommendations suggest that they will only approve of gradual change. But as Gorbachev's experience showed, leaders of Communist states are often reacting to conditions beyond their control when they launch democratizing reforms. A combination of economic crisis, political stalemate, and international changes can nudge avowed authoritarians toward democratic choices. Were that to happen, the investigation reports suggest that Hu Jintao and Zeng Qinghong—pragmatists with a genuine concern to make the system work better—might be open to nonorthodox solutions, and might gain the support of some of their colleagues.

For now, the self-confidence of the new elite appears real. It remains to be seen whether they will be able to do what they claim they can: surmount the country's challenges and solve the Party's problems without fundamentally restructuring the political system.

8

CHINA'S PLACE IN THE WORLD

ALTHOUGH THE LEADERS of the Fourth Generation are better educated and more technically proficient than their predecessors, they have less international experience. Only one member of the new Politburo Standing Committee, Luo Gan, studied outside China, compared with three members of the preceding PBSC, Jiang Zemin, Li Peng, and Li Lanqing. The preceding leadership traveled extensively, made diplomatic visits, attended summits, and entertained a ceaseless stream of visitors from abroad. The Fourth Generation leaders have not yet had equally rich opportunities for foreign contacts, with the exception of Hu Jintao as a member of the outgoing PBSC.

The new leaders are nonetheless well briefed on China's foreign relations. Like members up and down the Party hierarchy, they have internalized the Party's view of the world and are skillful at repeating it to many different kinds of audiences. We cannot expect the investigation reports to reflect as much diversity in foreign policy views as they do in domestic politics. Responsibility for foreign policy and national security issues in China is tightly held by specialists and a few top-level decision-makers. Others in the political elite are expected to close ranks around whatever decisions have been made. But we can look for differences of emphasis, as well as for common themes in how the new leaders present the leadership's policies to audiences within Party circles.

In any case, it seems plausible that Hu Jintao's generation sees less need to make changes in Jiang Zemin's foreign policies than in his domestic policies. When Jiang took office in 1989, China was subject to sanctions by many countries and had to contend with a resolution lodged against it at the UN Human Rights Commission because of widespread horror at the bloody repression of the Tiananmen pro-democracy movement. With much effort Jiang maneuvered the nation back to full international respectability. He was able to restore normal relations with Japan and Europe in the early 1990s. He went on to preside over the reversion of Hong Kong to Chinese sovereignty in 1997, and to attend summits with President Clinton in 1997 and 1998. In 2001 the International Olympic Committee awarded the 2008 Olympics to the city of Beijing and China entered the World Trade Organization. In October 2002, Jiang visited George W. Bush's ranch in Crawford, Texas. China sees itself today as a respected leader among countries.

Jiang's most impressive achievement in the eyes of the new elite was to create a degree of strategic stability in political relations between China and the United States, despite what the Chinese see as a wildly fluctuating, often irrational, American policy toward China. Jiang managed to keep three US presidents with divergent ideas about China policy committed to a set of central principles in US–China relations that served Chinese interests reasonably well. Central among them were America's support for China's entry into the world trading system and America's lack of support for Taiwanese independence. This is the legacy that Hu's generation will seek to preserve. Since the rest of China's foreign policy turns on the relationship with the US, we do not see signs of major change in relations with other nations and regions.

Judging from the excerpts contained in *Disidai*, Hu Jintao's foreign policy views are the most systematic and sophisticated of the new leaders. As a two-term PBSC member and vice-president for one term, Hu has been a close observer of foreign policy making even though he is not known to have exerted much influence on foreign relations and remains little known on the international diplomatic circuit. As general secretary and president, he will likely become the dominant figure in foreign policy, seconded by Wen Jiabao, who, as premier, will oversee day-to-day administration of diplomatic and trade relations. Still, as in the past, major decisions will be made by the collective leadership.

Western governments may find Hu's earnest and businesslike style a welcome change from that of Jiang Zemin. While Jiang tended to devote large parts of diplomatic meetings to small talk and atmospherics, Hu typically gets past formalities quickly and sets out an agenda for the meeting. This way of doing things has partly reflected the fact that he ranked below Jiang. But it has also showed something of his personal style. Hu may be dull but he is businesslike.

China as a status quo power. In their internal remarks, many made after September 11, 2001, the new Chinese leaders present their country not as a dissatisfied power, as some in the West portray it, or as a challenger to the United States for regional preeminence; they see China as a pillar of the global community, a force for stability and peace. According to Hu Jintao:

> Today, with the cold war over, international society should be based on a new security concept centered on mutual trust, mutual benefit, equality, and cooperation.... We resolutely oppose expanded military preparations, because military preparations cannot protect security, but lead instead to new instability. International security in the twenty-first century should be established on the basis of international cooperation and a system of international law.

China supports the United Nations, according to Hu Jintao: "To solve global issues requires that the United Nations and the Security

Council play their roles in full." China supports multipolarity (many nations having a say in world affairs), which is described by Hu as "beneficial to the establishment of a fair and rational new international political and economic order." Multipolarity is the right framework, Wen Jiabao adds, for solving global issues like environmental degradation, global poverty and illness, drug trafficking, and refugees. And all the leaders' statements portray China as an active partner in the fight against international terrorism.

Seeing China as a good world citizen, its leaders accept the concept of "globalization"—which they understand as intensified participation in the world economy and acceptance of its rules for international trade and investment. They interpret its benefits as contrasting with the isolationist nightmare of the Mao years. In 2001, China attracted $47 billion in direct foreign investment (excluding financial investments) and exported goods worth $266 billion, figures equivalent to 4 percent and 23 percent of its GDP for the year. That reflects a remarkable volume of interactions with the rest of the world for a continent-sized economy which only began to allow foreign trade and investment in the early 1980s (the comparable proportions for the US were 1 percent for direct foreign investment and 10 percent for exports). In short, judged from Beijing, globalization has been good to China, even if further changes in the global rules are needed to improve the distribution of benefits to China and other poor countries as well as to create the conditions for sustainable growth.

According to Hu, globalization is "an irresistible developmental tide." China, he has said, intends to be a rule-abiding member of the World Trade Organization. Wen Jiabao will continue Zhu Rongji's policy of promoting domestic compliance with World Trade Organization commitments. He says that China, moreover, must change its approach to investments from abroad; instead of subjecting foreign investors to arbitrary bureaucratic decisions, it should act according to reliable timetables and should obey the provisions of international agreements.

Of course, Wen says, China will "make full use of the transitional period" that it was granted under the accession agreement for entering the WTO, "especially being careful about the [pace of] opening [Chinese markets] and [withdrawing state] oversight and management of sensitive sectors like services.... We should provide reasonable protection for domestic production and markets."

In view of China's good global citizenship, the rise of China is a threat to no one, according to Hu and the other leaders. As China develops, says Hu, "we will simply have more resources to oppose hegemonism and power politics." This view of China as a status quo power defending the established world order rests on the idea that world politics is conducted among states who are sovereign in their internal affairs. It is American-style attempts to undermine state sovereignty on grounds of human rights abuses or imminent threats that undermine the status quo. In Chinese eyes, then, the chief obstacle to global stability and international law—the source of the hegemonism and power politics that China is sworn to oppose—is the US.

The US relationship. Because of the United States' global dominance, the relationship with America is, as Hu Jintao puts it, the "central thread in China's foreign policy strategy." Managing relations with the US is seen as a problem of dealing with a looming threat.

America's "strategic eastward movement has accelerated," Hu Jintao says. Looking around China's periphery, he notes:

> [The United States has] strengthened its military deployments in the Asia-Pacific region, strengthened the US–Japan military alliance, strengthened strategic cooperation with India, improved relations with Vietnam, inveigled Pakistan, established a pro-American government in Afghanistan, increased arms sales to Taiwan, and so on. They have extended outposts and placed

pressure points on us from the east, south, and west. This makes a great change in our geopolitical environment.

Such a US attempt to contain China was inevitable because of American strategic interests, according to Wen Jiabao:

> The United States is trying to preserve its status as the world's sole superpower, and will not allow any country the chance to pose a challenge to it. The US will maintain its global strategy based in Europe and Asia, and the focus will be on containing Russia and China and controlling Europe and Japan. The core of American policy toward China is still to "engage and contain." Some conservative forces in the US are sticking stubbornly to their cold war thinking, stressing that the rise of China must harm American interests. The US military is planning to move the focus of military planning from Europe to the Asia-Pacific region. The US will continue to exert pressure [on us] on Taiwan, human rights, security, and economics and trade [issues].

Zeng Qinghong agrees:

> China and the US can find points of convergent common interest, but these will also objectively become latent points of conflict.... In the process of China's rise, the US will [contribute] much capital and advanced technology, and if the two sides can cooperate it will benefit America's maintaining its position as number one in the world. But the Americans constantly worry that a strong China will threaten their position of primacy. So the US wants both to dominate China's market and to find every possible way to contain its development. This contradictory attitude determines that US–China relations develop in a zigzag pattern, so different from [the smooth development of] Sino–European relations.

Zeng adds that the CIA and FBI have made the containment of China a top priority, while Luo Gan warns that "the US wants to use the war in Afghanistan to have a permanent military force in Central Asia, which will have a big impact on our national security."

On the whole, the leaders' statements suggest that they give credence only to one side of the China policy debate in the United States. Their views parallel those of American strategic "realists" who believe that China and the US must inevitably come into conflict. None of the leaders' statements even alludes to another American view—in fact, the official one expressed repeatedly by American presidents and other high officials since Nixon—that American interests are served by a stable and prosperous China. Evidently Chinese analysts consider such statements to be too obviously deceptive to deserve attention, even though American policy over the decades has often been consistent with them.

No matter how difficult, keeping US–China relations on an even keel is a strategic imperative for China. American hostility can damage China's economy and threaten its security all around its borders. Therefore Hu Jintao states, using a quotation from Jiang Zemin, that China will accentuate the positive: "Increase understanding, reduce trouble, don't act oppositional, develop cooperation." Despite their dark diagnosis of American intentions, the leaders claim to believe that common economic interests will moderate American behavior. It is this argument that makes it possible to construct an optimistic view for the long term, since China in the foreseeable future would not have the power to compete militarily with a resolutely hostile United States.

Such thinking also reflects the Chinese leaders' instrumental view of foreign policy, in which common interests trump ideological differences. They argue that the US will eventually shape its policies to obtain both economic gains and the help it will need from China to deal with such international problems as the war on terror and the tensions on the Korean peninsula. According to Wen:

What determines the direction of development of US–China relations is the two countries' basic interests. In strategy, foreign policy, economics and trade, culture, education, science and technology, and people-to-people ties, the two countries have a broad basis for cooperation. They have common interests and goals on a host of global issues such as anti-terrorism, anti-proliferation, anti-corruption, and attacking drugs and organized crime. The two countries have even broader room for cooperation on maintaining peace and stability in the Asia-Pacific region, especially the Korean peninsula. All this goes to show that common interests are greater than the divisions between the two countries.... US–China relations have an inherent, automatic forward dynamic. When US–China relations encounter a setback, we should not and need not lose confidence.

Zeng Qinghong says, "Bush and Clinton are both clear—that to form bad relations with China is against their long-term basic national interest. Therefore, the United States will not develop bad relations with China in the long term, and US–China relations cannot evolve into [something similar to] the former US–Soviet relations."

As the Chinese leaders see it, the risks of failure should be equally compelling on both sides. According to Hu, "Neither side gains if relations deteriorate." Zeng Qinghong adds, "This is not to say a conflict is inevitable, only that avoiding conflict is a long-term task for both sides."

Russia, Europe, and Japan. China's leaders think of every other foreign policy relationship and problem in the context of US relations. For example, they value their new friendship treaty with Russia, and cooperation with Russia in the six-member Shanghai Cooperation Organization, for contributing to peace and stability on China's northern and western borders. The organization, which consists of

China, Russia, and four Central Asian states, holds annual summits and has set a common policy opposing terrorism, fundamentalism, and separatism. China shares an interest with Russia in trying to restrain American unilateralism—hence, for example, the two countries' co-operation in early 2003 to block UN Security Council authorization of the American invasion of Iraq. But the Chinese leaders know that the potential for broader Sino–Russian cooperation is limited by Russia's overwhelming interest in a good relationship with the United States. As Hu Jintao puts it:

> Given the historical lessons of the past, Sino–Russian relations will follow the ancient [Confucian] saying, "Relations between gentlemen should be as thin as water."[1] We should mutually keep a certain distance, mutually respect the other side's principles and interests. When it comes to relations with the United States, we should not use each other as cards to play against the Americans.

Europe is a diplomatic bright spot because of a similar compatibility of strategic interests and the strong potential for economic coopera-tion. In 2001, the European Union issued a policy statement asserting that China had strong prospects and global importance. "With Europe," says Hu Jintao, "we have no direct conflicts of interest and we have broad common interests." Most of Western Europe shares China's aim of checking overly assertive American power, and joined in Chinese and Russian opposition to the 2003 US war in Iraq. The Chinese leaders therefore believe that they can magnify China's influence by cooperating with the European powers. As Wen Jiabao explained to one Party audience, European Union diplomats are often able to modify American positions in ways that are consistent with Chinese interests. Consequently, Wen said, "If in the coming years we can

---

1. Implying that one should not presume or make demands.

maintain even more cooperation in various respects with the EU...we will get even more respect in the world, and will play an even more important role on the international stage."

For the Chinese leaders the only blemish on the European relationship is the issue of human rights, but it is a minor one. Referring to France, Wen says:

> Of course, due to differences in social system, economic development, historical background, and cultural traditions, China and France still have some disagreements and differences. The most important is human rights. Such disagreement and differences are normal, unavoidable. French people's human rights concepts are really very different from ours, and France has historically given great prominence to human rights.

It is interesting to compare Wen's comments about French culture with Hu Jintao's remarks about cultural issues in China's relations with the United States. Hu said:

> On the surface [US–China conflict] is a political and ideological conflict, but in fact it is a conflict of national interests. This is why Russia cannot completely enter into the US-led Western camp, even now that its political system has changed, because it is a question of national interests and has nothing to do with the political system.

It seems that the leaders see French human rights criticisms as growing out of understandable cultural differences while American strictures are seen as cynical instruments of a containment strategy. As avowed cultural relativists (at least for the purposes of diplomacy), the leaders are more willing to compromise on issues that they see as genuinely cultural than on those that they believe are used by practitioners of power politics as pretexts to further instrumental objectives. This means that they are more disposed to make concessions to concerns about human rights that emanate from Europe than from America. Says Wen:

> Acknowledging differences in human rights is beneficial to the communication between the two sides [China and France]. Even more important, we ourselves must correctly see the problems that we actually have on the human rights side. We still have a lot of work to do [in this area].

Japan is a sad contrast to Europe in Chinese eyes, a tool of American power rather than a counterbalance to it and hence a threat to Chinese interests. Zeng Qinghong is quoted at length on this issue. "The Japan–US alliance," he says, "is the focus of Japanese national interest, and its purpose is to contain China and Russia." "In the Western Pacific the US and Japan have a common interest in containing China. And the core is the Taiwan question." Zeng does not place much hope on rising Japanese nationalism to loosen Japan's tie with the US: "Even though anti-American nationalist sentiment has been increasing in recent years, the Japanese government has strengthened strategic cooperation with the US." He argues that Japan's economic troubles are only strengthening its links with the US: "In the past decade the decline of Japan's economy and the increasing tension in its relations with neighboring Asian countries have made it even easier for the US to control this chess piece."

A series of problems therefore overshadows China's dealings with Japan: these are "Japan's denial and glossing over of its history of invading China, Japan's violation of the one-China principle in regard to Taiwan, the problem that the Japan–US alliance threatens Chinese security, the conflict over rights over [the island group of] Diaoyutai and its surrounding sea, and conflicts in the area of trade and economic cooperation." The potential for economic cooperation remains the major reason for optimism, however, and Zeng counsels that leaders on both sides should keep trying to create a basis for friendly neighborly relations in the new century.

Disidai does not contain any quotations covering leaders' views on the rest of Asia—the Korean peninsula, Southeast Asia, and India and Pakistan—even though this is the region where China's influence is greatest and its impact most felt. This may reflect the belief that in China's grand strategy to resist the expansion of American power these countries are not major chess pieces comparable to Russia, Europe, and Japan. In addition, the complexities of the Asian scene—where most conflicts are multisided and internal to the region—may not concern policymakers at the highest level until they affect relations with other Great Powers.

Taiwan, Tibet, and Xinjiang. The relationship with the United States also provides the perspective in which Chinese leaders analyze three problems that, strictly speaking, they consider to be domestic, rather than foreign policy, issues—their relations with Taiwan, Tibet, and Xinjiang, the vast northwestern region bordering on Tibet and Central Asia, where China faces separatist resentment among Muslim ethnic groups. Domestic opposition to Chinese rule is not, in the leaders' view, the real source of difficulty in Taiwan and Tibet. Instead, that opposition has been manipulated, exaggerated, even created by the Americans as part of their strategy of containing China.

Zeng Qinghong describes Taiwan and Tibet as "bargaining chips" of America's China strategy. As he puts it:

> When the US believes that improvement in US–China relations suits its interest, Taiwan becomes unimportant; when America believes that conflict between the two sides is necessary, the Taiwan question is placed on the White House's table. The

Americans never consider Taiwan's interests, only their own. Don't you think the Taiwanese are clear on this point? Of course they are—but they cannot say so.

Hu Jintao comments that "the root of the delay in solving the [Taiwan] problem is the US. The US should not get involved in this matter. The Chinese people on the two sides of the strait can properly handle this family matter."

The military option for solving the Taiwan problem must be preserved, the new leaders agree—otherwise, Hu says, "peaceful reunification would be impossible." But, since a possible military action against Taiwan is a national security matter, there is no specific discussion of it in the investigation reports.[2] The reports emphasize China's nonmilitary strategy: to rely on the attractions of the mainland's economic growth to draw the Taiwanese people toward unification. As Li Ruihuan put it, as recorded in his investigation report:

> [The Taiwan problem] will eventually be resolved; this is an objective fact that doesn't depend on human will. Regardless of how much the Taiwan authorities refuse to accept the one-China principle,...people's contacts across the Taiwan Strait have developed into a tide, and economic and cultural transactions are constantly increasing. No one can deny this.... As our comprehensive national strength increases, the Taiwan independence path can only get narrower and narrower.

The leaders optimistically believe that the rise to power in Taiwan of

---

2. Some of the details are discussed in Zong Hairen's earlier book, *Zhu Rongji in 1999*. That book quotes military leaders as discussing weaknesses in China's current preparedness for a military assault on Taiwan, but as guaranteeing that a military victory will be possible by a certain deadline, which is x'd out in Zong's account.

the independence-minded Democratic Progressive Party, which captured the presidency under Chen Shui-bian in 2000 and became the largest party in the Taiwanese legislature in 2001, will be a passing phenomenon. Zeng Qinghong's dismissive evaluation of Chen is typical:

> He has power but no idea of how to use it; he is not a skillful politician. The Taiwanese support him for the time being only out of a certain emotionality, but emotion has to be sustained for a long time [to be of any importance]. For now, Chen is relying on the economic prosperity built up under the [former regime of the] Kuomintang to survive [and cannot provide continuing prosperity]. So the Taiwan people's emotions toward him cannot be sustained for long.

Hu Jintao summarizes: "Chen Shui-bian is temporary." This no doubt explains the mainland leaders' lack of urgency in seeking to negotiate with Chen.

Several members of the new leadership believe that Beijing should play down official talks and concentrate on building up economic and social exchanges to entice Taipei to the bargaining table. Those holding this view include the Politburo members who are most knowledgeable about Taiwan: PBSC member Jia Qinglin, who worked for eleven years in Fujian, the province most involved with Taiwan, former Taiwan Affairs Office Director Wang Zhaoguo, and Politburo alternate Wang Gang, who served in the Taiwan Affairs Office in the early 1980s. Their views are shared by Xi Jinping, who dealt with Taiwan matters as Fujian governor.

In contrast to a widespread view in the West, therefore, the Fourth Generation leaders do not see the development of democracy in Taiwan as a real obstacle to reunification. They see expressions of popular wishes for autonomy from China as manifestations of "plots" and "interference" in the island's affairs. Hu Jintao has said, "Taiwan affairs should be decided by the Taiwan people," but he quickly added, "This does not mean they can hold a referendum and then declare independence." The new leaders anticipate that the current leaders in Taiwan will be replaced by a more pro-Beijing group as Taiwan's economy becomes more integrated with the mainland's and its international isolation, enforced by Beijing, drives home to Taiwan's residents the impossibility of independence. "For now the Taiwan people respect Chen Shui-bian and thank him, but this will not last," concludes Zeng. In view of the DPP's popularity in Taiwan and the possibility that Chen will win another term in the next presidential election, scheduled for 2004, these statements could turn out to be dangerously misinformed.

The Fourth Generation leaders see Tibet, like Taiwan, as a proxy battlefield in China's relations with the US. For half a century China has engaged in a campaign to repress religious and cultural freedoms in Tibet while promoting economic development, in order to consolidate its control over what it sees as a strategically crucial territory. According to Zeng Qinghong, international criticisms of Chinese policies in Tibet "fully reveal the hidden psychology of the Dalai [Lama] clique and international enemy forces to use the so-called 'Tibet problem' to damage China's stability, divide Chinese territory, and contain China's development and strength." "Tibet is China's Tibet, not America's Tibet or Europe's Tibet," Zeng adds. "Everyone knows that the US native Indians suffered cultural genocide and the US and Europe are always having problems with racial discrimination, so what right does the US have to beat others with human rights? They should solve their own problems first."

Li Ruihan's views on Tibet are significant, even though he did not make it into the new leadership, because their harshness indicates how little flexibility there is on this issue even among liberal members of the elite. In one speech, Li said that unrest in Tibet was a result of excessively liberal policies by the central government:

> From 1951 to 1959 the central government basically implemented autonomous rule there. The result was a rebellion. From quelling the rebellion in 1959 through to the end of the Cultural Revolution, the central government ran Tibet under tight management and as a result stability was ensured and ethnic conflict was minimized. In the reform era, Tibet has enjoyed more freedom and prosperity than ever but it has also become more unstable and also more internationalized.

Li did note, however, that alongside tight management inside Tibet, Beijing needs to adopt a flexible attitude in dealing with the Dalai Lama:

> The Dalai Lama and the few separatist activities [being carried out] there can at most create some troubles, but cannot form a major threat. Looking back on history and forward into the future, we have at all times to take Tibetan independence as the issue that we are addressing and come up with countermeasures to this. In dealing with the Dalai Lama we don't have to take a hostile attitude and use excessive measures. Just as long as he doesn't engage in Tibetan independence [activities], we can talk with him. We should be clear, under present conditions, that no plan can last for long that doesn't include the Dalai Lama.

Similar views were expressed by Zeng Qinghong, who said:

> Everyone can see the advancing development in Tibetan society. In pushing forward the modernization of Tibet and opposing

the separatist activities of the Dalai [Lama] clique, China has followed the trend of the times and has won the hearts of the [Tibetan] people. [But] our propaganda work is not good enough and today in foreign countries there are many purposeful distortions as well as unintentional misunderstandings about Tibet.

Perhaps attitudes such as Li's and Zeng's lay behind Beijing's willingness to receive delegations from the Dalai Lama in July and September 2002, and again in June 2003, although only for the avowed purpose of seeing Tibet's progress and not for negotiations. In any case, the new generation views the situation within Tibet as manageable. Zeng Qinghong says that "for historical reasons, religious faith is the most important thing for the Tibetan people.... Upholding the autonomy system in the ethnic region, fully guaranteeing to the various ethnic groups in Tibet, especially the Tibetans, the right to autonomously manage the region's affairs in accordance with law, fully respecting their cultural traditions, habits and customs, their language and their religious beliefs—this is an important guarantee for the healthy development of Tibetan modernization." Hu Jintao advocates keeping the war of words with the Dalai Lama at a level that is "beneficial, reasonable, and restrained." He expects that Tibet's next spiritual leader will be more amenable to Beijing's wishes. "The Dalai Lama is over sixty. He does not have many more years left," Hu has stated, no doubt alluding to persistent reports of the Dalai Lama's ill health.

Of all China's problem regions, the one to which the West has paid least attention, Xinjiang, is the one that the Fourth Generation leaders seem to worry about the most. Xinjiang is an ethnically diverse region of some 19.25 million people in northwest China. Nearly half of the population is made up of Turkic-speaking Uigurs, who are largely Muslim. For years China has restricted the building of mosques there and arrested hundreds of people for peaceful dissent. The region came into the international spotlight after September 11, when Beijing attempted to justify repression of pro-separatist activities as part of the international war on terrorism.

Most foreign specialists believe that Xinjiang separatist activities have been infrequent and mostly nonviolent. As head of the security apparatus, Luo Gan describes the situation in far more serious terms. His investigation report quotes him as saying that pro-independence groups conducted over two hundred violent terrorist incidents between 1990 and 2001, mostly against government and police offices and infrastructure, leaving 162 dead and 440 injured,[3] and that 130 "terrorist elements" were arrested in Xinjiang after September 11 who had received training in Afghanistan. Luo Gan reported, "There always have been and probably always will be terrorists in Xinjiang."

Luo Gan believes that Tibet, with a single unified minority mostly committed to nonviolent protest, is easier to manage than Xinjiang, where multiple ethnicities and fractures among the Uighur population are compounded by the greater recourse to violence as a form of protest. "To guarantee long-term stability [in Xinjiang] we have to unite with the great majority of ethnic groups there," he says. Luo also points out that Xinjiang's strategic location is more complicated since it borders on the unstable Central Asian republics that emerged from the breakup of the Soviet Union. According to his account, the East Turkestan separatists, as the Party calls them, intensified their use of violent and terrorist tactics in the 1990s with the aid of foreign groups, including al-Qaeda. The investigation report praised Luo for

---

3. The figures for violent incidents quoted in *Disidai* (200 incidents, 162 dead, 440 injured) were also given in a public report on terrorism in Xinjiang issued by the State Council on January 21, 2002, and were later cited by the US government as a reason for classifying the East Turkestan Islamic Movement—one particular Uighur organization—as a terrorist group.

carrying on the fight against terrorists in Xinjiang "with unprecedented determination and thoroughness."

Hu Jintao has called for installing a detailed control system, from bottom to top, in the parts of the autonomous region where there have been political problems:

> We must grasp the basic levels to protect stability. We can realize political stability, economic prosperity, and long-term social order in Xinjiang only if we take hold of this "ox's nose."... We must select and send a large number of excellent young and middle-aged cadres, whose personnel lines and salaries are on the central government's budget,[4] to work in those villages where the situation is complicated, the economy is poor, and the task of upholding stability is difficult. We must definitely manage religious affairs in a way that relates to Xinjiang's reality, that is adapted to the situation on the ground, and that is firm and rational.

The government's policy should be

> "to protect what is legal, restrict what is illegal, and attack what is criminal," so as to bring religious activities to comply self-consciously with Party policy and state law. We have to send our best people to the front lines, the village and township Party committees have to play a core leadership role, the village Party branches have to become fortresses in the battle, and the police precinct offices, People's Armed Police, and basic-level militia must develop their roles as core cadres along with the advanced peasants.

---

4. The language implies that the cadres would be Han Chinese from outside the region, sent to work in Uighur villages.

Xinjiang, then, appears to the Fourth Generation to pose a more critical challenge than either Taiwan or Tibet. Only one member of the new Politburo has expressed any fresh ideas about the region, the alternate member Wang Gang, who spent four years up until 1981 as personal secretary to the then Xinjiang Party chief. Wang has attributed problems in the region in part to large-scale Chinese immigration. (Han Chinese are now 41 percent of the population, compared to 4 percent in 1949.) The central government, Wang has said, should grant real autonomy to Xinjiang, as its status as an autonomous region promises on paper, and limit Chinese immigration. The government should also privatize the military-run development body, the Xinjiang Production and Construction Corps (*bingtuan* for short), whose omnipresent mining and farming activities have caused widespread resentment. Set up in 1954, the corps has served as a symbol of the PRC's imagined beneficence to the Uighurs, so dismantling it would be tantamount to revising the official history of PRC policies there.

Military and security affairs. The documents offer only glimpses of the role of the military in defining and influencing foreign policy in China. The fact that there is no military member of either the outgoing or the incoming PBSC signifies the growing professionalization of the military and its relative withdrawal from politics. The last time a uniformed officer held a PBSC post was between 1992 and 1997, when Deng Xiaoping's friend and ally General Liu Huaqing held one. His successor as the top uniformed leader, General Zhang Wannian, joined the Politburo but not the PBSC, setting a precedent that was followed in 2002.

Two military men sit on the new Politburo—Guo Boxiong and Cao Gangchuan—while one, Xu Caihou, serves in the Party Secretariat. The role of the two uniformed Politburo members is to represent the concerns of the military in policymaking. One of them, Cao, serves as minister of defense in the State Council. The minister of defense has no direct role in military administration but uses his protocol status as a cabinet member to handle relations with foreign military organizations. Below Jiang Zemin, Hu Jintao, and the three senior generals, there are another three generals on the Central Military Commission. The six military members' average age is somewhat over sixty and all of them come from technical backgrounds.

At sixty, General Guo Boxiong is younger than most of the men who head the thirty-odd major PLA departments. Guo worked in a military armaments factory in Shaanxi in the late 1950s before joining the PLA in 1961. He served through most of his career in the Lanzhou military region, an area in the northwest which covers the restive Muslim region of Xinjiang and several nuclear weapons testing and production facilities. During a stint in the Beijing military region from 1993 to 1997, following the purge of the Yang faction in the military, he became known as a soldier loyal to Jiang. He has been the executive deputy chief of general staff and a CMC member since 1999. Guo is known for his emphasis on training and discipline. He is an advocate of combined force operations (*lianhe zuozhan*), the technically challenging strategy by which army, naval, and air forces fight jointly in a war. US forces excel at such coordination but China has only recently begun to train for it.

Cao Gangchuan represents a cohort of able, professionally minded officers who have been selected for their ability to keep pace with the increasing technological demands of modern warfare. He studied Russian in the mid-1950s before receiving training in Russia in missile science between 1957 and 1963. He remained in the armaments sector of the military, in 1989 reaching the position of head of the Military Affairs Bureau of the PLA's General Staff Department, which handles the acquisition of weapons and equipment. After further postings in defense technology and acquisitions-related departments, he was made a full general in 1998 and joined the CMC. He became the first director of the General Armaments Department set up in

1998. He will be the senior-ranking vice-chairman of the CMC under Hu Jintao.

Cao is considered a leading exponent of a slimmed-down high-tech military, a concept that faced some resistance from advocates of the old strategy of a "people's army" of millions of spirited low-tech recruits. His strategy is focused on Taiwan, which he believes could easily be overwhelmed through a carefully planned and quickly executed high-tech attack from the mainland. Cao has personally overseen some military drills aimed at Taiwan which involved new technology. He sees the Taiwan issue not as one of aggressive expansion, but as one of protective national defense: it is a problem that must be solved in order for the mainland to turn its energies inward to economic issues. According to Cao:

> Without a strong national defense, without a powerful military, we will not be able to put our energies whole-heartedly into economic development.... The more powerful our national defense, the more fully our country's security and the completion of unification [with Taiwan] is assured.

While the PLA ranks have fallen from 4 million at the beginning of Deng's reforms to 2.5 million today, Cao would like to see that figure fall further, to 1.5 or even 1 million troops. But smaller is not cheaper. Cao wants the PLA budget to continue its double-digit growth of the last decade so that new technology can be developed and acquired.

Hu Jintao seems to be in accord with Cao on this. The investigation report on Hu quotes him as expressing a commitment to invest in military modernization:

> We must place national defense modernization and construction in our overall strategy to develop comprehensive national strength, and continue without deviation on the road of build-

ing a Chinese-style army of excellent soldiers. We must actively promote quality construction of the army, and realize the transition from a quantitative-size model to a qualitative-capability model, from a labor-intensive model to a science and technology-intensive model.... We should as soon as possible narrow the gap between our military and those of the world's principal strong countries, constantly strengthening and developing our ability to balance the strength of other countries.

While the information on the military in *Disidai* focuses on technological and strategic issues, the army's political importance emerges in an intriguing passage in which Hu Jintao warns against any dilution of the army's political loyalty to the ruling Party. Hu says:

We must without exception uphold the absolute leadership of the Party over the military. We must resolutely oppose the corrosive influence of the erroneous ideas of "de-Partyization" [*feidanghua*], "depoliticization" [*feizhengzhihua*], and "republicanization" [*guojiahua*] of the military.

This quotation points to a different concern from the one about divided loyalties that has emerged since Jiang Zemin made his decision to remain in the military commission chairmanship. The division between Jiang's control of the military and Hu's of the civilian apparatus raises the fear of divided Party rule over the army. But the proposals to which Hu was alluding in his undated, but pre-transition, quotation called for the army to divorce itself from the Party and to give its loyalty only to the state.

Such a nationalized army would cease to indoctrinate troops in Party ideology and to promote officers for their Party loyalty. It would have more time and resources to devote to technical training. It might even expect to remain neutral in some future showdown between the Party and its challengers, in contrast to its behavior in the 1989 Tiananmen crisis.

Concerns about the spread of such ideas have surfaced in the military press in China in recent years, but their prominence in a senior leader's comments suggests that they are more than a passing concern. For Hu to have taken the trouble to refute them, such ideas must have been increasingly influential among younger, more technologically proficient officers. Thus from the Party's point of view, the threat of military intervention in politics is matched or even exceeded by the threat of its withdrawal from politics. The Fourth Generation leaders will have to try to find ways to encourage military professionalism without loosening the Party's grip on the army's loyalty.[5]

Former political commissar Xu Caihou may take the lead in this task in his capacity as a member of the Party Secretariat. General Xu, age fifty-nine, has been standing deputy director of the General Political Department and a CMC member since 1999. He spent most of his career as a political commissar, beginning with an assignment in the Jilin provincial military district in the 1970s. From 1993 to 1994, in the period immediately after the purge of the Yang cousins from the military, he served a brief period as editor of the *Liberation Army Daily* newspaper, when it was used by Jiang to instill a new sense of loyalty to the Party. Xu, who organized study sessions for Jiang's Three Represents in the military, was personally selected by Jiang Zemin for promotion in 1999.

Xu's job as liaison between the Party center and the military is to make sure that the army's line on propaganda and ideology reflects the views of the Party. He has spoken of the need for the military "resolutely to obey the Party and to take commands from the Party." He calls for an increase in ideological and political work in the military,

---

5. For more on this issue, see David Shambaugh, *Modernizing China's Military: Progress, Problems, and Prospects* (University of California Press, 2002), pp. 46–55.

and believes in "raising the military's ability to make political distinctions [*jianbieli*] and its political sensitivity [*minruixing*]." These phrases mean that Xu is a strong supporter of army loyalty to the Party.

Conclusion. Not surprisingly for the leaders of a great continental power, the foreign policy thinking of the Fourth Generation leaders is China-centered. International relations are important in their eyes first of all for how they affect China's territorial integrity, political stability, and economic development. Nonetheless the leaders' views of the world are well informed—probably more so than those of most American politicians—thanks to their years of exposure, as Party and government leaders, to the details of their country's foreign policy. They intend to continue what they see as successful foreign policies of the Jiang Zemin years, although adjusting their position toward the United States to reflect China's growing self-confidence.

In their view of the world the Sino–US relationship is the central problem that affects everything else; and their hopes of managing the American threat are centered on what they see as the possibilities for common gains between the two countries. While realizing that China is a relatively weak power, they are also aware of their strengths as a huge nation with influence in many regions and in important international institutions, and with an increasingly competent military establishment. Thus, in foreign policy as in domestic policy, the members of the new elite are aware of but not intimidated by the problems they face. They do not see themselves as isolated in the face of American power. In dealing with it, they hope to cooperate with the United States but they are also prepared to assert themselves against it. In either case they make it clear that they intend their actions to be based on a cool calculation of national interest.

9

THE PARTY LOOKS IN THE MIRROR

THE SECRET FILES used to choose China's new leaders bring us into a world which is unfamiliar in many ways. They introduce us to names and events which have been unknown or unremarked by the outside world, but which figure prominently in the cloistered life of high politics in China. They remind us how little we normally know about the perceptions and assumptions of Beijing's leaders. Perhaps most fascinating, the files tell us what the Chinese Communist Party sees when it looks in the mirror.

The Party sees itself differently from the way most outsiders see it. The view presented in the files may be only a part of the way the Party sees itself; and the Party's view of itself may be inaccurate or wrong. We do not endorse it, but we think it should be thoroughly understood. At a minimum, understanding how the Party sees itself will help us understand its actions in the coming years. It may also force us to rethink some of the conventional wisdom that shapes much Western commentary and policy on China.

An institutionalized succession. The Party sees itself—rightly, we think—as having carried out a more orderly, deliberate succession than ever before in its history. Succession presents a crucial challenge for all authoritarian states and has produced the worst political crises in the history of the People's Republic. In China, the Soviet Union, Eastern Europe, and elsewhere, struggles for power over the years exacted huge costs in political stability, economic development, and civil tranquility.

The Tiananmen events caused a reaction against this kind of political infighting. Deng Xiaoping, and the Party as a whole, wanted to put an end to destructive conflicts over succession to power. Therefore Deng summoned the other senior leaders and urged them to be loyal to Jiang Zemin, and with that in mind he labeled Jiang "the core of the Third Generation of leadership."

Jiang's ability to stay in power through a full two-and-a-half terms was one sign of the Party's new level of institutionalization. Although Deng himself came close to removing Jiang, as recounted in Chapter 6, in the end he did not do so. No one else tried to topple Jiang. Nor did Jiang attempt to purge his successor-designate, Hu Jintao. The military did not step in; nor did the new group of retired Party elders who were in place after Deng and his generation died. Jiang instead consolidated his power and lasted thirteen years in office. Other features that indicated a new degree of stability included the following:

- Jiang leaving civilian office when he said he would.
- The previously chosen successor coming into power.
- Acceptance of the rule that no one should accept a new term in the Politburo after reaching the age of seventy.
- Choosing every member of the new Politburo through consensus.

The institutionalization of Chinese politics, however, is not complete. Most conspicuously, Jiang Zemin's retention of the post of Central Military Commission chair was an exercise of pure personal power. Throughout the succession process factional interests were important even if they had to work within the boundaries set by rules about meritocracy, consensus, and retirement ages. The files, in short, purport to describe fair and objective institutional processes, but the same texts can be read as describing the workings of personal rivalry and factional loyalty.

Some bending of rules by people with power takes place in all political systems. It may remain more prevalent in China than in systems where power-holders are subject to scrutiny by independent media, supervision by courts, and competition from rival political parties. But the Chinese Communist Party's procedures for allocating power and making decisions have incontestably become more regular and reliable than they were before.

One traditional practice that has not changed is the Party's obsessive secrecy about its internal affairs. During the succession process, the regime embargoed information not only about the few details that were still being debated—such as the retirement of Jiang Zemin, the fate of Li Ruihuan, what to do with Fifth Generation leaders, and the role to be given to Li Changchun—but also about matters that had been fixed for a long time, such as Wen Jiabao's appointment as premier and Zeng Qinghong's promotion to the PBSC. During the autumn of 2002, staff preparing for the 16th congress were closeted in a Party-run hostel in Beijing's Western Hills and forbidden to see their families. The arrangements for the delegates' travel to the congress and hotel accommodations were made by central Party staff with high security clearances.

The information vacuum was filled with rumors circulated first in Beijing and then abroad that sometimes portrayed the succession process as comic opera. According to some reports, Jiang would stay on as both CMC chair and general secretary—some said, in all three of his posts. The Party constitution would be revised to create a new post of chairman so that Jiang could stay in power in that capacity. Hu Jintao would be premier. Li Peng would be state president. Zeng Qinghong would be left out of the Politburo. The congress would be delayed because the leaders could not agree. The picture was so confused that *The New York Times* warned in an editorial, "At the pinnacle of power, the culture of palace intrigue that has weakened China for centuries appears to have barely evolved at all."[1]

Secrecy created an aura of mysterious power. But because of it, the Party forfeited the chance for the outside world to see the succession as the deliberative, meritocratic process that it largely was.

A competent elite. Despite its acknowledged problems of discipline and corruption, the Party does not see itself as a decaying, demoralized, outdated organization. Rather, its self-image is of a tightly organized, smoothly functioning, dedicated, and disciplined group of politician-technocrats who face some problems at lower levels of the organization. The Party sees its Fourth Generation as a cohort of "revolutionary, young, knowledgeable, and specialized" cadres, carefully recruited and promoted over the course of twenty years, who possess multiple skills as policymakers, administrators, and political managers.

Much scholarly work has been devoted to showing that as the CCP transforms itself from a revolutionary party into a governing party, its leaders are changing from activists into technocrats.[2] The investigation reports support this view—the new leaders are mostly engineers, and most of them have managed factories, research institutes, bureaus, cities, and provinces. But the Party's documents do not portray the Fourth Generation leaders as narrow specialists or managers. Some of them, like Hu Jintao and Zeng Qinghong, have risen to the top as a result of their political skills, understood as the abilities to unite and motivate others, lead policy debates and forge consensus, change other people's views of their own interests, and articulate visions that will bring about change. The policy experts and administrators among them, like Wen Jiabao, Wu Bangguo, Li Changchun, and Luo Gan, are broadly

---

1. "The Chinese Labyrinth," *The New York Times,* August 18, 2002, p. WK-12.

2. E.g., Li, *China's Leaders.*

qualified administrators, able to integrate diffuse and complex matters of policy and carry out reforms while retaining economic and political control.

The Fourth Generation leaders look from the inside to be more unified and stable than the outgoing generation of leaders, who were thrown together by the disaster of Tiananmen and had to contend with an intrusive group of Elders, a politicized military, and an ambiguous distribution of power among themselves. The new group represents a balance of interests and personalities that has a real chance to maintain unity and work effectively. Hu Jintao takes office with an obvious need to share power and build consensus, particularly with Zeng Qinghong, who in turn has reasons to cooperate with him. Of course, the consensus could break down in the face of a domestic or international crisis, or could be eroded by rivalry, but these developments are not inevitable.

This is far from a demoralized leadership. In contrast to officials in late Communist Eastern Europe and the Soviet Union, the CCP leaders believe they can deal with the problems facing China while keeping their Party in power. Indeed, they believe that the fate of the country depends on continued CCP rule. As Wen Jiabao puts it, "The key to whether our country can handle its national construction well and can be managed well lies with our Party."

Wen's view sounds elitist, and it is, but it has some basis in fact. The Party has been able to co-opt talented people in all fields of life and has stifled the growth of organized opposition. In the new leaders' view, the only alternative to their own rule is social disorder and national humiliation. Contrary to occasional speculation in the West, nothing that the new generation undertakes will be intended as a way to put themselves out of business.

Answers to problems. Nor does the Party see itself as perched on top of a social and economic system that is out of control and heading into collapse. The Fourth Generation leaders know China's problems. During their earlier careers they grappled with failing state-owned enterprises, protesting workers, bankrupt banks, rural poverty, the collapse of the medical system, abusive prisons, weak courts, the deterioration of the environment—all the issues that lead some foreign observers to predict a "collapse of China."[3] The leaders are aware of widespread dissatisfaction with the Party and the need to combat corruption and reduce other causes of popular protest.

Whether China will collapse depends on many factors apart from the leadership, but the new leaders do not seem to consider collapse likely. They do not convey an air of hopelessness. They are not intimidated by China's problems. The solutions they propose may not be adequate, and they may not be as confident as they sound. But the excerpts from their speeches in the investigation reports leave the impression that the Fourth Generation leaders know the problems and have devised measures that they plan to try. Zong Hairen implies that most of them are pragmatic and flexible enough to consider more radical measures if the ones they describe in the excerpts fail.

Nor does the Party see China as fated to evolve into a liberal democracy. There is a prevalent view in the West that authoritarian political systems sooner or later have to make a transition to democracy in order to govern a complex modern society. Both of us, in fact, believe this.[4] But we think it is important to realize that the ruling Chinese elite holds a different view.

The Chinese leaders' views about the long-term future are not clearly stated in the documents. We know there are some informed Chinese who think China should eventually adopt some form of

---

3. E.g., Gordon G. Chang, *The Coming Collapse of China* (Random House, 2001).

4. See Andrew J. Nathan, *China's Crisis* (Columbia University Press, 1990) and *China's Transition* (Columbia University Press, 1997); and Bruce Gilley, *China's Democratic Future* (Columbia University Press, forthcoming, 2004).

liberal, constitutional democracy. But reading between the lines of the statements of the Fourth Generation leaders, we sense a different view. Some of them want to soften authoritarian rule, make it more responsive, and use the media and some political institutions, such as elections and courts, as tools to discipline the lower bureaucracy. But they think that their society is too complex and turbulent to be governable by a truly open, competitive form of democracy. They think Chinese society needs strong guidance both for domestic development and for foreign policy.

In Russia and the Western democracies the Chinese leaders see negative rather than positive examples—societies deprived of cohesion and elite guidance, functioning without benefit of a cadre of public-minded persons, dominated by selfishness and even gangsterism. They see themselves as a qualified managerial elite, uniquely able to manage their society's modernization. They believe the Communist Party should stay in power.

Implications for the world. Whether the Fourth Generation's self-confident and optimistic views of themselves, their Party, and China are well founded remains to be seen. But they will very likely be acting on the basis of those views. What does this counsel for an outside world concerned to bring about change in China that will make it a less repressive and more responsible world power?

Waiting for China to implode or for the CCP to reform itself out of office do not seem realistic options. Foreign governments and observers should not expect a complaisant or uncertain leadership that will passively succumb to a rising tide of problems or surrender graciously to liberal values infiltrated by means of economic globalization. Until events justify taking a different attitude, the outside world would be well advised to treat the new Chinese leaders as if they are here to stay.

Some of their views—in particular on Taiwan, Tibet, and Xinjiang —appear confrontational and misinformed. At the same time, the documents make it clear that China is affected, in some sectors quite deeply, by what the outside world thinks and does. Luo Gan shows himself sensitive to Western concerns about human rights, although he is mainly interested in how those concerns reveal inefficiency and disobedience within his police system than in principled issues of justice. In several of our quoted passages we see that the term "human rights" has entered Chinese elite discourse in a favorable sense. China wants to bring many of its practices into line with those of the advanced world, even if the world China thinks it is joining sometimes seems different from the world that we on the outside perceive. In short, there is an opportunity, as well as an obligation, for the outside world to engage with China for the better.

The question is how to do so. The information in this book suggests that unprincipled engagement, premised on the hope that China will naturally evolve as we wish as long as the world is trading and talking with it, is unfounded. Western engagement can be used just as well to reinforce Party dictatorship as to weaken it. Indeed, the Fourth Generation leaders see economic opening and participation in the UN and other aspects of the global system as critical to bolstering their legitimacy. But neither would a Great Wall of hostility toward the new leaders be effective. They are all prepared to resist when they feel that outside powers are threatening Chinese national interests.

An effective policy therefore must engage with China at all levels but with clear principles and purposes. The information on the new rulers provided here may, we hope, help people outside China to deal with that country as it is, and help it become what it should be.

ANDREW J. NATHAN is Class of 1919 Professor of Political Science at Columbia University. He is the author of *China's Transition, China's Crisis: Dilemmas of Reform and Prospects for Democracy*, and *Chinese Democracy*, the coauthor of *The Great Wall and the Empty Fortress: China's Search for Security*, and the co-editor of *The Tiananmen Papers*.

BRUCE GILLEY is a doctoral student in politics at Princeton University and a former contributing editor at the *Far Eastern Economic Review*. He is the author of the forthcoming *China's Democratic Future, Model Rebels: The Rise and Fall of China's Richest Village*, and *Tiger on the Brink: Jiang Zemin and China's New Elite*.

INDEX